EYEWITNESS ANTHOLOGIES

ANCIENT EGYPTIANS

Wooden figure of servant girl

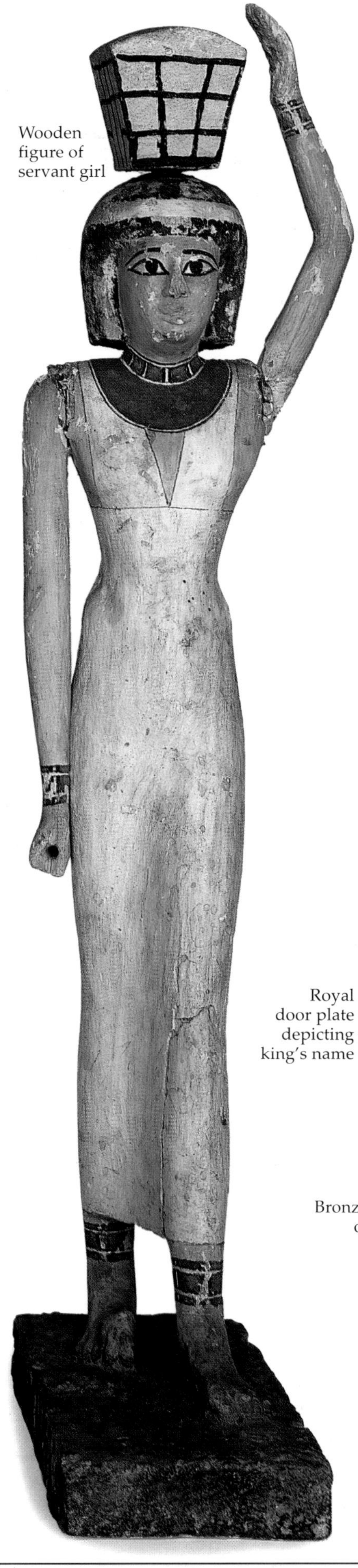

Good luck charm showing the god Heh

Royal door plate depicting king's name

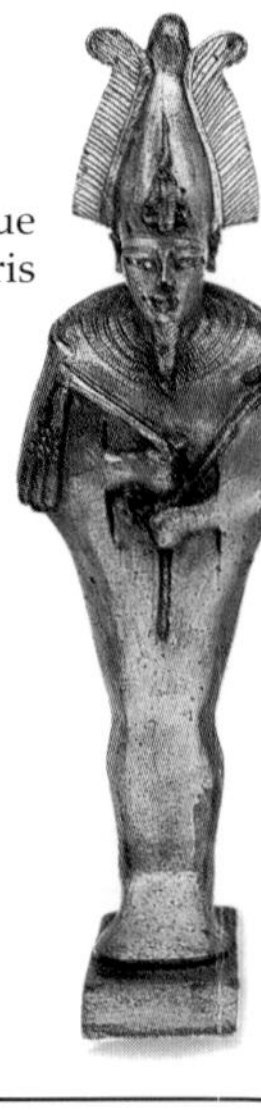

Bronze statue of Osiris

DK

A DORLING KINDERSLEY BOOK

Project editors Scott Steedman, Phil Wilkinson
Art editors Manisha Patel, Bob Gordon, Thomas Keenes
Managing editors Gillian Denton, Helen Parker, Simon Adams
Managing art editor Julia Harris
Research Céline Carez
Picture research Kathy Lockley, Cynthia Hole
Production Catherine Semark, Louise Barratt, Meryl Silbert
Editorial consultants Dr. I.E.S. Edwards and The Department of Egyptian Antiquities, British Museum

First American Edition, 1996
2 4 6 8 10 9 7 5 3 1

Published in the United States by
DK Publishing, Inc., 95 Madison Avenue
New York, New York 10016

Visit us on the World Wide Web at http: / / www.dk.com

Distributed by Houghton Mifflin Company, Boston

IBSN 0-7894-1409-0

Reproduced in Italy by G.R.B. Graphica, Verona
Printed in Singapore by Toppan

Woodern figure of Anubis, the ancient Egyptian god of embalming

Ceremonial axe with openwork head

EYEWITNESS ANTHOLOGIES

ANCIENT EGYPTIANS

Written by
JAMES PUTNAM & GEORGE HART

Photographed by
GEOFF BRIGHTLING & PETER HAYMAN

Pyramidion of Bugentef, New Kingdom

Cartonnage mummy mask, popular in Greek and Roman times

Mummy ready for burial

DK

Contents

Name tablets, placed in the foundations of pyramids

Bronze ram-headed sphinxes from Nubia

Lands of the Nile

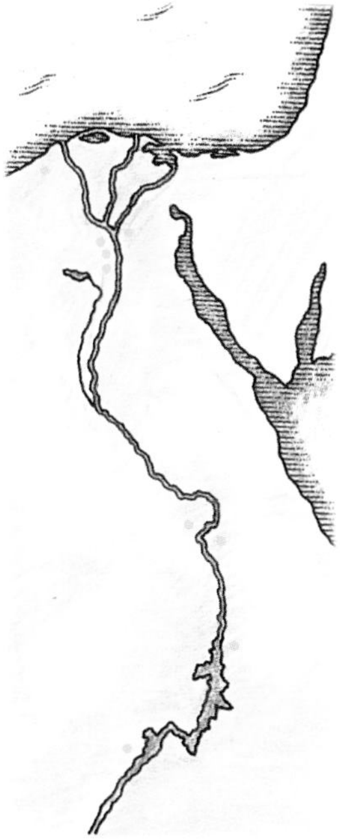

THE PERIOD WE CALL ancient Egypt lasted for 3,000 years - and the pyramids that the ancient Egyptians built have fascinated people ever since. How did they build these massive stone monuments, and why? The most famous pyramids are the three at Giza, near modern Cairo. But there are more than 80 others in Egypt, and another 100 farther south in the Sudan. The Ancient Egyptians went to great lengths to preserve their bodies (as mummies) and their worldy possessions, and to bury them beneath these huge structures. This has helped the world to rediscover the wonders of ancient Egypt and the people who lived there.

Stela tablet from the New Kingdom era

Egypt is mostly desert, and life has always been concentrated along the banks of the Nile River. In ancient times the land was often divided into two. The northern part, which included the fertile Nile Delta, was called Lower Egypt. In the south was Upper Egypt, which included a large area now flooded by the Aswan Dam.

The Three Kingdoms

Old Kingdom (2613-2160 BC)
when the massive pyramids at Giza and the Sphinx were built.

Middle Kingdom (2040-1750 BC)
when strong kings revived the tradition of pyramid building.

New Kingdom (1550-1086 BC)
when pharoahs such as Tutankhamun were buried in sacred underground rock tombs and pyramids were smaller with pointed roofs capped by a pyramidion, or capstone. (p.74)

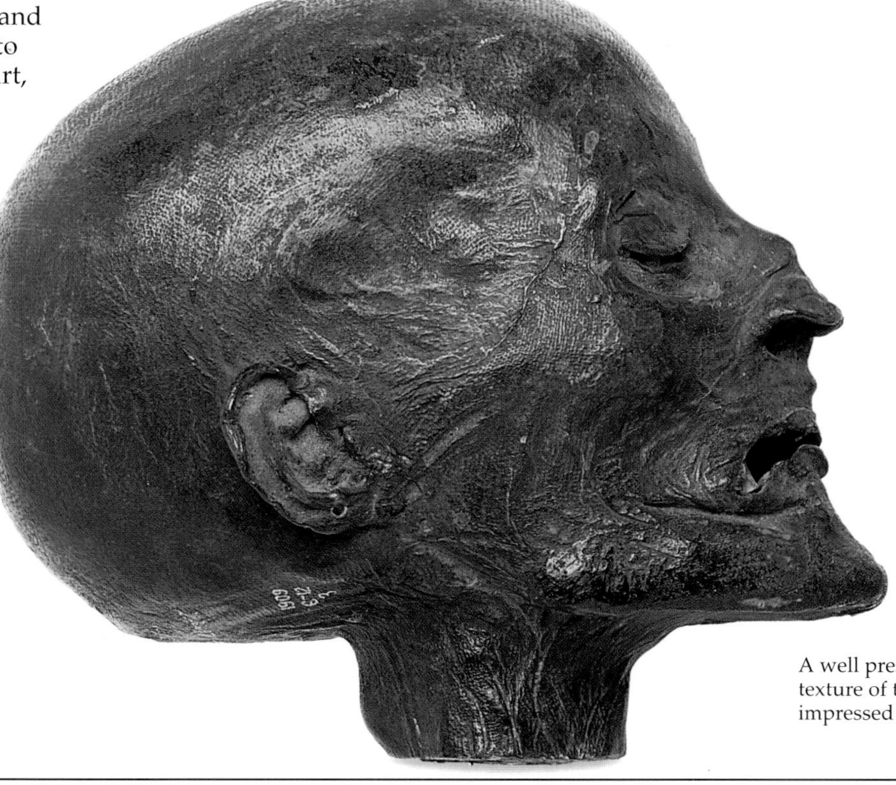

A well preserved face,with the texture of the linen bandages impressed on the skin

Egypt before the pharaohs

THE PERIOD we usually think of as ancient Egypt is the time when Egypt was ruled by the pharaohs - after c. 3000 B.C. But who lived in Egypt before the pharaohs? In the early Stone Age people in Egypt lived in areas fairly high above sea level near the Nile from the Delta to Aswan. Beginning in about 5000 B.C., settlers came to Egypt from Palestine and Syria, from the Libyan tribes living to the west, and from Nubia in the south. Shortly before 3000 B.C., traders from southern Iraq also sailed to Egypt, and some, attracted by the fertility of the country, stayed on. Soon these early settlers began to grow barley and to domesticate cattle, and to build villages of mud huts in parts of the flood plain that seemed safe from the annual Nile flood. Slate palettes and elaborately carved ivory objects, as well as fine pots, often buried with their owners in brick-lined graves, have been found dating from the period before 3000 B.C.

MACE HEAD
The mace was the kind of weapon used to give the death blow to a wounded enemy. But the smooth surfaces and superb carving of this example mean it was probably carried by a ruler or high commander on ceremonial occasions.

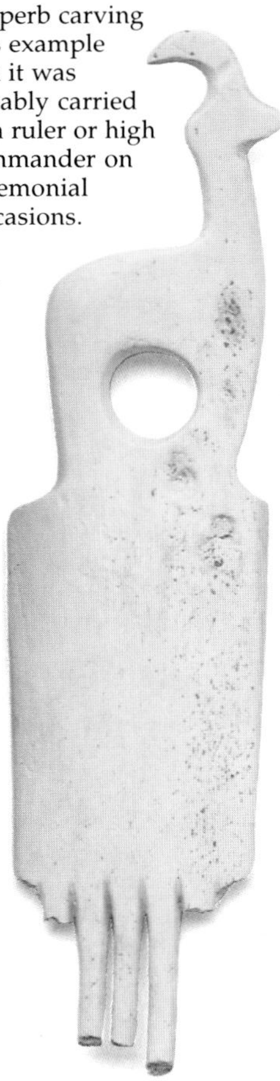

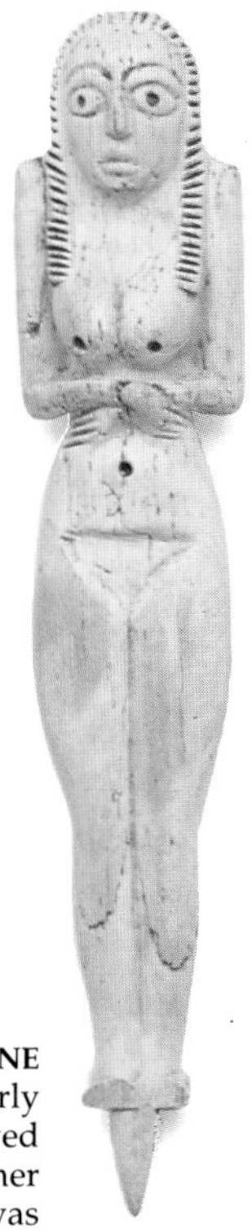

COMB AND CONCUBINE
The African elephant and hippopotamus provided early craftsmen with plenty of ivory. The comb handle is carved into the shape of a gazelle, perhaps because its owner enjoyed hunting this creature. The female figure was placed in a tomb and was meant to provide the owner with a female companion in the afterlife.

ANCIENT BODY
Before mummification evolved, burials involved arranging the corpse in a "sleeping" position with the elbows and knees drawn together. The body was placed in a pit with a selection of possessions, and sand was thrown on top of it. The sand absorbed all the water from the body, drying it out and preserving it, so the person's spirit would recognize it and inhabit it. Here you can see the fairly well preserved hair and features of a man who died about 5,000 years ago. When he was found, some people thought that he was still lifelike enough to warrant a nickname – Ginger, because of his red hair.

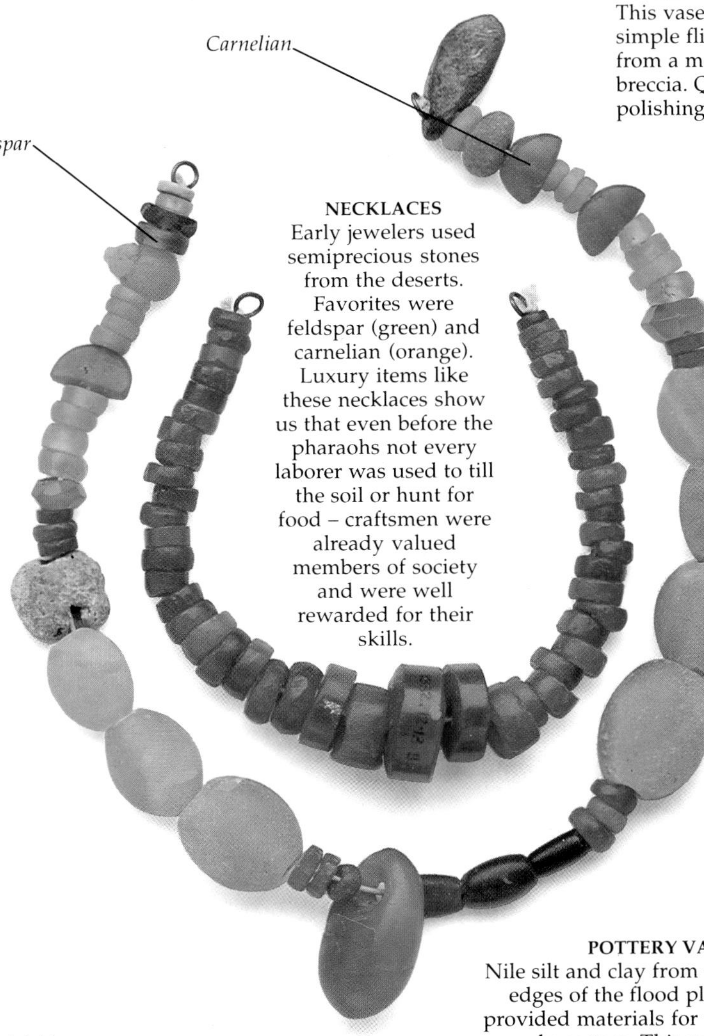

Carnelian

Feldspar

NECKLACES
Early jewelers used semiprecious stones from the deserts. Favorites were feldspar (green) and carnelian (orange). Luxury items like these necklaces show us that even before the pharaohs not every laborer was used to till the soil or hunt for food – craftsmen were already valued members of society and were well rewarded for their skills.

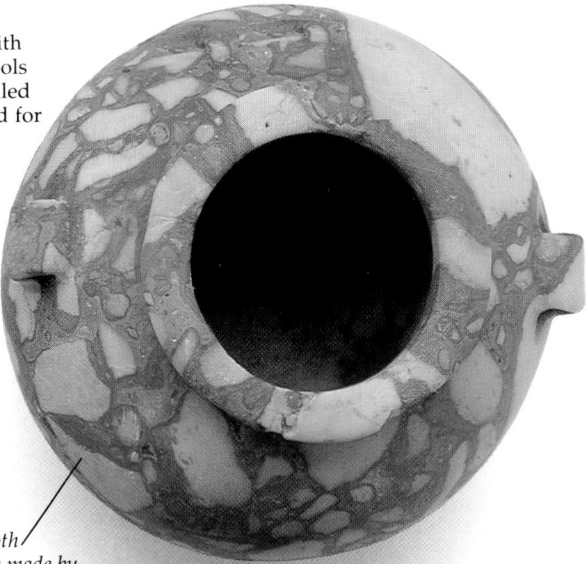

STONE VASE
This vase was carved with simple flint or copper tools from a mottled stone called breccia. Quartz was used for polishing the surface.

Smooth shape made by simple tools

POTTERY VASE
Nile silt and clay from the edges of the flood plain provided materials for the early potters. This pot's tapering base was designed to fit in a stand or to rest in a depression in the ground. The circular spirals are meant to give the impression of a vessel carved from stone.

Spiral design

Eye inlaid with ivory

COSMETIC PALETTE
Some of the oldest surviving Egyptian objects are slate palettes. Some are rectangular; others are carved in animal shapes like hippos, turtles, falcons, or this obese ram. The surface was used for grinding minerals for eye paint (p. 114)

On the banks of the Nile

THE DESERT, also called the Red Land, covers more than 90 percent of Egypt. The desert supported only small settlements in wadis (river valleys) and oases. The Egyptians lived on the banks of the Nile River or beside canals extending from it. The area near the Nile was Kemet, or the Black Land, named after the rich dark silt on which the farmers grew their crops. Without this fertility, there would have been no civilization in Egypt. From ancient times right up to today the pattern of life in Egypt for the majority of the population has depended on the exploitation of its fertile agricultural resources. The Nile flood began the year for the Egyptian farmer, when the river, rising from the swelling waters of the Blue Nile and White Nile, which converge just north of Khartoum in the Sudan, brought deposits of silt into Egypt. When the Nile waters subsided, the farmers went to work sowing barley and emmer wheat. The result usually was a good summer harvest.

FAMINE
In a climate of extremes, crops could sometimes fail and famine could hit the population hard. Statues of people like this beggar remind us of this problem in ancient Egypt.

A RIVERSIDE PEOPLE
The ancient Egyptians lived in a strip of land on either side of the Nile, where the Nile flood made the land fertile. The flood area is shown in green on this map.

Scribe with his palette

Herdsman driving cattle with a stick

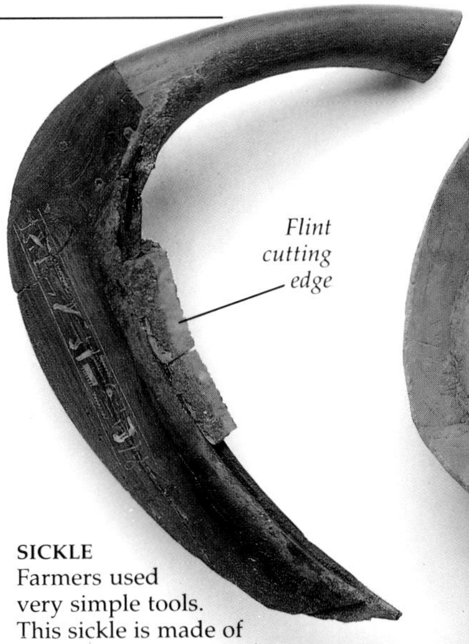

SICKLE
Farmers used very simple tools. This sickle is made of wood with flint teeth. In pictures of the harvest you can see groups of men cutting the crops using sickles like this. The stalks left behind in the field would eventually be gathered to make mats and baskets.

WINNOWING FAN
After donkeys brought the wheat to the threshing floor, two wooden fans like this were used to separate the grain from the chaff.

WINNOWING
The men gathered up the grain and chaff (husk) and threw it into the air. The breeze carried away the lighter chaff, leaving the grain to fall onto the floor. The winnowers wore linen scarves to keep the chaff out of their hair.

SHADUF
Water was still needed after the flood went down, so canals were dug, leading as far away from the river as possible to bring water to the more remote fields. To raise the water from the river to fill the canals, the Egyptians used a device called a shaduf, as they do today. It consists of a trellis supporting a pole with a counterweight. It could easily be operated by one man, who would lower the bucket into the river before pulling it up with the help of the weight.

CATTLE COUNTING
An important measure of a person's wealth in ancient Egypt was the number of cattle he owned. Here, in this tomb model of Meketre, mayor of Thebes in c. 2000 B.C., cattle are being counted as they are driven past the mayor and his top officials and scribes. The accounts recorded by the scribes were kept for tax purposes.

The oval enclosing the hieroglyphs that make up a royal name is called a cartouche. This one contains the name of King Tuthmosis III.

Famous pharaohs

THE KING was not only the most powerful and important man in Egypt – he was thought to be a god. He was known as the pharaoh – a word which derives from a respectful way of referring to the king by describing him as the "great house" (*per-ao*), meaning the palace where he lived. The Queen of Egypt was also thought of as a goddess but was usually given the title of "Great Royal Wife" – only rarely did women rule Egypt in their own right. There was an effective system of teaching a prince to become a pharaoh, which included training him to be an expert sportsman and potential war leader. Often the ruling pharaoh would adopt his heir as co-regent to enable a smooth takeover when the king died. Sometimes princes had to wait a long time. One pharaoh, Pepy II, holds the record for the longest reign of any monarch. Pepy II came to the throne when he was six years old. He was still king of Egypt 94 years later when he was 100. It is remarkable that in Egypt's long history there are only a few references to pharaohs being assassinated, usually as a result of a plot in the court to put a prince who was not the true heir onto the throne.

ARMLESS QUEEN
This statue of an Egyptian queen is from around 700 B.C. Her arms were attached separately but have been lost, as has her crown of plumes.

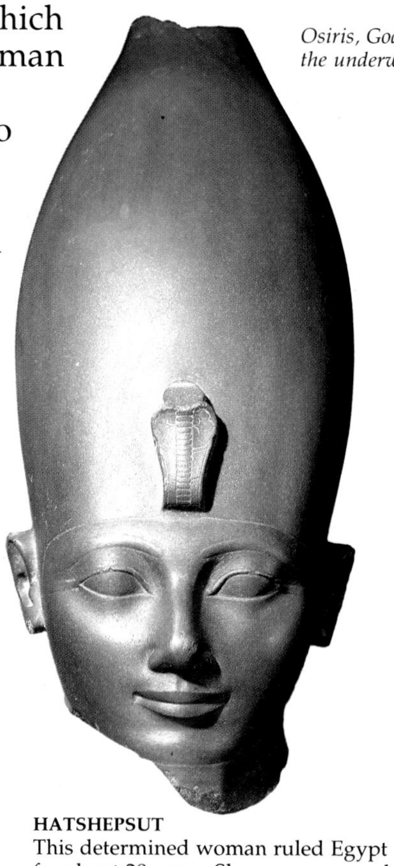

HATSHEPSUT
This determined woman ruled Egypt for about 20 years. She was supposed to be regent for her young stepson, but took over the reins of government. She wore the pharaoh's crown and royal ceremonial beard. In this sculpture she wears the crown of Upper Egypt, which bears the cobra goddess.

Akhenaten

Nefertiti

AKHENATEN AND NEFERTITI
In Akhenaten's reign the traditional Egyptian gods were banished – only the sun god was worshiped. To break the links with other gods, Akhenaten founded a new capital city and closed the temples of other gods. Queen Nefertiti helped her husband set up the cult of the sun god Aten and probably ruled with him. After their death Tutankhamun and his successors restored the old gods. The names of Akhenaten and Nefertiti became hated and were removed from inscriptions, and their temples were torn down.

The mystery of the sphinx

There has been a lot of confusion about sphinxes in ancient Egypt because of Greek legends. In the Greek myth of King Oedipus, the sphinx is a ferocious and deadly female creature who destroys men who are unable to solve the riddle she gives them. But the Egyptians saw the sphinx as a lion's body with the ruler's head. The lion was a creature of the sun god and so emphasized the king's role as son of Re (p. 78) The lion's strength also suggests the monarch's great power. Sometimes sphinxes combine other elements, such as the head and wings of a hawk, symbolizing the god Horus (p. 83).

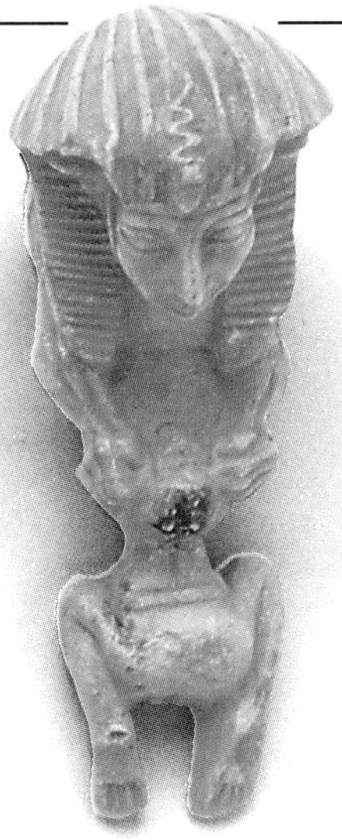

SPHINX AND PRISONER
The way that the sphinx represents the pharaoh's power is shown in this ivory statuette, carved over 3,600 years ago.

SPHINX AT GIZA
This sphinx was carved about 4,500 years ago for the pharaoh Khafre and guarded the way to his pyramid.

RAMSES THE GREAT
In the 13th century B.C., Ramses II reigned over Egypt for 67 years. He built more monuments and set up more statues than any other pharaoh. Among his buildings are the mortuary complex on the West Bank at Thebes, today called the Ramesseum, from which this statue comes. The king wears a royal head cloth called the nemes, above which is a crown of cobras.

TUTANKHAMUN
This ruler came to the throne when only nine years old. He was obviously guided by his high officials, but seems to have been determined to bring back the old gods who had been banished by Akhenaten (see left). This famous golden mask comes from his tomb (p. 69).

TUTHMOSIS IV
This king was famous because he freed the great sphinx at Giza from the desert sand that had blown around it. He is portrayed on his knees holding two jars of sacred liquid. He is protected by the cobra goddess Wadjet on his forehead. Only kings and queens were entitled to wear cobra goddesses, who it was thought would deal out instant death by spitting flames at any enemy.

The royal court

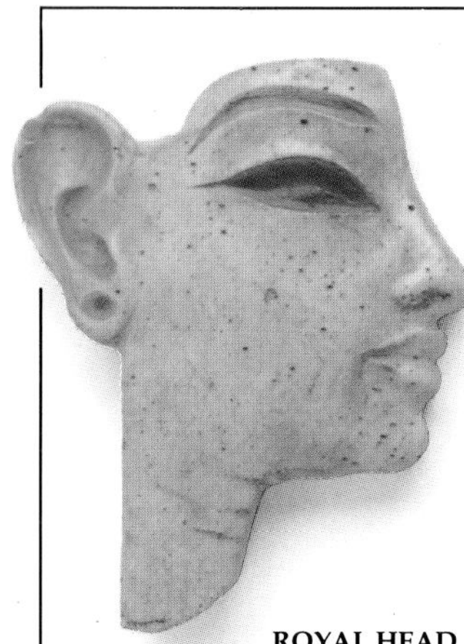

ROYAL HEAD
This portrait in glass was probably used as an inlay in a piece of palace furniture or as a decoration around a window.

AT GREAT STATE OCCASIONS like royal jubilee celebrations or the giving of gifts to favored courtiers, the king and court gathered together, and top officials, diplomats, and high priests would attend. Some of the courtiers were relatives of the king; some won high office through their ability as scribes. When people approached the king, they often kissed the ground at his feet. We know this because one courtier boasted that the pharaoh insisted that he kiss the royal leg and not the ground. Sometimes the pharaoh simply wanted to relax at court. King Sneferu was all set to watch 20 beautiful women from his harem row on the royal lake. It went well until one woman dropped her hair clasp in the lake, began to sulk, and stopped rowing; she refused even the king's request to carry on. The court magician had to part the waters and get the clasp from the bottom.

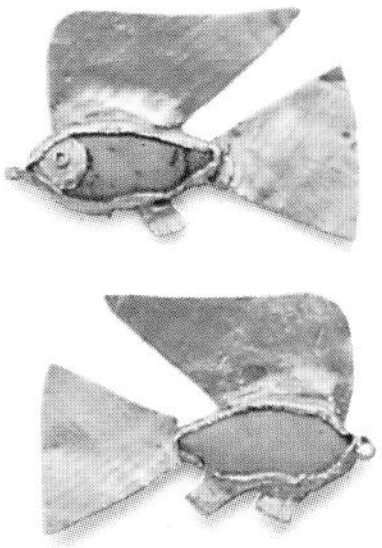

FISHES
Children sometimes wore fishshaped amulets in their hair, possibly to guard against accidents in the Nile.

OYSTER-SHELL PENDANT
The earliest jewelry in Egypt was often made of shells. Later jewelers imitated these shapes in gold. This one is carved with the name of King Senwosret.

AMULET CASE
Amulets, and protective spells written on papyrus, were put in containers like this one and hung from a necklace.

Lion's-paw legs

ROYAL THRONE
Queen Hetepheres was the mother of King Khufu (p. 42). Her original burial place was robbed but some of her splendid furniture was reburied near her son's pyramid. The court throne was made of wood overlaid with gold leaf. Insects ate the wood away but archaeologists were able to reconstruct the furniture.

CEREMONIAL THROW STICK
Courtiers used wooden throw sticks to catch birds. This one, made of brittle faience (pottery; see p. 103), had no practical use and it was carried during ceremonies. It bears the name of Akhenaten, the pharaoh who lived in the 14th century B.C.

ROYAL VASES
The pharaohs used the best-quality utensils and cosmetic containers, which were buried in their tombs for use in the next world. These two smoothly carved mottled stone vases have lids of gold adorned with imitation twine, also in gold. They were made for King Khasekhemwy.

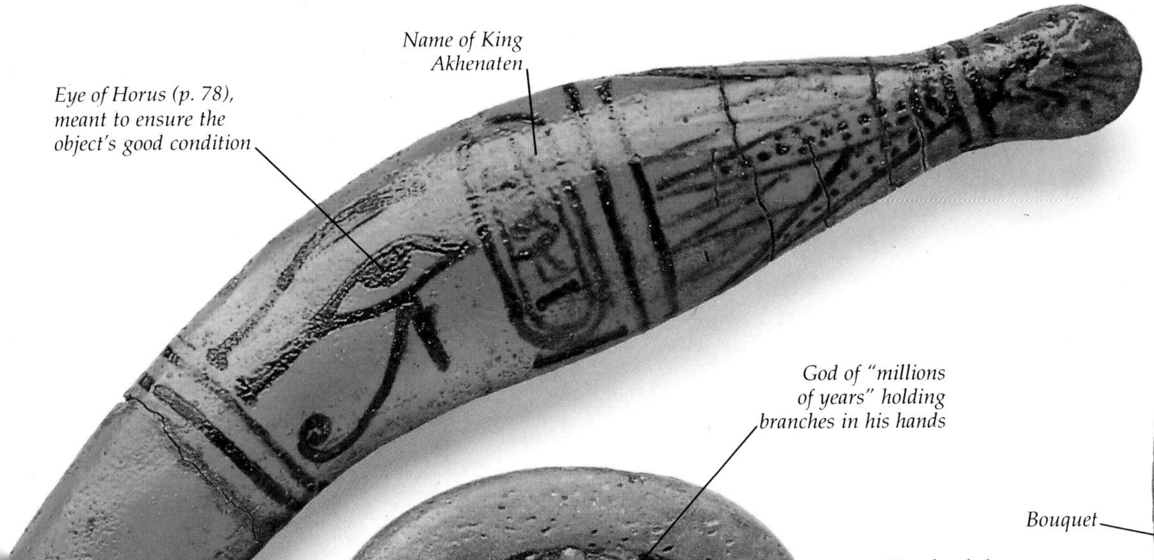

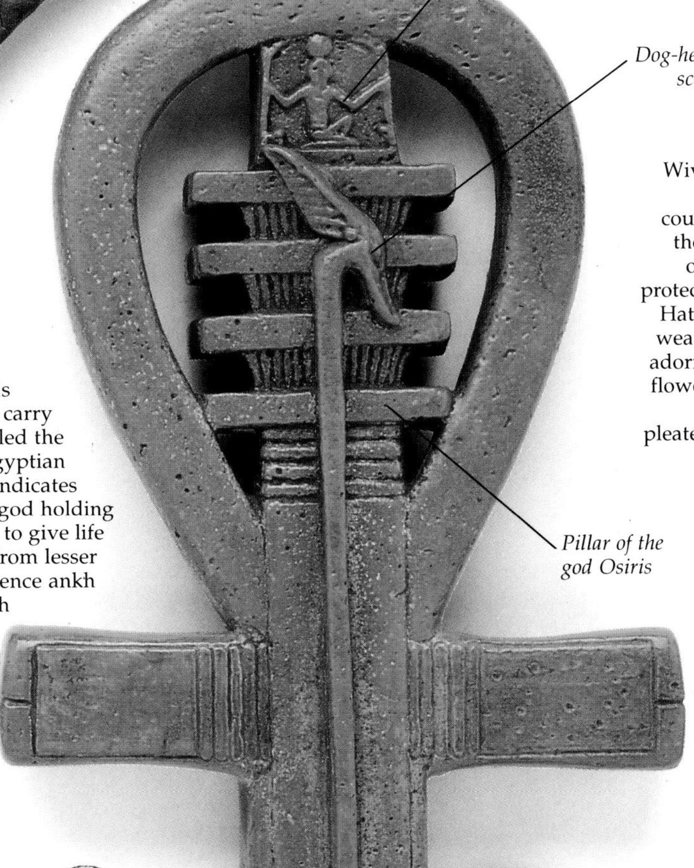

SIGN OF LIFE
Only kings, queens, and gods were allowed to carry this symbol. Called the ankh, it is the Egyptian sign of life and indicates that the king or god holding it has the power to give life or take it away from lesser mortals. This faience ankh is decorated with a dog-headed scepter symbolizing power.

NOBLEWOMAN
Wives of great officials held high status at court. They could form themselves into a sort of "guild" under the protection of the goddess Hathor. This court lady wears a very heavy wig adorned with a circlet of flowers; she also holds a floral bouquet. Her pleated dress is bordered with fringes.

PHARAOH
This gold figurine shows the royal studded crown, which could be worn at court or when the king was riding in his chariot, and the crook and flail, which represent kingship, as does the cobra goddess curled up on the king's forehead.

LOTUS TILE
This tile comes from a section of inlay on a wall, floor, or piece of furniture in King Akhenaten's capital. Surviving fragments like this give us an idea of the splendors of the royal courts.

This scarab was placed over the heart of a king to help him through the scrutiny of his past life which occurred in the underworld

Preparing for the tomb

THE EGYPTIANS dreaded the thought that one day their world might cease to exist. From their belief in the power of magic, they developed a funerary cult which, in their eyes, ensured their survival forever. This involved preserving the body of the deceased. The embalmers took the body to the Beautiful House, where they worked. They made a cut in the left side of the body with a flint knife and removed the liver and lungs. These were dried out and stored in special vessels called canopic jars. The brain was also removed, but the heart was left in the body so that it could be weighed in the afterlife (p. 35). Then the body was covered with crystals of a substance called natron, which kept it from decaying, packed with dry material like leaves or sawdust, and wrapped in linen bandages.

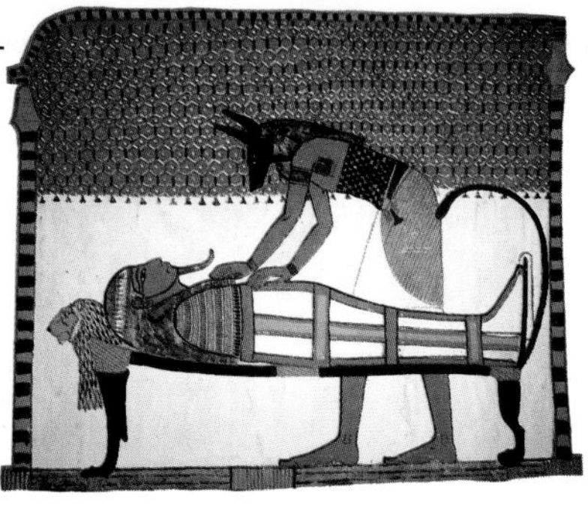

ANUBIS
The god Anubis was supposed to be responsible for the ritual of embalming. His titles included "He who is in the place of embalming." Here he is putting the final touches on a mummified corpse.

WAX PLATE
Plates like this were used to cover cuts made in the flesh of the corpse. The protective eye of Horus (p. 78) symbolized the soundness of the body on which it was placed.

UTENSILS FOR "OPENING THE MOUTH"
"Opening the mouth," one of the most important of all funerary rites, restored a dead person's living faculties, allowing the mummy to eat, drink, and move around. Egyptians hated to die abroad because they knew that their corpse would not receive this rite and their afterlife would be in jeopardy. This model kit contains some of the instruments for the opening the mouth ceremony. There are vases and cups for holding and pouring sacred liquids, and a forked instrument for touching the mouth of the mummy.

OPENING THE MOUTH
A priest wearing the mask of Anubis holds the coffin upright. Behind the grieving wife and daughter, priests scatter purified water and touch the mouth of the mummy case with the ritual instruments. The eldest son burns incense and a spell is recited.

CANOPIC JARS
Any part of the body could be used in a spell against a person, so the inner organs removed during mummification were protected in special containers called canopic jars. The intestines, stomach, liver, and lungs were dried out, wrapped up in linen, and each placed in a separate jar.

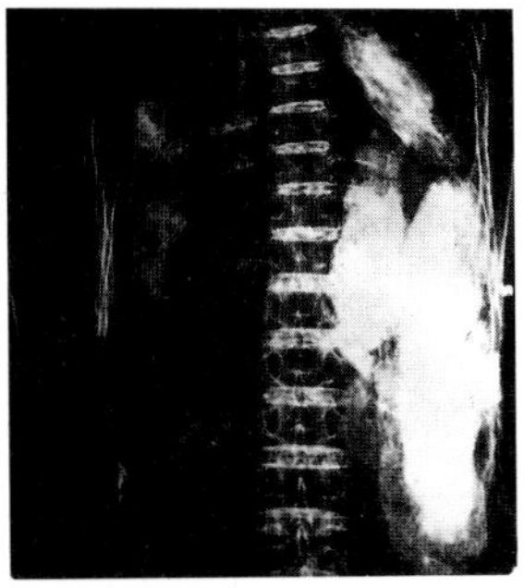

WHAT'S INSIDE?
An X-ray of a mummy reveals the stuffing that replaced some of the organs.

MUMMY LABELS
Small wooden tags attached to mummies identified the body and gave protection. Anubis is shown on the tag on the left. He is black because black is the color of life in ancient Egypt (from the color of the fertile Nile mud).

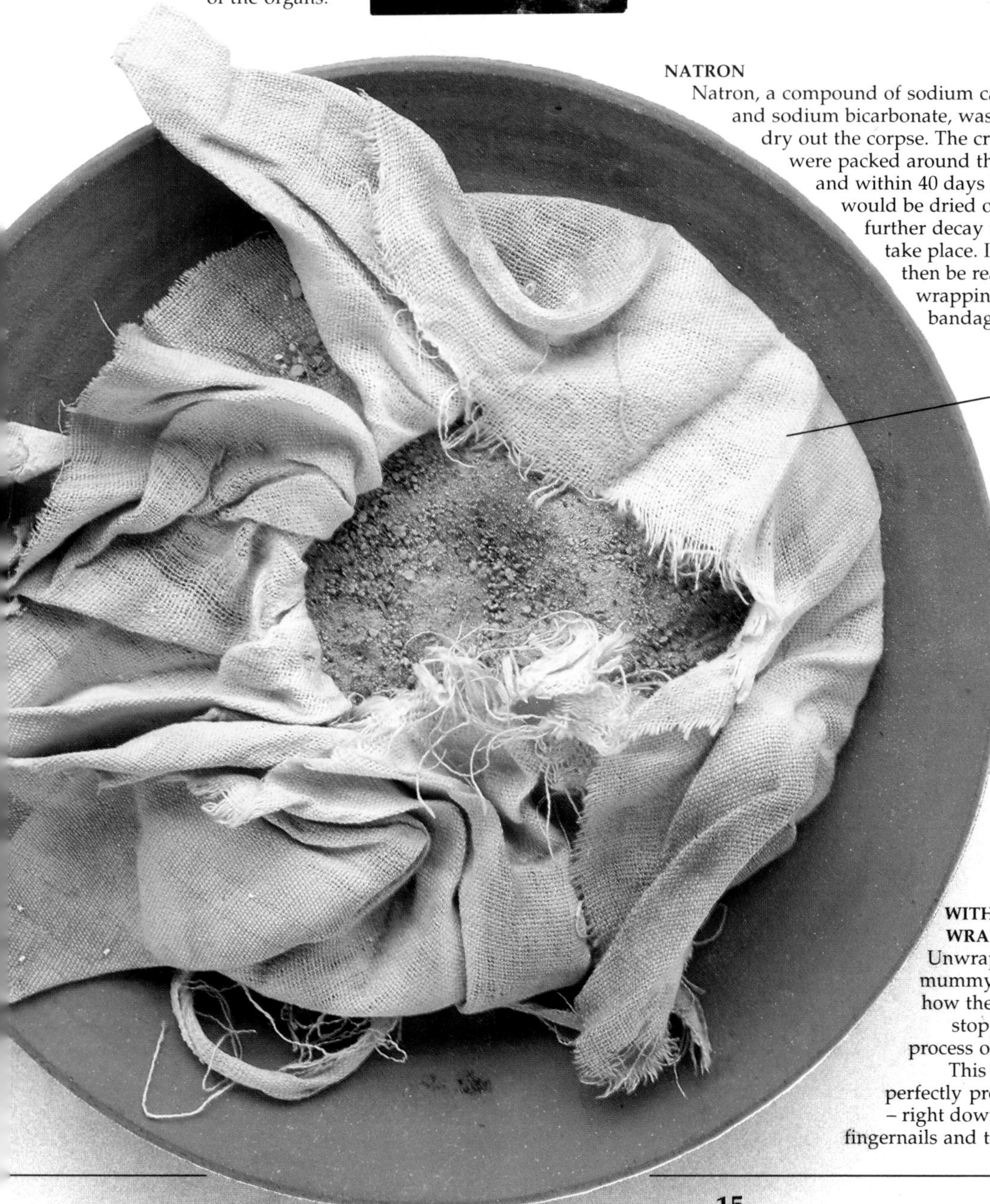

NATRON
Natron, a compound of sodium carbonate and sodium bicarbonate, was used to dry out the corpse. The crystals were packed around the body, and within 40 days the corpse would be dried out and no further decay would take place. It would then be ready for wrapping in linen bandages.

Ancient linen wrapping

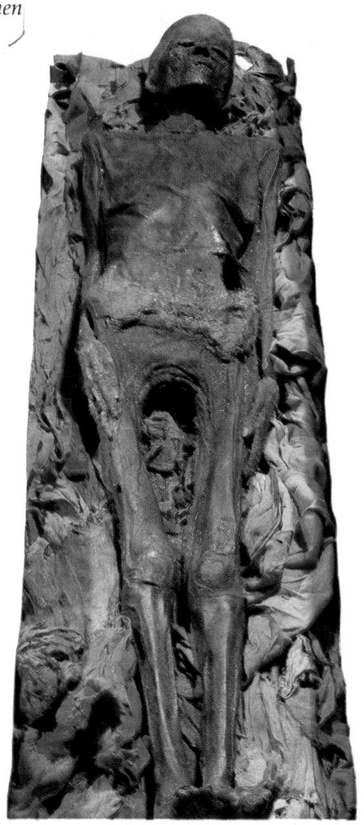

WITHIN THE WRAPPINGS
Unwrapping a mummy shows how the natron stopped the process of decay. This body is perfectly preserved – right down to the fingernails and toenails.

Making a mummy

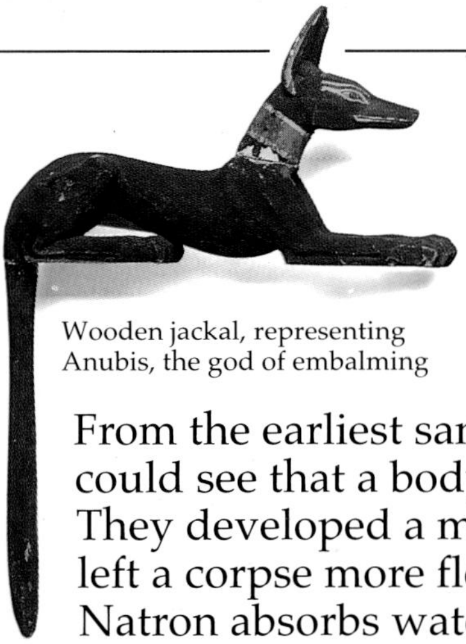

Wooden jackal, representing Anubis, the god of embalming

"MY CORPSE IS PERMANENT, it will not perish nor be destroyed in this land for ever." So ends spell 154 in the Book of the Dead (pp. 34–35). From the earliest sand burials 5,000 years ago (p. 6), the Egyptians could see that a body had to be dried to stop it from rotting away. They developed a method of drying with natron, a natural salt that left a corpse more flexible and lifelike than drying with hot sand. Natron absorbs water. It also dissolves body fats, and is a mild antiseptic that kills destructive bacteria. Embalming traditionally took 70 days, of which 40 used to dry the body. But first of all the vital organs, which decay the fastest, had to be removed. Only the heart, which the mummy would need when it was judged in the next world (p. 35), was left. The body was then washed with palm wine and spices and covered in natron. Later, molten (liquid) resin, taken from trees, was poured over the body to help preserve it. To stop it from cracking, the skin was rubbed with a mixture of cedar oil, wax, natron, and gum. Then the body was packed with wads of linen, sand, or even sawdust, to give it shape. Finally the mummy was ready to be wrapped in layers of linen bandages.

EMBALMING EYEWITNESS
The Greek historian Herodotus visited Egypt in 450 B.C. and wrote the only eyewitness account of embalming. "In the best treatment" he observed, "first of all they draw out the brains through the nostrils with an iron hook… Next they make an incision in the flank with a sharp obsidian blade through which they can extract all the internal organs. Then they clean out the body cavity, rinsing it with palm wine…(then) they cover the corpse with natron for seventy days, but for no longer, and so mummify it. After the seventy days are up they wash the corpse and wrap it from head to toe in bandages of the finest linen anointed with gum."

Imsety, with a person's head, guarded the liver

Qebehsenuef, a falcon, held the intestines

Hapy, a baboon, kept an eye on the lungs

Duamutef, a jackal, guarded the stomach

FOUR DUMMIES
The mummy's internal organs were embalmed separately. By about 2000 B.C., they were then placed in containers called canopic jars. These little coffins had heads, either of gods or the dead person. By 1000 B.C., the wrapped organs were put back in the mummy. But dummy canopic jars with nothing in them were still put in the tomb. These dummy jars have the heads of the four gods known as the Sons of Horus (p. 22).

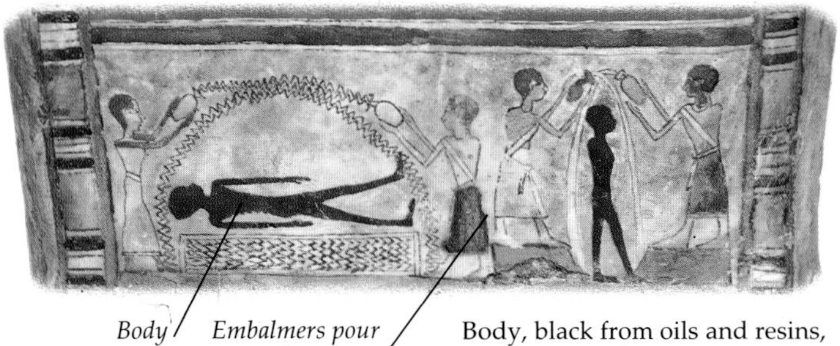

Body / *Embalmers pour water from jugs* / Body, black from oils and resins, is purified with streams of water

Embalmers / *Head embalmer wearing Anubis mask* / Lying on bier (couch), body is covered in dry crystals of natron

CANOPIC CHEST
This wooden chest belonged to a doctor called Gua, who died c. 2050 B.C. It contains his four canopic jars. They have human heads – it wasn't until 1500 B.C. that the Sons of Horus (p. 22) became common as stoppers.

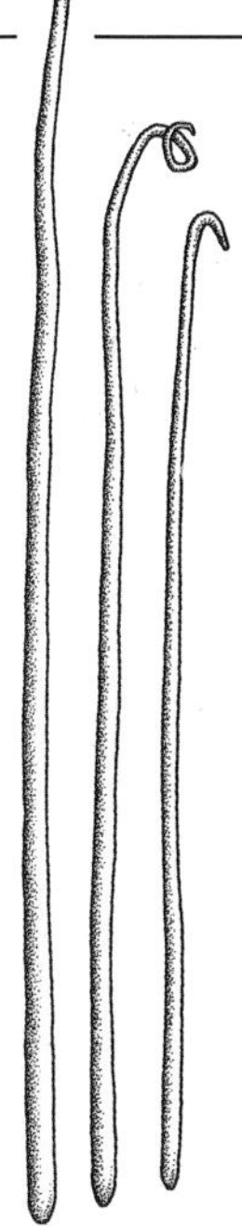

BRAIN HOOKS
A rod was usually pushed up the nose to punch a hole into the skull. Then bronze hooks or spoons could be poked in to scoop out the brain.

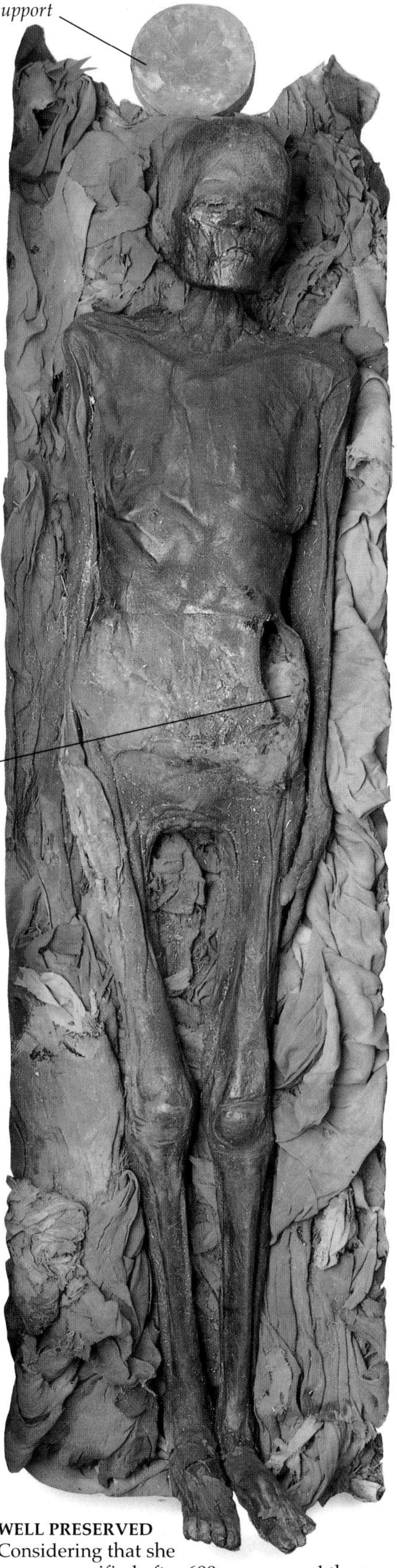

BOWL OF NATRON
A natural salt, natron was found around the edges of desert lakes near Cairo.

Wax embalming plate with wedjat-eye decoration

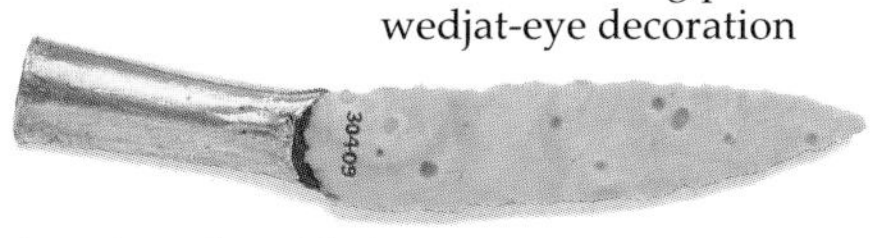

Ritual knife with gold handle and flint blade

EMBALMING TOOLS
The embalming incision was usually made on the left side of the body. Herodotus says the knife blade was made of obsidian, a kind of volcanic glass that had to be imported from Ethiopia. But all the ritual knives that have been found have blades of flint. After the organs had been removed, the incision was covered by a plate decorated with a wedjat eye (p. 22).

WHERE THE SUN SETS...
Cemeteries, tombs, and embalmers' workshops were usually on the west bank of the Nile. The Egyptians believed this desert area where the sun set every evening was the land of the dead.

STEP BY STEP
The best pictures of embalming are painted on the mummy case of Djedbastiufankh, from about 600 B.C. This case is now in the Hildesheim Museum, Germany.

Mummy, bandaged and wearing a mask (pp. 20–21), is attended by Anubis

WELL PRESERVED
Considering that she was mummified after 600 B.C., around the time Herodotus visited Egypt, this woman has been remarkably well embalmed. By then, the empire was collapsing and the art of embalming was in decline. Embalmers still made sure the mummy looked good on the outside, but they didn't bother much with the insides. Usually bodies were simply coated from head to toe in resin.

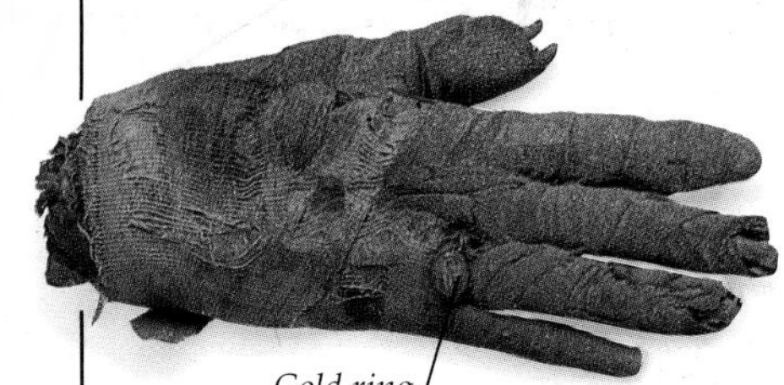

NEED A HAND?
Each finger on this 3,000-year-old mummified hand has been individually wrapped. It is wearing a gold ring set with a scarab beetle (p. 118). Rings and other jewelry were often specially made just to be worn by mummies.

Wrapping up

HUNDREDS OF YARDS OF LINEN were used to carefully wrap a mummy. The linen didn't just come in the well-known rolls of bandages. Mummies were also wrapped in shrouds, large sheets of material which were thrown over the body like a cape. Each shroud had to be long enough to be knotted at the top, behind the mummy's head, and also underneath the feet. As many as 20 alternating layers of bandages and shrouds have been counted on one mummy. The exact arrangement of the rolls and shrouds of linen varied a lot from period to period, and can be helpful in dating mummies. The first layer was usually a shroud. Then each finger and toe was wrapped up separately. Next a long strip of linen beginning at the right shoulder was crisscrossed over the head. To hold the head up, a strap was then passed under the chin and knotted on top of the head. As more bandages were added, they were kept very tight, to maintain the mummy's distinctive shape. Protective amulets (pp. 22–23) and sometimes the dead person's jewelery were placed between the layers. At the same time the linen was constantly brushed with sticky, liquid resin. This glued the bandages together and made them slowly stiffen as they dried. Around 15 days were set aside for the wrapping, and the whole process was accompanied by much prayer and ritual.

THE FINAL SHROUD
The wrapping was completed by a shroud. This covered the entire mummy and was held in place by a long bandage running from head to toe and crossed by horizontal bands.

SHROUD FRAGMENT
Numbers had many meanings to the ancient Egyptians. Traditionally, mummies were wrapped in seven shrouds, as this was a magical number. The outer shroud was often painted with magical writings and spells to protect the mummy within.

IT'S A WRAP
In this imaginative picture of a wrapping, an assistant is busy pouring the resin used to hold the bandages together. Lying on a special bier (couch), the mummy is being wrapped in stages, supervised by the chief embalmer. Priests kneel at the feet of the mummy, reciting sacred spells. In the background, more assistants are trying to get the mummy case (pp. 24–29) down the stairs.

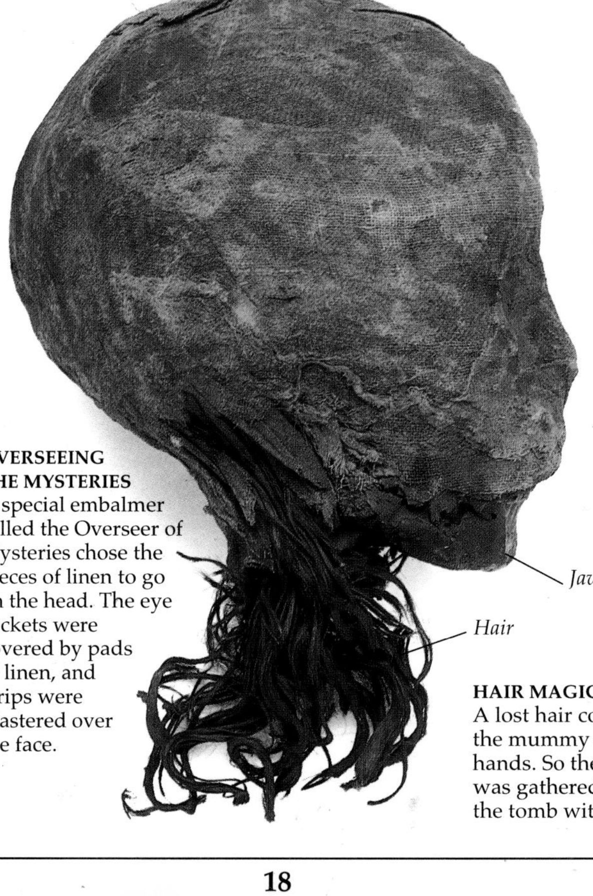

OVERSEEING THE MYSTERIES
A special embalmer called the Overseer of Mysteries chose the pieces of linen to go on the head. The eye sockets were covered by pads of linen, and strips were plastered over the face.

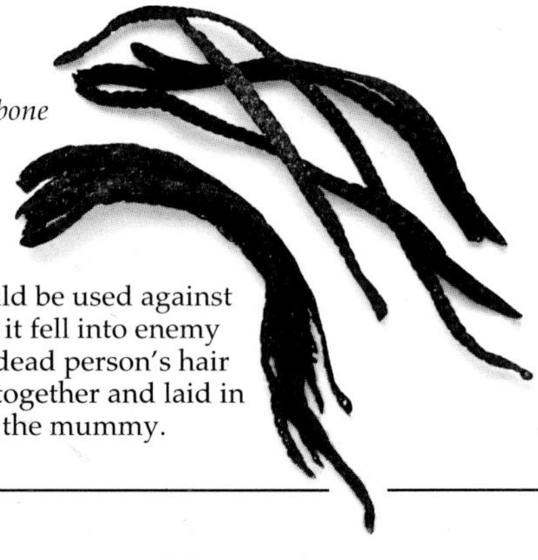

HAIR MAGIC
A lost hair could be used against the mummy if it fell into enemy hands. So the dead person's hair was gathered together and laid in the tomb with the mummy.

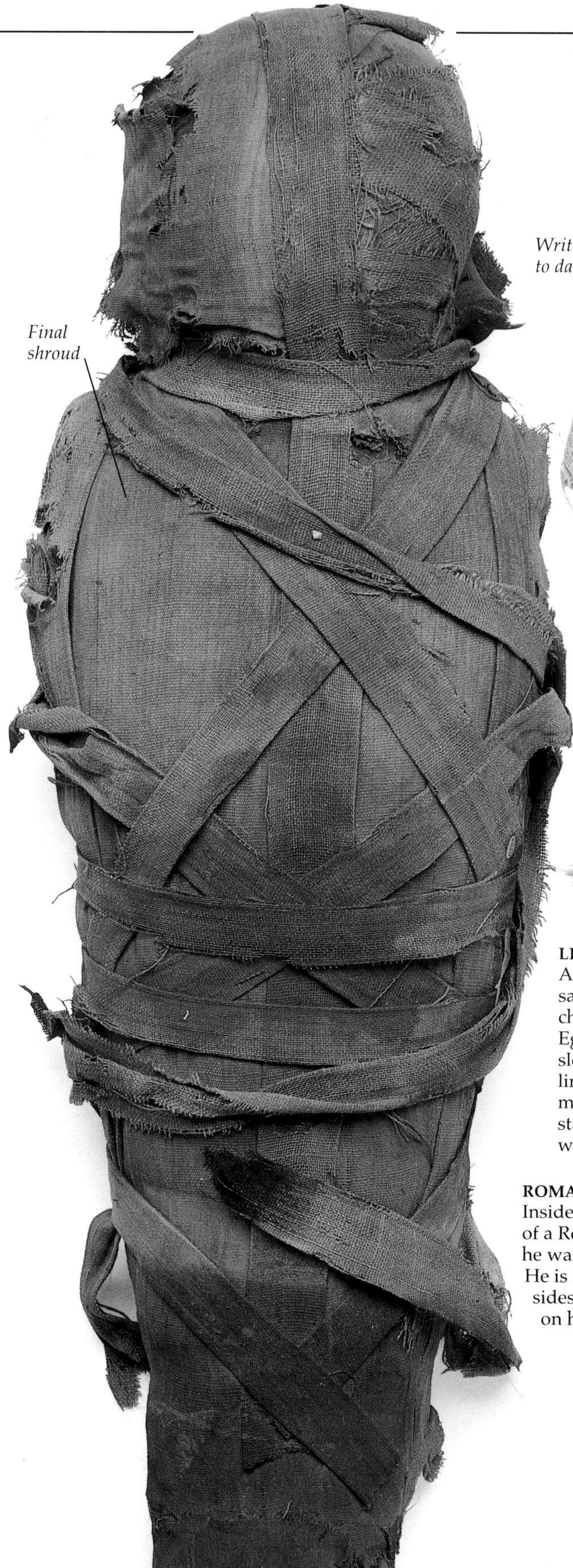

LINEN OF YESTERDAY
All the wrappings above were unrolled from the same mummy. The linen varies a lot in quality. The cheapest was old household cloth. This explains a sad Egyptian funeral song in which the dead person is said to be sleeping in the "cast-off linen of yesterday." This domestic linen is well worn and has often been darned. The best mummy wrappings were clothes used to dress statues of gods in the temples. Writing on wrappings can be used to date mummies.

ROMAN BOY
Inside these wrappings is the body of a Roman boy. X-rays show that he was about eight when he died. He is lying with his hands by his sides and is wearing a bracelet on his right wrist.

TOOTSIES
Even the toenails on this beautifully bandaged foot have been individually wrapped.

A French archaeologist discovers a mummy in the ruins of Antinoe, 1896

Mummy masks

A BEAUTIFUL MASK did more than protect the mummy's face – it could also act as a substitute head if the mummy's real head was lost or damaged. When the dead person's spirit (the *Ba*, p. 28) returned to the tomb, it could recognize the mummy by its mask. One of the most famous works of art in the world is the stunning gold mask found on Tutankhamun's mummy (pp. 11, 73). The masks of pharaohs may all have been made of solid gold, often inlaid with beautiful gemstones. The use of gold was connected to the belief that the sun god, with whom the mummy hoped to be united, had flesh of pure gold. Less important mummies wore masks made from cartonnage, a sort of paper-mâché of linen or scrap papyrus gummed together with plaster or resin. The wet cartonnage was molded to fit the mummy. Once it had hardened, it could then be gilded (covered in gold leaf) or painted in rich colors.

ALL DRESSED UP AND NOWHERE TO GO
This Roman mummy mask shows a woman dressed up in her best clothes and wearing her favorite jewelry. She is even wearing make-up so she will look her best for the gods.

FIT FOR A PRINCESS
This cartonnage mask from about 1900 B.C. belonged to a wealthy woman. She has not been identified, but the beautiful vulture headdress she is wearing suggests that she may have been a princess.

GREEK GOLD
Cartonnage mummy masks were particularly popular by Greek and Roman times (pp. 21,124). This elegant gilded mask is rich in raised decoration, a typical feature of the period.

Floral wreath

Curly wig

SPITTING IMAGE
Ancient Egyptian masks were usually idealized, with perfect features and a calm and noble expression. Greek mummies (above) wore more personal masks with realistic features and vividly painted details. These masks seem to represent real people.

WOODEN FEATURES
This mask was carved from wood and then painted. It comes from 1350 B.C. – the same period in which Tutankhamun was pharaoh (pp. 72–73).

Pierced ears for wearing studs

Collar of lotus petals

Eye of Horus (wedjat)

Ba *(soul) bird*

EVERY PICTURE TELLS A STORY
This cartonnage mask from the Roman period is gilded and painted with many religious scenes. Glass eyes were added to create a more lifelike appearance.

Gods holding the Feather of Truth

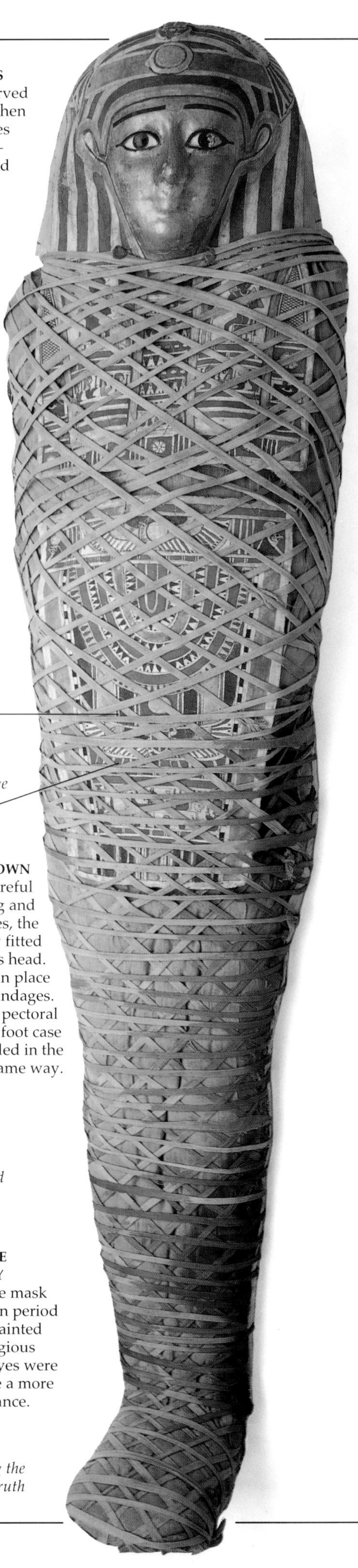

Linen strips holding mask and pectoral in place

Pectoral, a painted cartonnage chest decoration

TIED DOWN
After the careful embalming and wrapping processes, the mask was finally fitted over the mummy's head. It was then lashed in place with more bandages. Often a decorated pectoral (chest plate) and foot case (p. 29) were added in the same way.

Amulets and magic charms

ANCIENT EGYPTIANS WORE AMULETS, or charms, after they died, just as they did in life. They believed these charms had magical properties to protect the body from evil or bring good luck. Many different kinds of amulets, often representing plants, animals, or parts of the body, were placed inside a mummy's wrappings. Several hundred amulets have been found on a single mummy. They were positioned on the body according to the Book of the Dead (pp. 34–35), and many were inscribed with excerpts from these sacred writings. The particular stone or material used for the amulet was believed to give it extra power. Priests often spoke spells and prayers as the sacred amulets were placed on the mummy.

Clenched fist, to give power of action

Two finger amulet laid on embalming incision

THE THREE GRACES
Between them, the mother goddess Isis (right), her son Horus (center), and her sister Nephthys (left) gave powerful overall protection to the mummy.

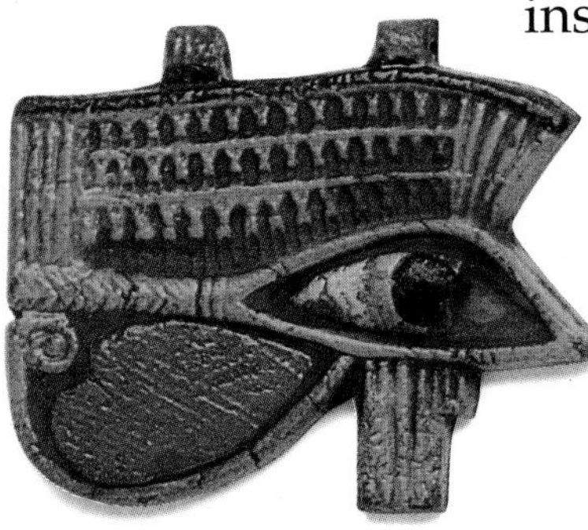

EYE OF HORUS
According to an ancient legend, the god Horus had his eye miraculously restored after he had lost it in a fight with evil. This eye symbol, known as the wedjat eye, became connected to healing. It was thought to protect the mummy's health and give the body new vitality.

Taweret

Bes

ODD COUPLE
Taweret the pregnant hippopotamus was the goddess of childbirth. Her lion-maned assistant, Bes, was a dwarf who protected women and children.

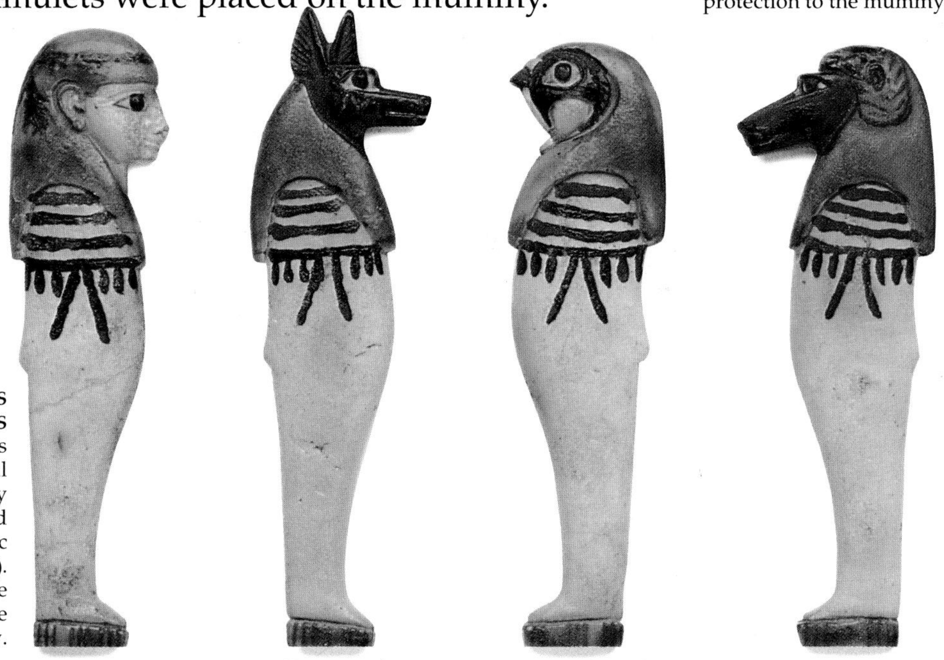

FOUR SONS OF HORUS
These amulets guarded the vital organs, usually removed and placed in canopic jars (pp. 16–17). They are made from faience, a type of glazed pottery.

Imsety (human head)

Duamutef (jackal head)

Qebehsenuef (falcon head)

Hapy (baboon head)

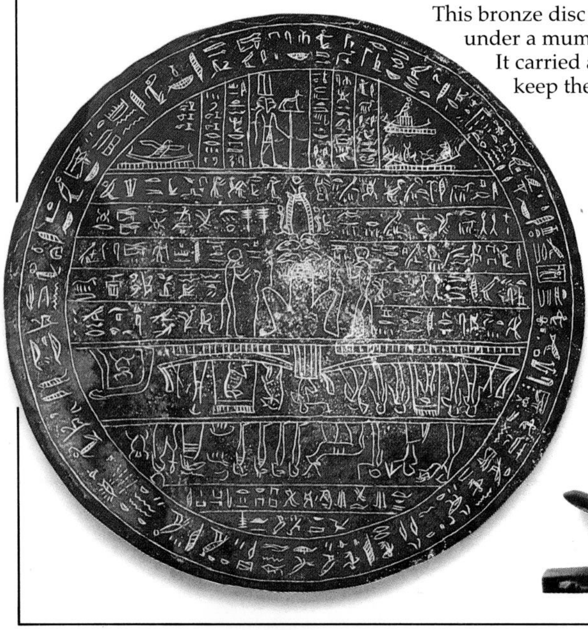

HEAD WARMER
This bronze disc was tucked under a mummy's head. It carried a spell meant to keep the head warm.

Headrest amulet made of obsidian

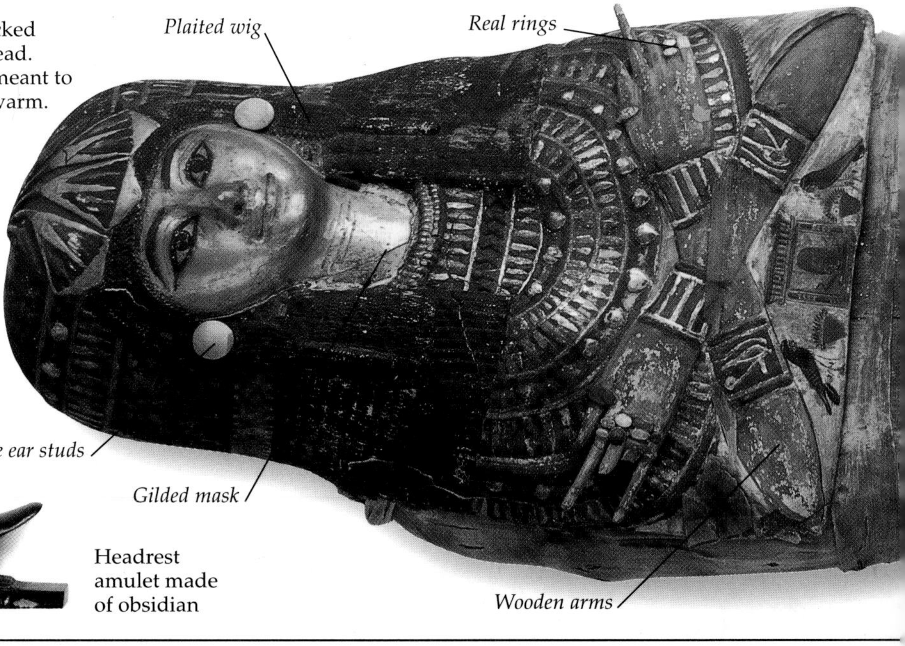

WINGED HEART SCARAB
Egyptians thought that intelligence dwelled in the heart, not the brain. This heart amulet made sure that the mummy went into the afterlife with all of his or her wits intact.

Falcon head

GIRDLE OF ISIS
This knot amulet represents Isis, the mother goddess. It is made of red stone, to represent her blood. Placed on the chest, the girdle was a powerful symbol that protected the mummy.

STAIRWAY TO HEAVEN
These steps symbolize the stairs on Osiris' throne, which every mummy's spirit would have to climb (pp. 80–81).

Papyrus reed (p. 32)

Counterpoise, made of blue faience

Heart, made from a red-and-white stone called breccia

CLOSE TO THE MUMMY'S HEART
This heart scarab has no wings. These important amulets were often set in a frame and sewn on top of the mummy's wrappings. The ancient Egyptians thought that the scarab beetle (p. 118) was born magically from a ball of dung. So it was not surprising that they associated it with rebirth after death. A spell from the Book of the Dead that would help in the Weighing of the Heart (p. 35) was written on the other side of the amulet.

Shen, a circle of cord, a symbol of completeness and eternity

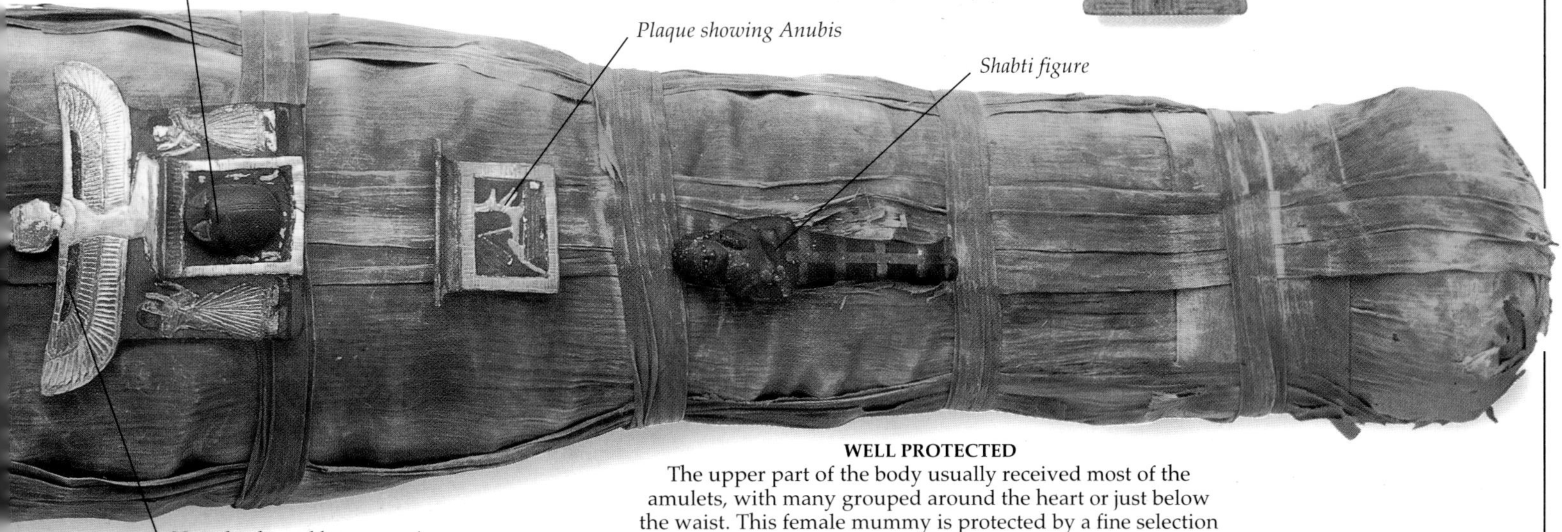

WELL PROTECTED
The upper part of the body usually received most of the amulets, with many grouped around the heart or just below the waist. This female mummy is protected by a fine selection of amulets – though most are still hidden among her bandages. She is also wearing some of her favorite jewelry.

A MUMMY'S NEST
This nest of mummy cases was made for Henutmehit, a priestess in the Egyptian capital of Thebes around 1250 B.C. The fine gold decoration suggests that she was very important. Her mummy, which has not been found, would have been protected by the mummy cover. This has an upper and lower part, both made of cartonnage. The mummy was then laid into two wooden cases, with the inner case fitting inside the outer one. Both have eyes and eyebrows made of a black volcanic glass called obsidian.

Mummy cases

AFTER AN ANCIENT EGYPTIAN HAD BEEN EMBALMED and bandaged, his or her body was placed in a coffin or mummy case. The case protected the mummy from wild animals and tomb thieves. More importantly, it was regarded as a substitute body and a house for the dead person's spirit. Mummy cases changed a lot through ancient Egypt's long history. The first ones were usually just plain rectangular wooden boxes. By the Middle Kingdom, about 2000 B.C., wealthy people were being placed inside two mummy cases for extra protection. Around the same time, the first mummiform (mummy-shaped) cases began to appear. By the New Kingdom, from 1567 to 1085 B.C., both inner and outer mummiform coffins were popular.

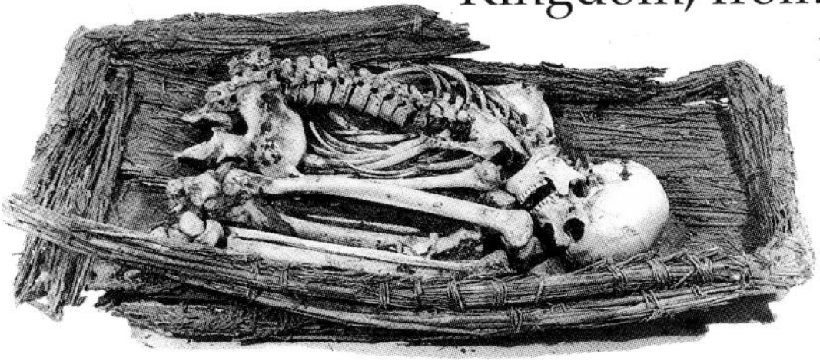

EARLY MUMMY CASE
About 5,000 years ago, an ancient Egyptian was placed in this reed basket and buried in the hot sand. Like a sand mummy (p. 6), he or she was laid in a hunched-up position with the knees tucked up by the face. But the basket stopped the sand from preserving the body, so only a skeleton remains.

FINISHING TOUCHES
This painting comes from the walls of the tomb of Ipuy, a sculptor during the reign of Ramesses the Great (pp. 70, 122). It shows workers putting the finishing touches on Ipuy's wooden mummy cases.

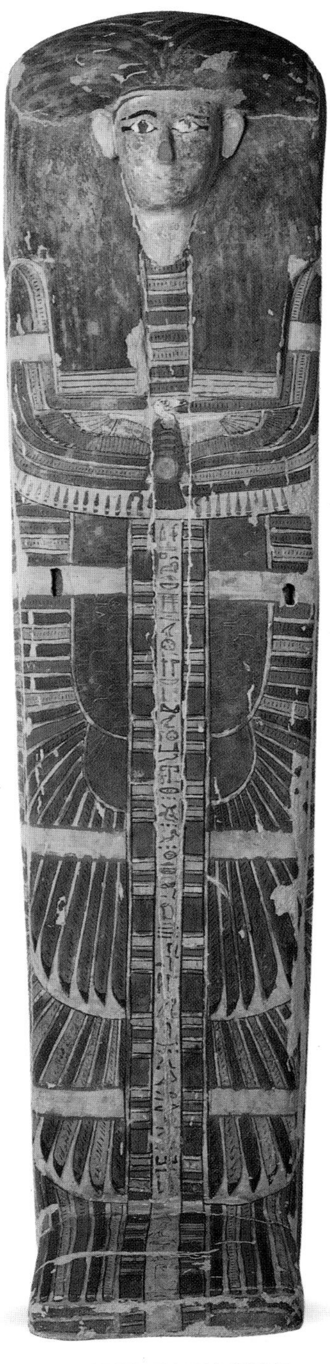

WRAPPED IN FEATHERS
A vulture's feathers protect the owner of this mummy case lid. It is known as a *rishi* case, from the Arabic word for feathered.

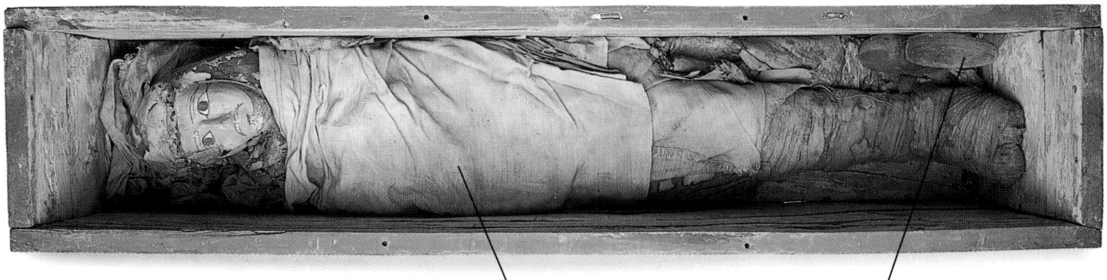

FACING THE RISING SUN
A masked man called Ankhef lies in his rectangular coffin from around 2020 B.C. At some point he must have been turned around, because he should be lying on his left side, with his head on the headrest, which is now by his feet. Mummies often faced east, so they could see the sun, a symbol of rebirth, rise over the desert each morning.

PAINTED EYES
False eyes were painted on the east side of this wooden inner coffin (c. 2000 B.C.). Lying on its side, the mummy could "look out" through the eyes. Below them is a painted door, for the mummy's spirit to leave and reenter the coffin.

Continued on next page

Outer coffin lid — Inner coffin — Masked mummy — Unwrapped mummy

TINY NEST FOR A TINY MUMMY
This is one of two tiny nests of coffins found among all the treasures in Tutankhamun's tomb (pp. 72–73). It contained the mummified body of an unborn child, probably the king's daughter. The wrapped mummy was wearing a mask and lying inside a gilded inner coffin. All this fitted inside a second, outer coffin less than 19.5 inches (50 cm) long.

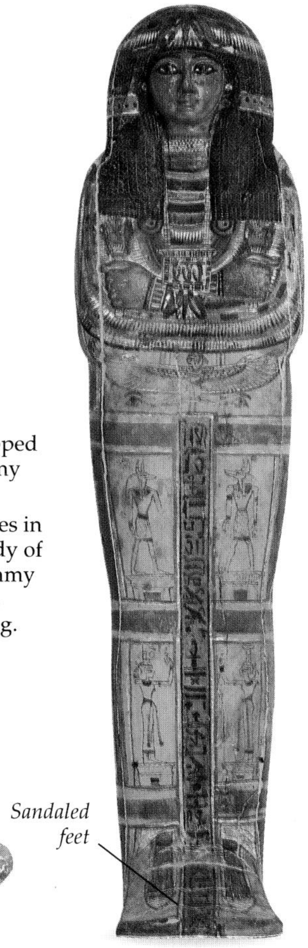

Wooden case of priestess Katebet, c. 1300 B.C.

RED BRACES
The red braces on this inner case are a common feature of the period from 1000 to 800 B.C. They show that the owner was a priest or, as in this case, a priestess. The decorations in her hair are lotus blossoms (p. 82).

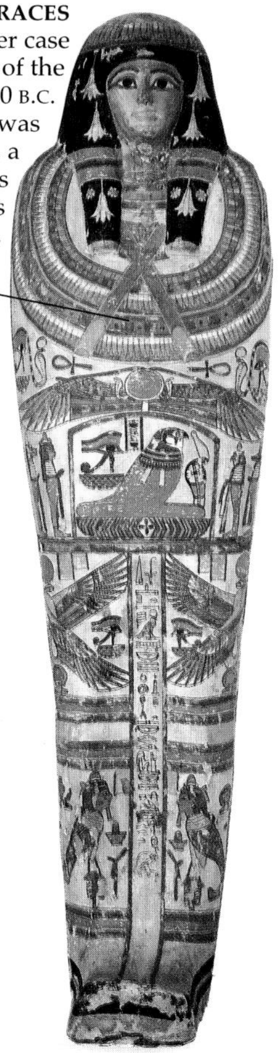

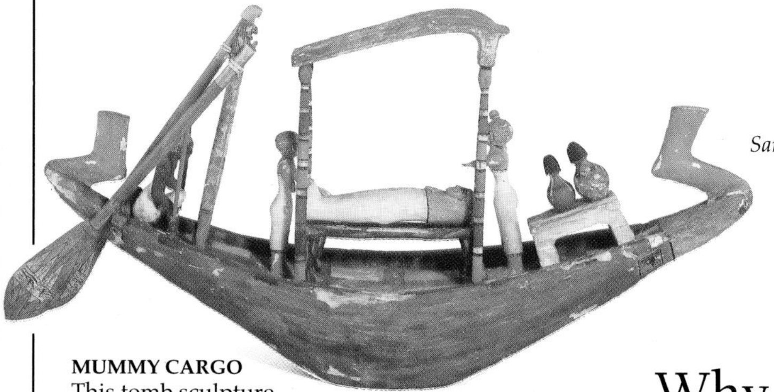

MUMMY CARGO
This tomb sculpture shows a mummy making the symbolic journey to Abydos, the city of the god Osiris (pp. 80–81).

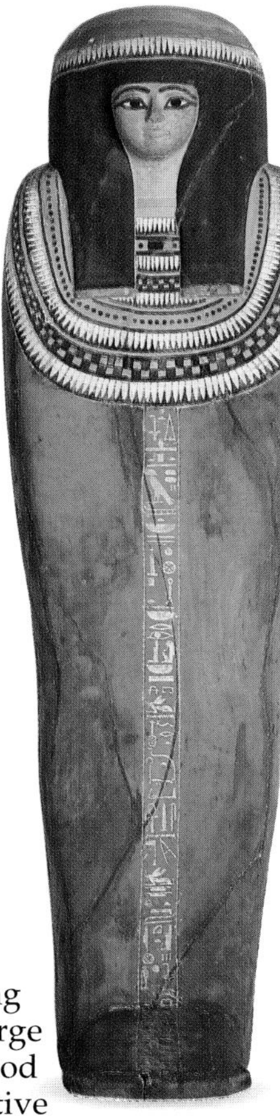

SEX CHANGE
This coffin's pink face shows that it was made for a woman. But the inscription says the owner was a man, an official called Nesperennub, who lived around 800 B.C. Egyptians often took over other people's coffins in this way.

Why cartonnage?

Wood was the ideal material for making mummy cases. But there are very few large trees in Egypt, and the best pieces of wood had to be imported. An excellent alternative was cartonnage (p. 20), which was cheap, light, and easy to shape and paint.

OFF TO FRANCE
Napoleon's army (p. 51) removed many mummy cases from their tombs and carried them back to France. Most are now in the Louvre Museum in Paris.

Detail from Léon Cogniet's paintings on the ceiling of the Campana room in the Louvre, showing one of Napoleon's soldiers transporting a mummy case

MAGIC SYMBOLS
The symbols painted on cases were meant to protect the mummy or help it on the difficult voyage to the afterlife. Apart from gods and magic symbols, decoration included floral wreaths, elaborate wigs and collars, and jewelery. This is a selection of the most popular symbols.

Mummy case decoration

There is nothing sad or depressing about Egyptian mummy cases, which are painted in bright and joyful colors. This is because the Egyptians were confident that the dead person had left for a better world. Skilled artists painted the surfaces with beautiful hieroglyphs and religious images. Scenes from the Book of the Dead (pp. 34–35) were common. Other scenes show the sun god, Re, whom the dead person was thought to join in heaven, or the scarab beetle, a symbol of rebirth (p. 118). The various gods associated with Osiris, in particular the four Sons of Horus (p. 22), were also painted on many coffins. Another popular figure was the sky goddess, Nut, who is often seen on the lid or floor of the coffin, with her feathery wings wrapped around the mummy in protection.

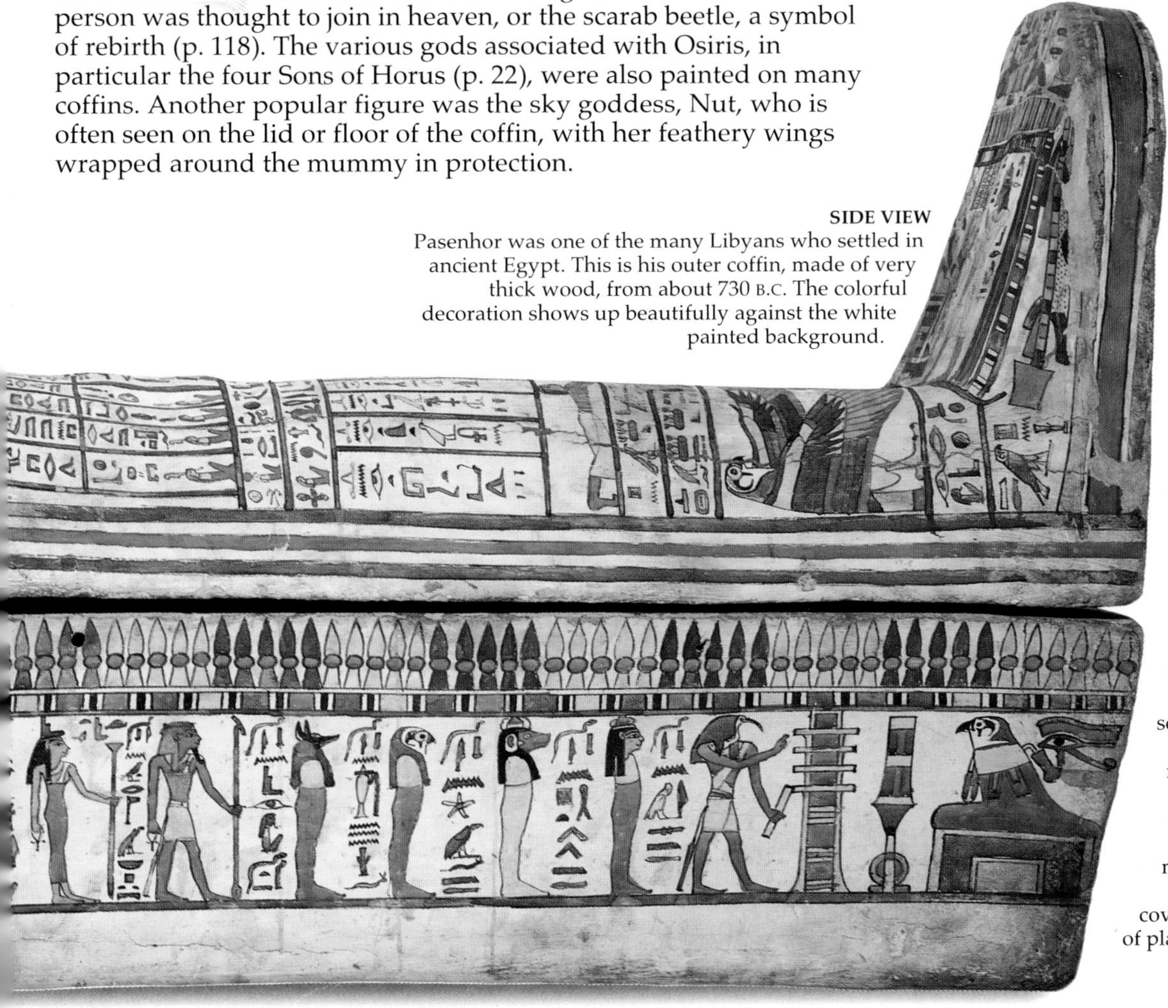

SIDE VIEW
Pasenhor was one of the many Libyans who settled in ancient Egypt. This is his outer coffin, made of very thick wood, from about 730 B.C. The colorful decoration shows up beautifully against the white painted background.

MUMMY BOARD
Mummiform boards were sometimes put on top of the mummy. This board of a priestess from 950–900 B.C. is made of carved wood. This is covered by a layer of plaster painted in raised relief.

Continued on next page

Later mummy cases

By the Late Period of ancient Egyptian history, mummy case production was a thriving industry. Ready-made coffins could be bought off the rack in a range of sizes and styles. Usually an inner, cartonnage case was fitted inside one or two outer cases made of wood. The surface decorations became more and more complicated, and large gods and goddesses were painted on the insides. Designs and hieroglyphs naming and praising the owner were often added, to give each coffin a personal touch.

WHAT'S YOUR SIZE?
The largest outer cases are massive. Under three cases and layers of linen, the person was tiny in comparison.

BIG HEAD, BIG WIG
The outer coffin lid of Nesmin, from about 350 B.C. has a huge head. This is sunk into rounded shoulders carrying a big wig and collar.

Mummy with Ba *bird*

Hieroglyphs read "all life and power"

SURROUNDED BY GODS
A woman named Seshepenmehit was buried in these two wooden coffins around 650 B.C. The floor of her outer coffin is decorated with a figure of the god Ptah-Sokar-Osiris, a symbol of birth, death, and the afterlife. Both coffin lids are covered in columns of hieroglyphs and scenes from the Book of the Dead (pp. 34–35).

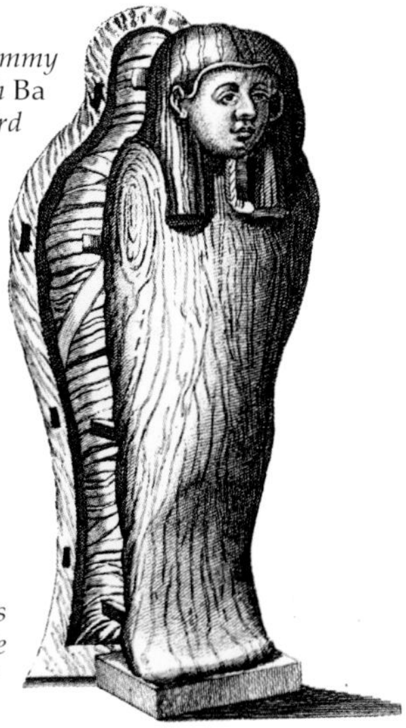

AND ON THE INSIDE...
One of the earliest European pictures of an Egyptian mummy, this engraving was published by a French consul to Egypt in 1735. It shows how the pegs in a wooden mummy case join the lid and base.

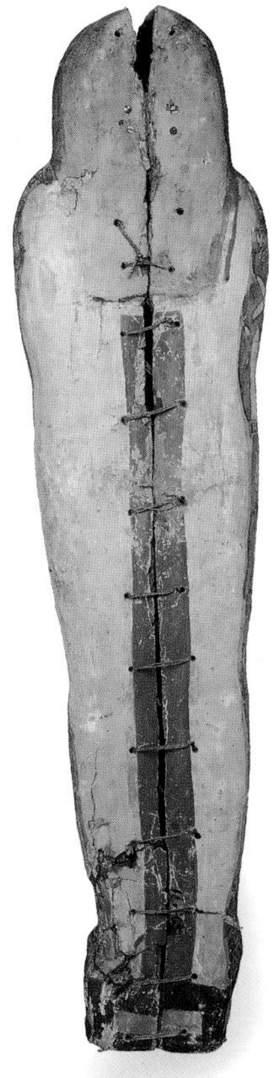

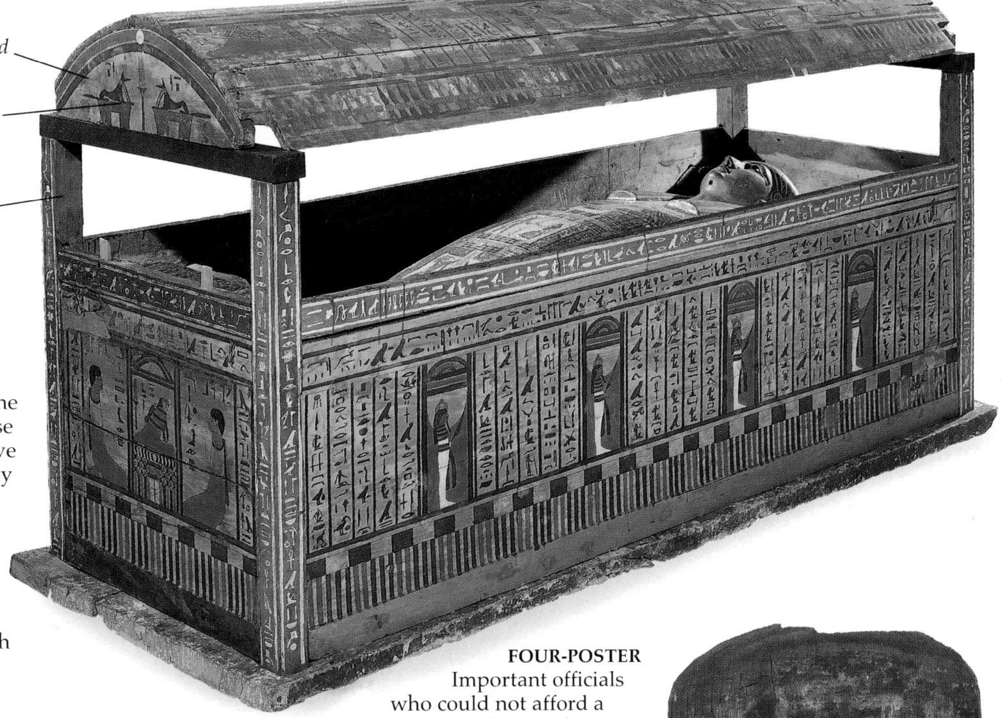

Curved lid

Figures of Anubis

Corner posts

LACED FROM BEHIND
Wooden mummy cases came in two parts, the lid and the base. But inner cases made of cartonnage were normally made in one piece. This cartonnage case from c. 850 B.C. would have held the wrapped mummy of a young girl. The mummy must have been placed inside while the linen was damp and flexible. Once the case had dried, its back was laced up like a corset, with thongs that sealed the mummy in. Only then was the case painted.

FOUR-POSTER
Important officials who could not afford a sarcophagus might stretch to an extra outer coffin. The priest Hor (c. 680 B.C.) had two mummiform cases, which lay inside a large rectangular box. Also made of wood, this third coffin has a curved lid held up by four corner posts. Every inch of the cases is covered with gods, hieroglyphs, and magic spells.

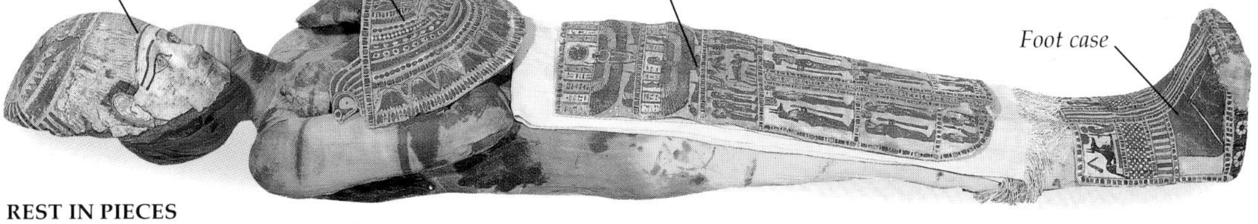

Face mask

Cartonnage collar with falcon head at both ends

Apron, a painted body decoration

Foot case

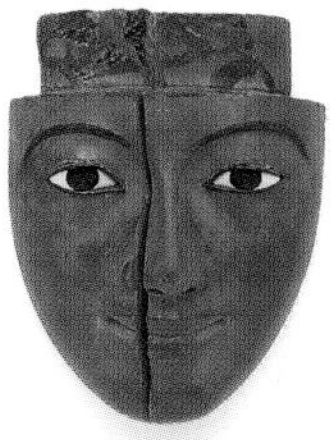

NOT MASKS
These faces were carved from wood and pegged onto mummy cases.

REST IN PIECES
The Ptolemaic period began in 323 B.C., when Egypt was conquered by Alexander the Great (p. 31). The inner cases of Ptolemaic mummies consisted of four pieces of cartonnage – the face mask, collar, apron, and foot case. These were placed directly onto the shroud and then held in place with a last layer of bandages.

Ba *bird*

Hieroglyphs

SACRED BULL
The ancient Egyptians worshiped many animals (pp. 118–119). The sacred Apis Bull was the largest and most important. There was only one Apis at any one time. He was kept in great luxury beside the temple, where he was attended by servants and a harem of cows. This painting on a foot board shows the bull carrying a mummy to its tomb.

UNDER MY TOES
Gilded sandals like these were sometimes painted under a mummy's feet. The figures painted under the mummy's sandals are tiny enemies, symbolizing the dead person's victory over evil.

THE LATEST FASHION, A.D. 200
In the Roman period, from 30 B.C. to A.D. 323, coffins were painted with their owners wearing daily clothes. This Roman woman left for the next world in a bright toga, worn with a stepped wig and a lot of jewelry, including gold rings.

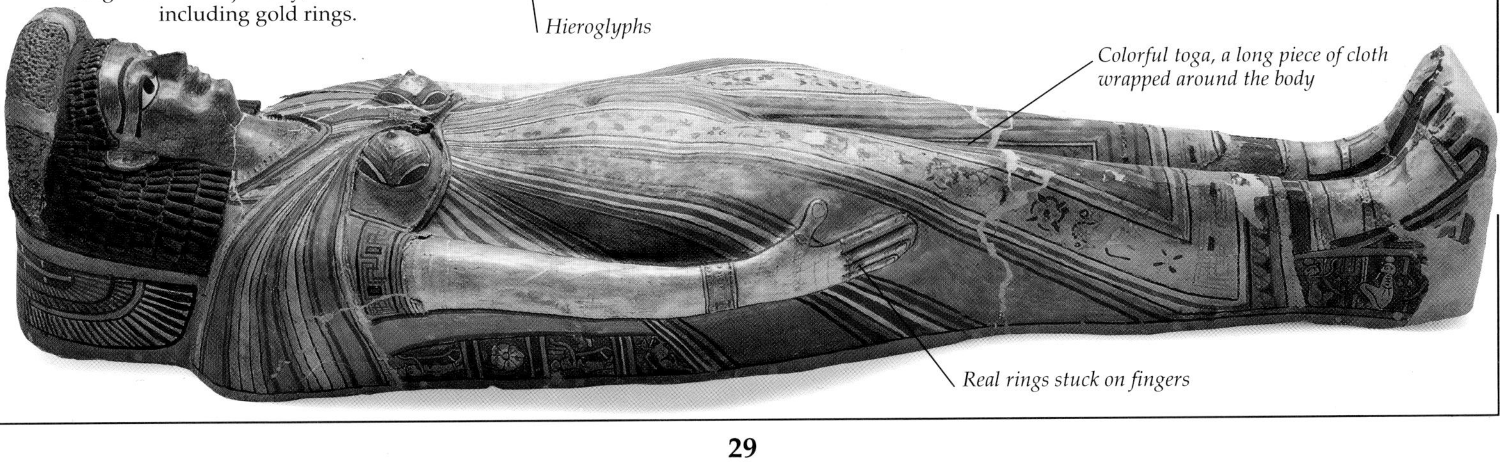

Colorful toga, a long piece of cloth wrapped around the body

Real rings stuck on fingers

Into the sarcophagus

A SARCOPHAGUS IS A COFFIN made of stone. The word means "flesh eater" in Greek, for the Greeks believed that the stone would dissolve a dead body. Sarcophagi were expensive, and only pharaohs, noblemen, or important officials were buried in them. They were also incredibly heavy, and had to be positioned in the tomb by gangs of workmen. During the funeral, the mummy was carried into the tomb and sealed in the sarcophagus. The first sarcophagi were plain rectangular boxes, but later ones were rounded to look like the mummies lying inside them.

HEAVY WEIGHT
This huge sarcophagus of basalt is nearly 9 ft (3 m) tall and weighs 4.5 tons. It belonged to Wahibra, an inspector of scribes.

DIGNIFIED IN DEATH
One of the most beautiful royal sarcophagi belongs to Seti I, a great warrior and the father of Ramses the Great (pp. 70, 122–123). His tomb, found in 1817, is cut deep into a cliff in the Valley of the Kings (p. 70). The pharaoh's sarcophagus was in the burial chamber over 330 ft (100 m) below ground. It is made of calcite, a semi-transparent stone. Seti I's mummy, found separately in the royal cache of 1881 (pp. 70–71), was remarkably well-preserved.

VICEROY'S COFFIN
This is the inner sarcophagus of Merymose, the Viceroy of Nubia, c. 1380 B.C. It is one of the first stone coffins made for an important person who was *not* a pharaoh.

Feathered rishi *decoration*

Hieroglyphs, once inlaid with blue-green pigment

Fragment from lid of Seti I's sarcophagus, which shattered when lifted

Alexander the Great

ROYAL BATHTUB
The last real Egyptian pharaoh, Nactanebo II, was buried in this huge sarcophagus. It ended up in Alexandria, where the Greeks used it as a public bathtub. Before the hieroglyphics were translated, it was thought to have belonged to the Greek ruler Alexander the Great. Alexander's body has never been found, but ancient writings claim that he was preserved in a glass sarcophagus full of honey.

Drain holes added for use as bathtub

BACK AT REST
Tutankhamun (pp. 11, 73) is the only pharaoh still lying in his tomb. His mummy has been returned to its outer gilded coffin and laid back in the huge sarcophagus. This stone coffin was originally housed inside four gilded shrines large enough to drive a car into. Behind it are wall paintings showing sacred funeral rituals.

PROFESSIONAL WEEPERS
Important Egyptians hired mourners for their funerals. These women would cry, wail, wave their arms, and throw dust in the air as the mummy was dragged into the tomb and laid in the sarcophagus.

Howard Carter (far left) watches as Tutankhamun's outer mummy case is lifted out of the sarcophagus

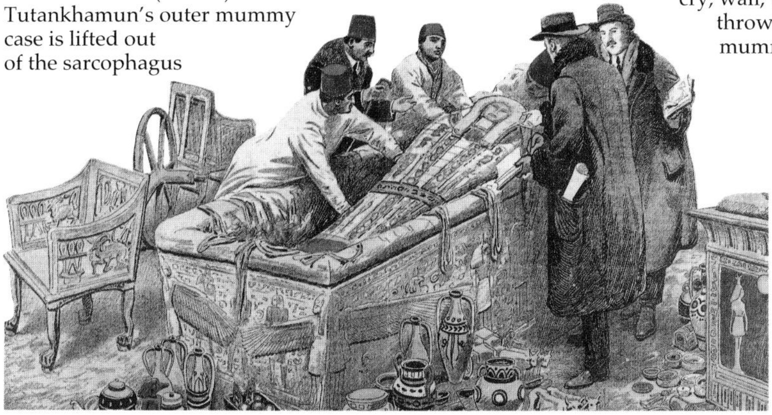

WELL ARMED
This sarcophagus lid, made of red granite, covered the mummy of Setau, the Viceroy of Nubia. He was buried at Thebes around 1230 B.C. In his hands he holds two magical symbols, the girdle of Isis (p. 23) and the djed pillar (pp. 80–81).

HOUSE OF SPIRITS
Like the oldest mummy cases, early sarcophagi were regarded as palaces for the dead. This rectangular sarcophagus made of red granite comes from the Old Kingdom, around 2500 B.C. At either end are false doors, for the mummy's spirit to pass through when it leaves and reenters the coffin.

False door

Workers for the afterlife

THE ANCIENT EGYPTIANS were an agricultural people, and every year they were all required to do some farming and irrigation work for the government. But rich Egyptians could avoid this work by paying someone to do it for them. When the mummy got to the Field of Reeds, as the Egyptians called heaven, he or she would have to do similar work, sowing and reaping for the god Osiris (pp. 80–81). So from early on, wealthy people were buried with shabtis (worker figures) to do their work after death. Shabtis were inscribed with Chapter Six of the Book of the Dead, which promised "O shabti, if the deceased is called upon to do any of the work required there…you shall say 'Here I am, I will do it.'" In the early New Kingdom (about 1500 B.C.), a single shabti seemed to be enough to guarantee an easy afterlife. But by 1000 B.C., rich Egyptians were being buried with 401 shabtis, one for every day of the year, plus 36 bosses, armed with whips to keep the workers from slacking as they sweated in the heavenly fields.

Overseer or boss shabti wearing skirt and carrying whip

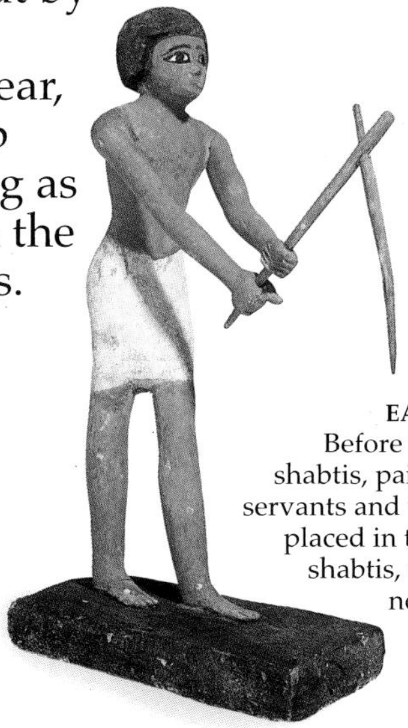

EARLY DIGGER
Before the custom of shabtis, painted wooden servants and workers were placed in tombs. Unlike shabtis, this worker is not shaped like a mummy.

BOX OF WORKERS
Shabti figures were often packed up in beautifully painted wooden boxes. This shabti box belonged to the priestess Henutmehit, whose golden coffins are on page 24.

Dead priestess gives offerings of food to gods

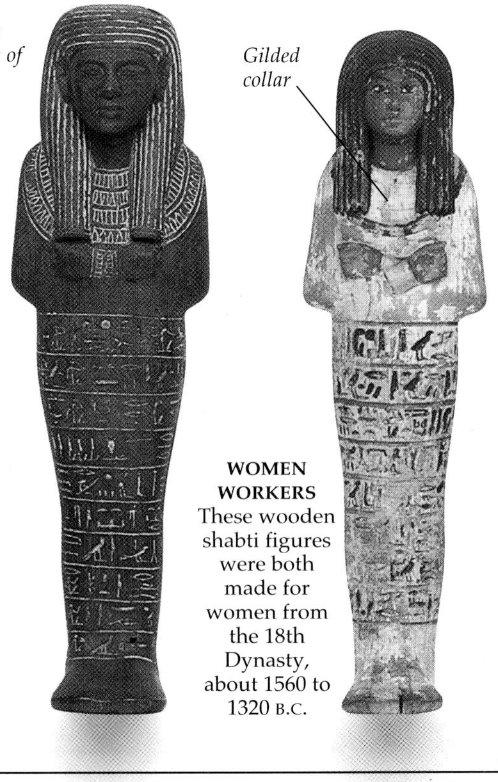

Gilded collar

WOMEN WORKERS
These wooden shabti figures were both made for women from the 18th Dynasty, about 1560 to 1320 B.C.

Royal cartouche

Shabti of Pharaoh Seti I

Nemes *headdress*

Shabti of Pharaoh Amosis

Cartouche, oval-shaped inscription with king's name written in hieroglyphs

Shabti of Pharaoh Amenhotep III

ROYAL SHABTIS
The earliest surviving royal shabti (above) belonged to Amosis, a pharaoh who died in c. 1546. It is wearing a *Nemes* headdress made from cloth folded over the hair. Other royal shabtis, like this one of Amenhotep III (left), wear the domed crown of Upper Egypt.

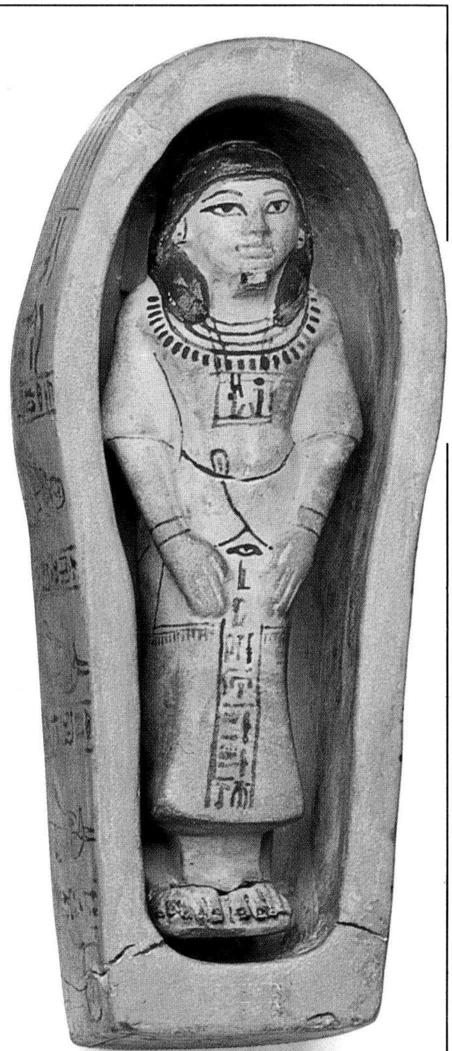

MODEL COFFINS
Shabtis were sometimes put in elaborate cases made to look like real mummy cases. This one is made of blue faience.

WELL EQUIPPED
Many shabtis carry hoes, picks, seed baskets, and other tools. These tell us a lot about farming in ancient Egypt.

ALL SORTS
Stone, wood, clay, wax, bronze – shabtis were made of all kinds of materials. But the most common was faience, a type of glazed ware.

Pick

Hoe

Lid of inner wooden case on right

Stone shabti in wooden mummy case and square outer coffin

Journey to the afterlife

THE ANCIENT EGYPTIANS imagined there existed an underworld below the earth, which they called Duat. Parts of it were full of perils, like poisonous snakes, lakes of fire, and executioners. Spells to counteract these dangers were often written on coffins, together with a map of the underworld. Eventually the spells and map were put on ornate scrolls of papyrus instead, which are now known as the Books of the Dead, since many were discovered on or near mummies. The book was a passport through all the dangers lurking in Duat. If you could recite the correct spells, you could pass through unharmed. The ultimate danger was to fail the test set for you in the Hall of the Two Truths, where your heart was weighed against your past deeds. The papyrus helped you as much as possible to pass the examination and reach a land that was just like Egypt itself.

Outspread arms show that the god's power extended beyond its own body

Ram-headed god statue covered in black resin

RAM-HEADED GOD
Sometimes statues of underworld gods were placed in the tombs in the Valley of the Kings (p. 68). With their power to ward off evil, they were meant to protect the king as he traveled through the underworld. These gods had heads of creatures such as tortoises, hippos, and rams. They are very different from other animal-headed deities (p. 78), who flourished above ground.

HIRED MOURNERS
The more mourners at a funeral, the higher was the status of the deceased. Sometimes the family hired women to mourn at funerals. They would wave their arms, throw dust over their hair, and weep.

Dead man

Anubis, jackal-headed god of mummification

Devourer of the Dead

Thoth, ibis-headed god of wisdom, with scribe's palette

Horus, falcon-headed sky god

Osiris, god of the underworld

WEIGHING THE HEART
The heart of the dead man, bearing a record of all his past deeds, is placed on scales. Forty-two assessor gods, one for each district of Egypt – some of whom are shown at the top of the papyrus – interrogate the dead man, accusing him of various crimes, which he denies. If he has told the truth, the ibis-headed god of wisdom, Thoth, writes that he is "true of voice" and can go through to the kingdom of Osiris, who is shown enthroned under the canopy. The awful punishment for the untruthful is shown next to the scales – the goddess called the Devourer of the Dead will eat up the heart, and the deceased will not survive into the afterlife.

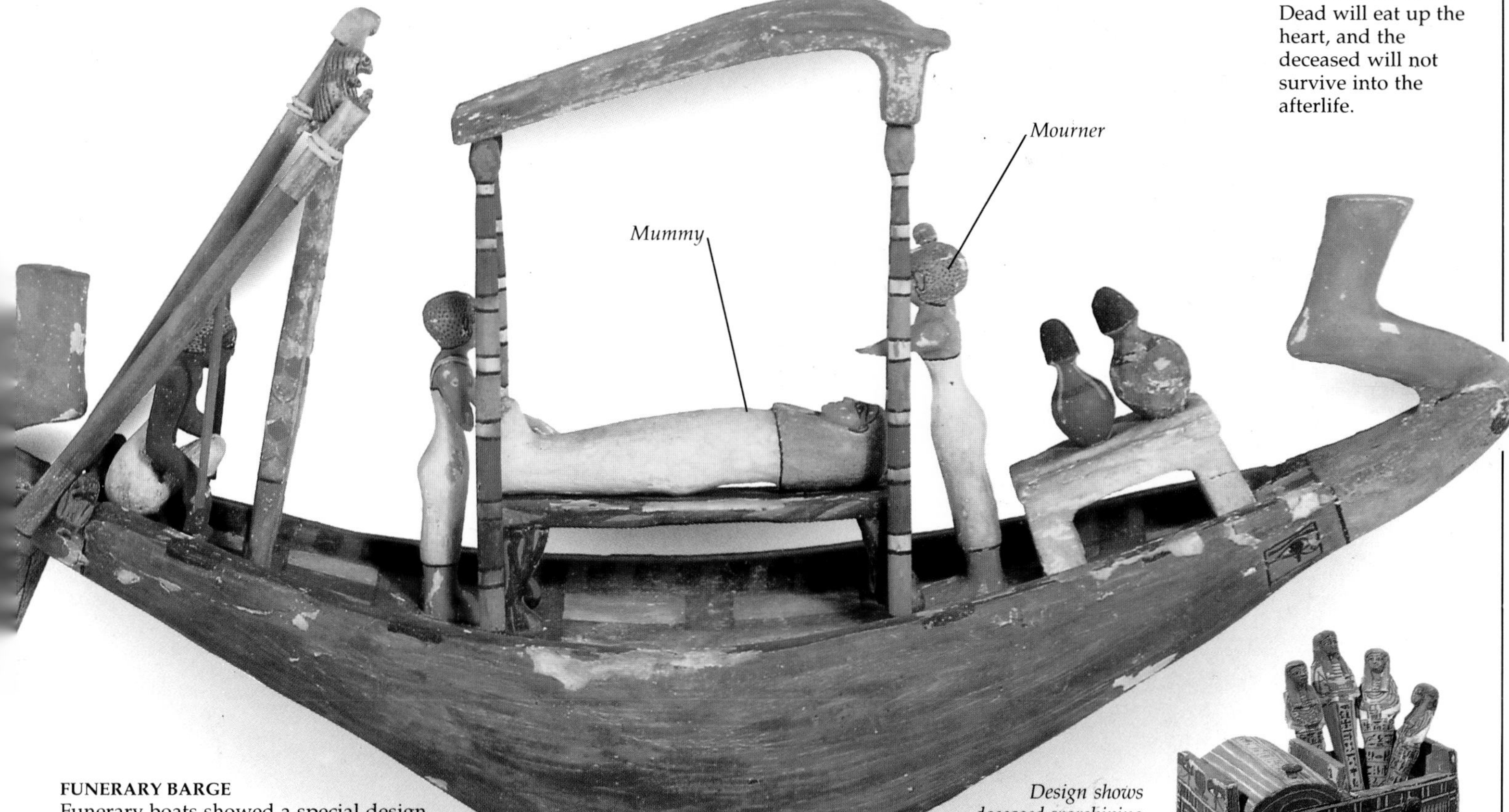

Mourner

Mummy

FUNERARY BARGE
Funerary boats showed a special design, imitating the boat used by the sun god for his journey through Duat. The curved end pieces are similar to those on boats made of bundles of papyrus stalks (p. 94). The mummified corpse travels under a canopy with two female mourners with shaven heads. These women represent the goddesses Isis and Nephrhys mourning for the murdered god Osiris. At the stern there are two large steering oars held by a seated sailor. The color green on the side of the boat (the color of crops before they ripen) symbolizes resurrection in the afterlife.

Design shows deceased worshiping the sons of Horus

MODEL SERVANTS
In the afterlife it was possible that the god Osiris would require you to do manual work in the fields. If you were a scribe or a priestess you would not want to do manual work, so you would be buried with shabti figures. These were thought to leap to life at the command of Osiris and do the work required. Some people were buried with hundreds of shabtis. Even pharaohs played safe by having them in their tombs.

Built for a king

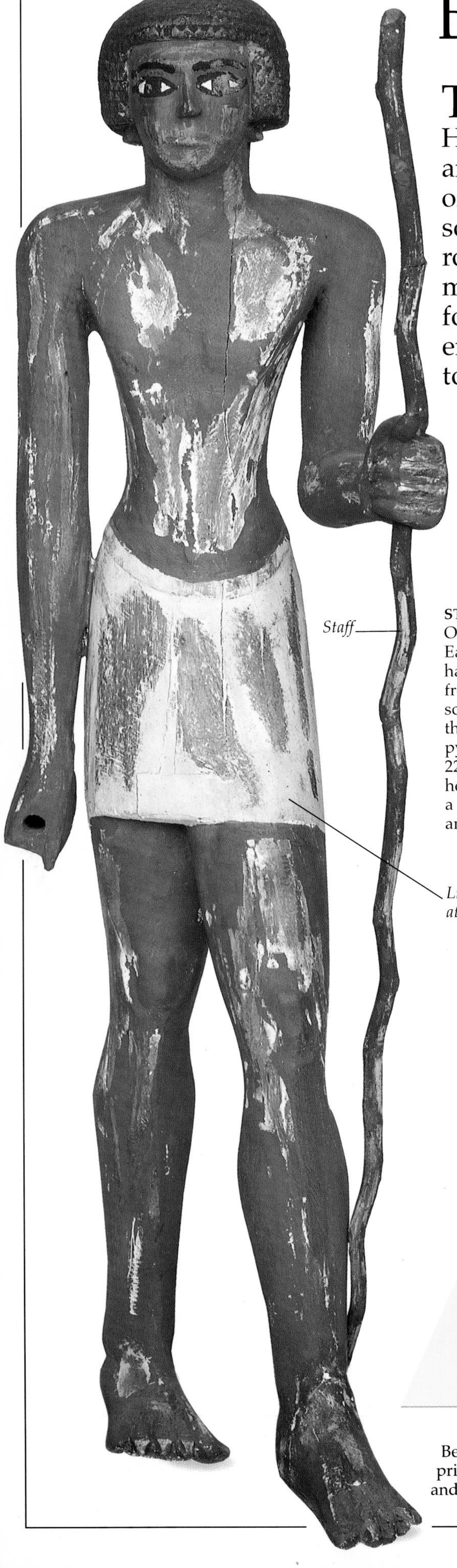

THE EGYPTIANS BELIEVED THEIR PHARAOH was a living god. He led the army in battle, passed judgment on criminals, and controlled the treasury. He also represented the unity of Egypt. In early times, most people lived in the north or the south, called Lower and Upper Egypt. It was the pharaoh's role to keep the two regions together. The centralized government meant he had all the resources of Egypt at his disposal for building his pyramid. The finest sculptors, masons, engineers, and countless workers spent years building the tomb. The laborers who dragged the stones were not slaves. They were farmers who believed that if they helped their king get to heaven, he would look after them in the next world.

STAFF OF OFFICE
Officials were very powerful. Each government department had many workers, ranging from the chief official to the scribes. Officials often built their tombs around the king's pyramid. This statue from 2250 B.C. shows an official holding a wooden staff, a sign of his rank and authority.

PYRAMID SITES
There are more than 80 pyramids in Egypt. They are all on the west bank of the Nile, where the sun sets. In the Old Kingdom, pyramids were grouped around Memphis, the capital. In the Middle Kingdom, the capital was moved upriver to Lisht, so most pharaohs built their pyramids farther south.

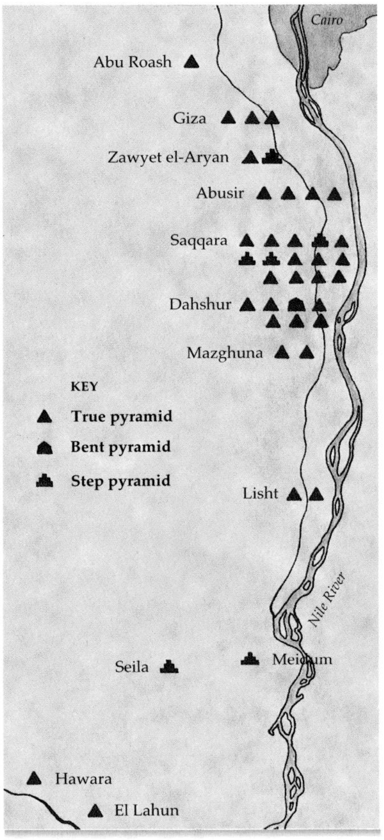

THE SOCIAL PYRAMID
Beneath the pharaoh were the royal family, nobles, and important priests, soldiers, and officials. The middle class included merchants and skilled craftsworkers. But most Egyptians were peasant-farmers.

SON OF THE SUN GOD
The pharaoh had many official titles, including Lord of the Two Lands and Son of Re, the sun god. This huge head of Radjedef was found near his pyramid at Abu Roash. The king is wearing the royal *nemes* headcloth. A cobra is poised on his brow, ready to spit fire at the king's enemies. Radjedef ruled only for eight years, between Khufu and Khafra, who built the two massive pyramids at Giza. His pyramid is ruined.

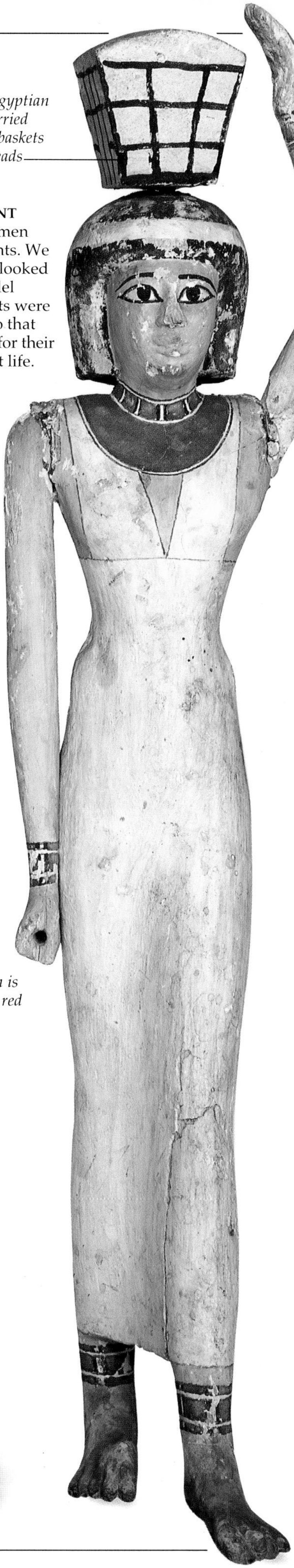

Ancient Egyptian women carried trays and baskets on their heads

HUMBLE SERVANT
Many young women worked as servants. We know what they looked like because model figures of servants were put into tombs so that they could work for their bosses in the next life.

MODEL COUPLE
In Egyptian statues, pharaohs usually have elegant, perfect features. Ordinary people are more natural and realistic. This is the court official Katep and his wife Hetepheres. He has a suntan, but his wife has pale skin, suggesting that she spent most of her time indoors. The statue was found in Katep's tomb near the Giza pyramids.

Hetepheres with her arm around her husband

Katep, who lived around 2500 B.C.

Wig

Her skin is painted a pale yellow

His skin is painted red

The great Step Pyramid

THE FIRST PYRAMID – probably the first large stone structure in human history – was built for the pharaoh Djoser at Saqqara around 2680 B.C. It was designed by the architect Imhotep, who became more famous than Djoser. The Step Pyramid is really a series of six mastabas, flat-roofed buildings with sloping sides set one on top of the other. Beneath it, cut deep into the underground rock, lie the burial chambers of Djoser and five members of his family. The king's vault was lined with granite and sealed with a three-ton plug. But it was robbed long ago – only a mummified foot was found inside.

IN THE SHADOW OF THE STEP PYRAMID
Over the following centuries, many important officials built their mastaba tombs around the mighty Step Pyramid. The walls are mostly decorated with everyday scenes. This carving comes from the tomb of the official Mereruka, c. 2300 B.C. It shows men carrying offerings of food, including ducks.

A BUILDER'S SKETCH
This is an ancient architectural drawing, probably made by builders working on the Step Pyramid. The vertical lines allowed them to figure out the exact angle of the building's sloping sides.

BUILT IN STAGES
The Step Pyramid was built around a core of desert stones. Imhotep changed his mind five times as the building progressed. He enlarged the original mastaba form twice before building a four-tiered pyramid structure on top. Then two more tiers were added by expanding the entire structure. It was finally faced with polished limestone to give a smooth finish.

The body of the pyramid is made of small stone blocks laid like bricks

Imhotep

More than 2,000 years after his death, the ancient Egyptians worshiped Imhotep as a god of wisdom. One writer called him "the inventor of the art of building with hewn stone." He is said to have written many books and became a sort of patron saint of scribes. He is often shown seated with a papyrus unrolled across his knees. He was also thought to be the son of the god Ptah, whose magic gave him the power to heal the sick.

Bronze statue of Imhotep, New Kingdom

UNFINISHED STATUE
This is one of three unfinished life-sized statues of Djoser found in his pyramid complex. Even in this worn state, the king's stern expression shows through. The spirit of a dead king was thought to emerge from the burial chamber and inhabit statues like these.

DISCOVERING THE WHEEL
How were the pyramids built? Did the Egyptians have building machines? There are many theories, but little hard evidence. This painting shows soldiers climbing a ladder on wheels. It is the only known image of a wheel from the Old Kingdom. At that time the Egyptians did not have pulleys for lifting stones.

Fine Tura limestone facing was stolen for later buildings

THE KING'S PORTRAIT
The first life-sized portrait in history is this seated statue of King Djoser. It was found in a closed chamber attached to the north side of his pyramid. Two round holes in the wall allowed the pharaoh to see the offerings left by his worshipers. The king is wearing a *nemes* headcloth, a sign of royalty, oddly poised on top of a bushy wig. His eyes were once inlaid with rock crystal. The wear and tear of 4,700 years cannot hide the king's strong personality, seen in his fierce face, prominent cheekbones, thick lips, and heavy jaw.

Nemes *headcloth*

Thick wig

False beard

One of Djoser's name in hieroglyphs

HIS LIFE'S WORK
Born in 1902, Jean-Philippe Lauer is a French architect and Egyptologist. He spent 50 years reconstructing the Step Pyramid complex at Saqqara. When he began, in 1926, the ruined columns and shattered blocks of stone lay buried in the desert sand. The model on this page is the fruit of his life's work.

The Step Pyramid complex

THE SAQQARA STEP PYRAMID was part of a large complex. Surrounding the pyramid is a series of courtyards and ceremonial buildings. Although they are small next to the pyramid, these were probably among the first large stone buildings ever made. Many are shaped and decorated like earlier structures of mud bricks, rushes, reeds, or wood. Though they are carved to look like real buildings, most of them are dummies, complete with fake doors. One courtyard was used for the special *sed* festival, held after Djoser had been king for many years. Crowds from all over Egypt came to watch the pharaoh run a course in the *sed* court. This makes the Step Pyramid the world's first sports arena! The race was a symbolic renewal of the king's power. Afterward, he was re-crowned as king of Upper and Lower Egypt on two thrones next to the *sed* court.

KIND OF BLUE
A small underground chamber lies to the south. The king was certainly buried under the pyramid, so the purpose of this second tomb is a mystery. The carvings and blue tiles may be a copy of the decoration in Djoser's palace at Memphis.

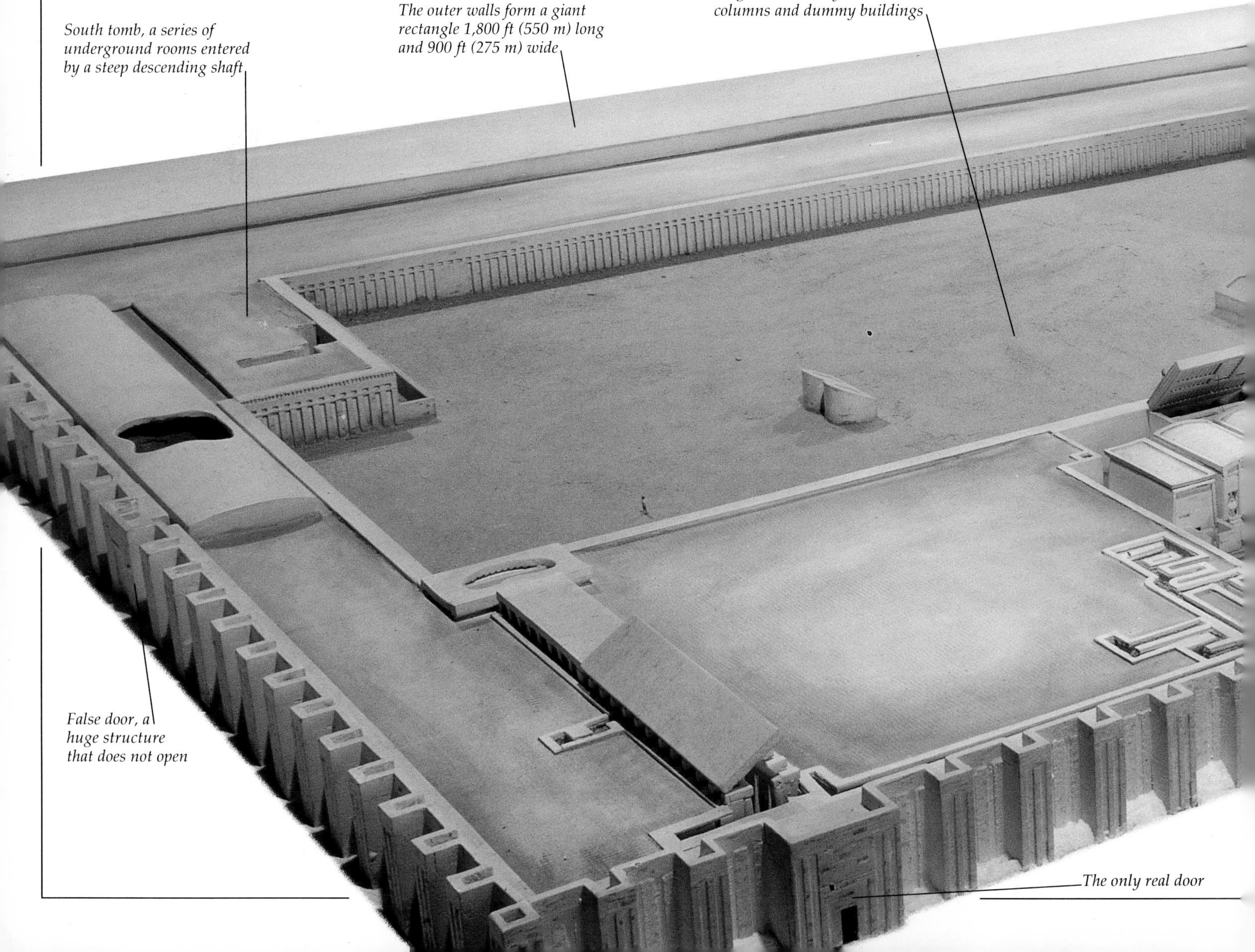

South tomb, a series of underground rooms entered by a steep descending shaft

The outer walls form a giant rectangle 1,800 ft (550 m) long and 900 ft (275 m) wide

Large south courtyard lined with columns and dummy buildings

False door, a huge structure that does not open

The only real door

Blue glazed tiles from the underground passages in the south tomb

STONE FLOWERS

These columns are along one wall of the House of the North. They were carved to look like papyrus plants, with triangular shafts like real stems. The capitals (tops) are shaped like open papyrus flowers. The Egyptians often copied nature in their architecture, so that it would blend into the living world.

STERN SUPPORT

A pavilion in the south courtyard was held up by these three columns. Statues may have stood in the alcoves between them.

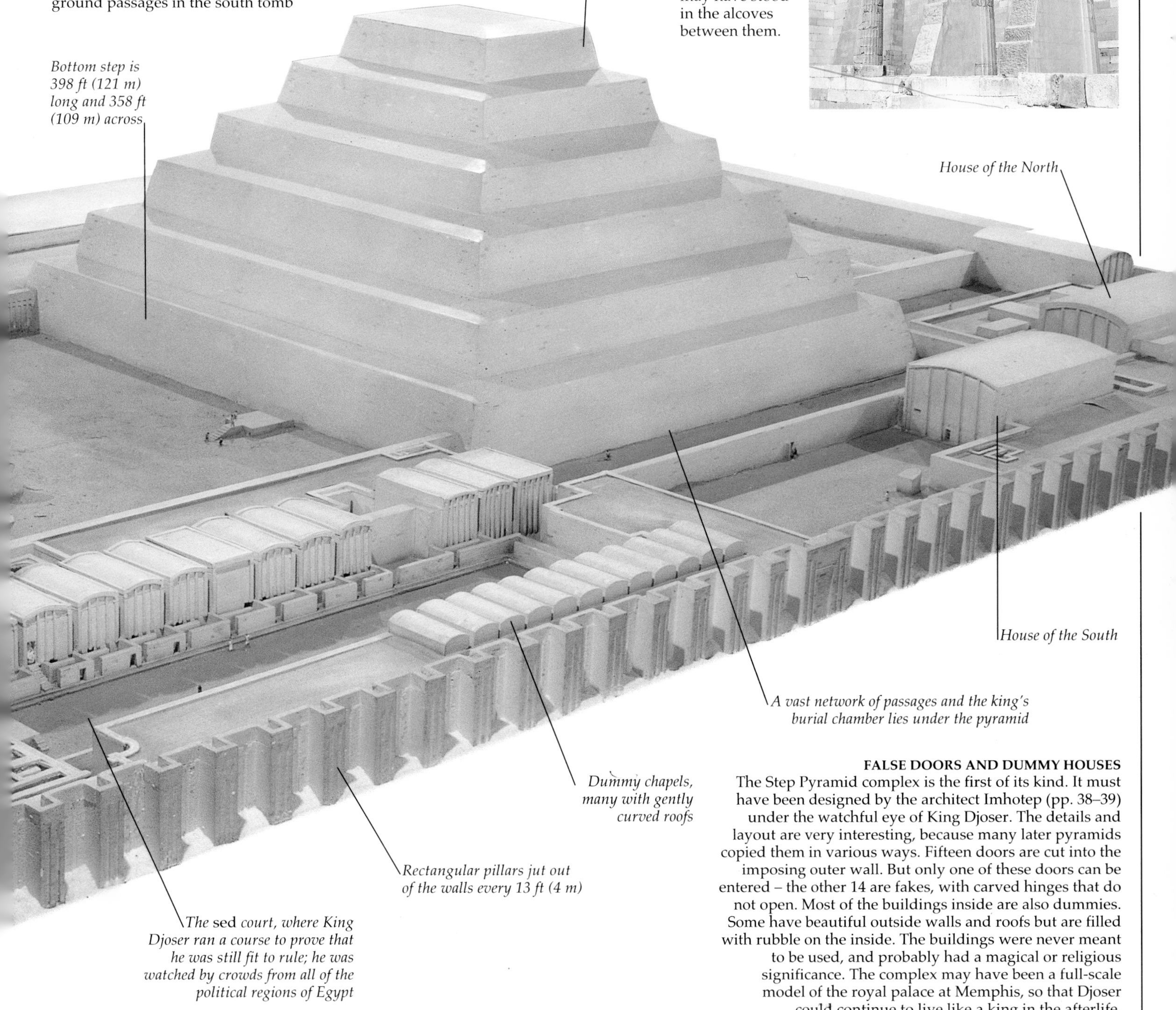

FALSE DOORS AND DUMMY HOUSES

The Step Pyramid complex is the first of its kind. It must have been designed by the architect Imhotep (pp. 38–39) under the watchful eye of King Djoser. The details and layout are very interesting, because many later pyramids copied them in various ways. Fifteen doors are cut into the imposing outer wall. But only one of these doors can be entered – the other 14 are fakes, with carved hinges that do not open. Most of the buildings inside are also dummies. Some have beautiful outside walls and roofs but are filled with rubble on the inside. The buildings were never meant to be used, and probably had a magical or religious significance. The complex may have been a full-scale model of the royal palace at Memphis, so that Djoser could continue to live like a king in the afterlife.

First true pyramids

THE PHARAOHS who followed King Djoser also built step pyramids. The familiar smooth pyramid shape was not developed until the reign of King Sneferu. In his 24 years as pharaoh (2575–2551 B.C.), he won wars in Libya and Nubia and built many new temples, fortresses, and palaces. Sneferu also built at least three – maybe even four – pyramids. His first, at Meidum, shows how building had progressed by that time. The construction of the core and outer casing is similar to Djoser's Step Pyramid. But the Meidum builders had made great advances in the handling of large blocks of stone. The main structure is made of huge slabs, not many small blocks. The builders had also devised a new way of roofing the burial chamber so it held the weight of the pyramid above and used improved methods of sealing the entrance against robbers. All these features were employed by Sneferu's son, Khufu, who built the biggest pyramid of all, the Great Pyramid of Giza. But in total tons of stone, Sneferu's four pyramids were an even bigger building project.

PYRAMID PROFESSOR
W. M. Flinders Petrie (1853–1942) was a brilliant English archeologist. Over 41 years, he excavated almost every major site in Egypt. He pioneered new scientific methods and published more than a thousand books and papers. Petrie made the first detailed study of the Giza pyramids, in 1881 and 82. He also figured out how the strange-looking Meidum Pyramid had been built.

THE DAHSHUR PYRAMIDS
Sneferu built two large pyramids at Dahshur. It is impossible to visit them now, because they are in a military zone. This old photo shows the Bent Pyramid, which the Egyptians called "the Gleaming Pyramid of the South." It has more of its fine stone facing than any other pyramid. The builders started at a very steep pitch. But halfway up they changed angles, probably because cracks appeared. The Bent Pyramid is also unusual in having two entrances, and two burial chambers – both empty. The northern pyramid was built later. It is a true pyramid that rises at a very flat angle.

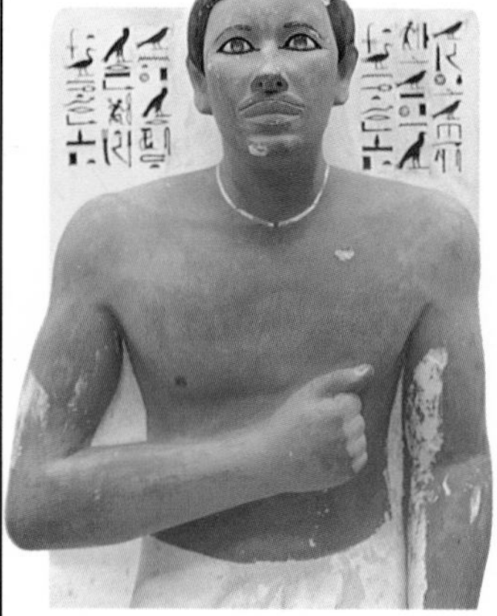

PRINCE...
Some of Sneferu's family were buried by the Meidum pyramid. One tomb held these superb statues of Sneferu's son Prince Rahotep and his wife, Nofret.

...AND PRINCESS
The eyes are real glass. The statues are so realistic that when the workmen saw them for the first time, they dropped their tools and fled!

KILLER KING
Sneferu was the first king of the Fourth Dynasty. He was an ambitious pharaoh. This carving celebrates a raid on the turquoise mines at Maghara in the Sinai Peninsula. It shows Sneferu killing an enemy. The text calls him "a great god... who conquers the foreign lands."

FAMOUS GEESE
Sneferu's eldest son was called Nefer-Maat. He was buried with his wife, Atet, in a tomb next to the Meidum pyramid. The walls are painted with colorful scenes of daily life. This famous detail shows geese eating grass. Roasted geese were a great delicacy for the ancient Egyptians.

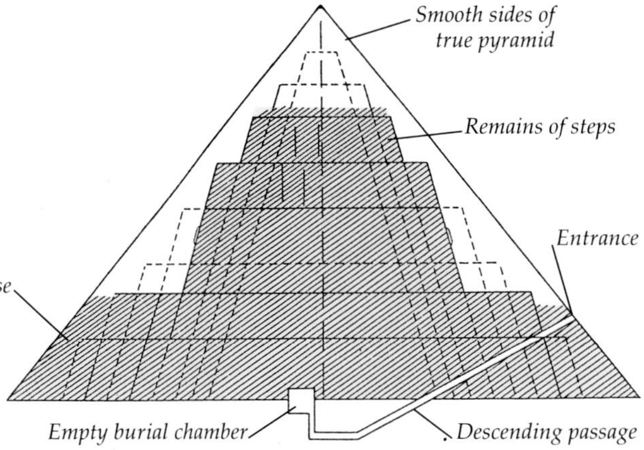

AND ON THE INSIDE...
It is usually very hard to tell how a pyramid was made without taking it apart. But the Meidum Pyramid has collapsed enough to reveal its inner structure. It started off as a step pyramid with seven steps but was later enlarged to eight. Both versions have traces of fine limestone casing and were meant to be final. But in a final change of design, the steps were filled in to produce a true pyramid with smooth sides.

The Meidum Pyramid stands on the border between green farmland, the land of the living, and the desert, the land of the dead

DESERT TOWER
The Meidum Pyramid rises like a tower against the desert landscape. Only the inner core is left, surrounded by a pile of rubble. This picture shows the causeway leading to the entrance. This was the first pyramid Sneferu built, and it might have been started by an earlier king. Sneferu may have decided to convert it into a true pyramid when the Bent Pyramid started to crack. But the burial chamber was never finished. As it is farther south than any other Old Kingdom pyramid, it may have been a cenotaph – a memorial to the dead king.

The pyramids of Giza

TOMBS BY THE NILE
Like all the major tombs of ancient Egypt, the Giza pyramids were built on the west bank of the Nile River. The Egyptians believed that this was the land of the dead. When the sun set in the west each day, they thought it traveled into another world where the spirits of dead kings lived.

"TIME LAUGHS AT ALL THINGS: BUT THE PYRAMIDS laugh at time." This old Arab proverb pays respect to the great pyramids of Giza, which have sat on a high plateau by the Nile for more than 4,500 years. By the time of Tutankhamun, they were more than a thousand years old, and even the Egyptians thought of them as ancient wonders. To the Arabs, who invaded Egypt in A.D. 639, the pyramids were unbelievably old. From a distance, they are an awesome, majestic sight. Up close, they are massive. The largest of the three, the Great Pyramid of King Khufu, was built around 2550 B.C. At its peak it was 481 ft (147 m) tall, with a square base 756 ft (230 m) on a side. It is made of about 2,300,000 blocks of solid limestone, each weighing 2.5 tons on average. Its neighbor, built 70 years later for King Khafra, is 9 ft (3 m) shorter. The third great pyramid was made for the pharaoh Menkaura. It is the smallest of the three, standing only 218 ft (66 m) high.

THE RIDDLE OF THE SPHINX
The Great Sphinx (pp. 54–55) looks east toward the rising sun. Carved from a huge outcrop of limestone, it has the body of a crouching lion and the face of a king, probably Khafra. Some workers building Khafra's pyramid may have seen the shape in a piece of leftover rock. They probably carved it as a tribute to their king.

The Giza pyramids seen from the south

BY CAMEL AROUND THE PYRAMIDS
For 4,500 years, people have come to see the great tombs of the pharaohs. Today millions of tourists from around the world visit the pyramids every year.

A GREAT VIEW
The best view of the Giza complex is from the top of the Great Pyramid. This picture comes from *Views in Egypt*, published by the Italian adventurer Luigi Mayer in 1804. It shows European travelers admiring the scenery from the summit. They are wearing Turkish dress, a common custom for travelers at the time.

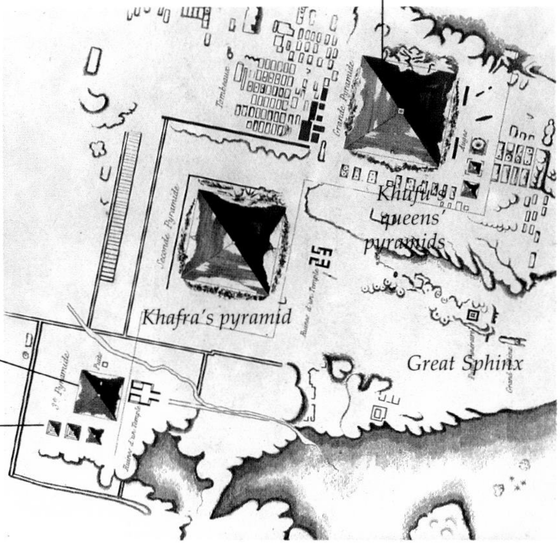

THE WHOLE COMPLEX
This is an aerial view of the Giza pyramids. There are 10 pyramids in all, because all three pharaohs built at least one small pyramid beside their big pyramids. These smaller structures are usually called queen's pyramids, though only some of them were built for the pharaohs' wives (p. 47).

The pharaohs of Giza

THE PHARAOH HAD TOTAL authority. His subjects thought of him as a god and would do anything for him. Without this absolute power, the pyramids could never have been built. The word *pharaoh* means "great house," and originally referred to the palace rather than the king. Khufu, Khafra, and Menkaura had their palaces at Memphis. From there they could admire their massive tombs being built nearby at Giza. The building process took many years – if the pharaoh was lucky, his pyramid would be ready before he died. These huge projects must have put an enormous strain on Egypt's economy. When they were finally finished, the Giza pyramids were given names which celebrated the majesty of the kings who built them. The Great Pyramid was called "Khufu is one belonging to the horizon." The other two were known as "Great is Khafra" and "Menkaura is divine."

RARE PORTRAIT
Khufu was probably the most powerful pharaoh ever to rule Egypt. Yet the only portrait of him to survive is this tiny ivory statue. When it was found, it had no head. The English archeologist Flinders Petrie had to sift through mounds of rubble before he finally found the missing head.

FALCON POWER
A falcon perches on Khafra's throne, its outstretched wings wrapped around his throat. The bird represents Horus, the god associated with the supreme power and strength of the pharaoh.

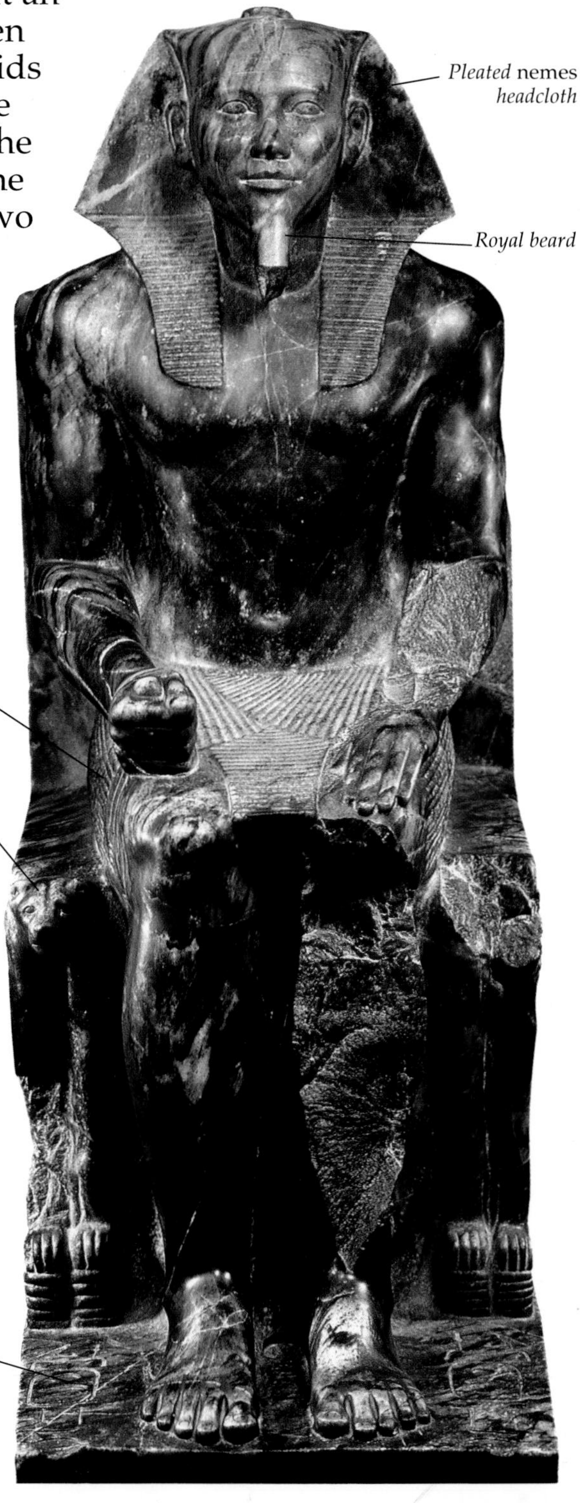

LION THRONE
One of the most striking Egyptian statues is this portrait of the pharaoh Khafra. He succeeded Khufu as king, and may have been Khufu's younger brother The statue is carved from a shiny, mottled stone called diorite. The king is shown larger than life size sitting on a lion throne. The statue was found deep in a pit in Khafra's valley temple, part of his pyramid complex. It may have been hidden there to save it from destruction by thieves or enemies.

HEAD IN THE SAND
The Great Sphinx (pp. 54–55) crouches in front of Khafra's pyramid. Its massive head is thought to be a portrait of the pharaoh. For most of its history, the Sphinx has been covered up to the neck in the drifting desert sands.

WE THREE KINGS
These are the cartouches – hieroglyphic names – of the three Giza pharaohs. Each name is framed by an oval loop of rope with a knot at the base. The loop represented eternity. By placing his name inside it, the pharaoh hoped to live forever.

WHO'S YOUR FATHER?
Ancient Greek historians, writing 2,000 years after the pyramids were built, claimed that Menkaura was Khufu's son. But he looks like Khafra, and many experts now believe Khafra was his father. This painting shows Menkaura as he may have looked in life.

The king has a muscular physique; his queen has much softer curves

The fine grain of the stone graywacke gives the sculpture a smooth finish

MODEL COUPLE
Most Egyptian pharaohs had many wives. But only two or three were queens, and the king usually had a favorite. This is the earliest known statue of a king and queen together. They are Menkaura and his favorite wife, Khamerernebty. The queen is hugging her husband in an affectionate way. Human touches like this are rare in Egyptian art, which is very formal. There are no records about Menkaura from his own age. But Greek historians say he was a fair and just pharaoh. In contrast, they describe Khufu and Khafra as wicked tyrants who forced the whole country to work on their pyramids.

Menkaura's cartouche

ANCIENT REPAIRS
A broken wooden coffin was found in Menkaura's pyramid. But the style and writing show that it was made nearly 2,000 years after the king's death. Later Egyptians must have tried to repair his coffin after it was damaged.

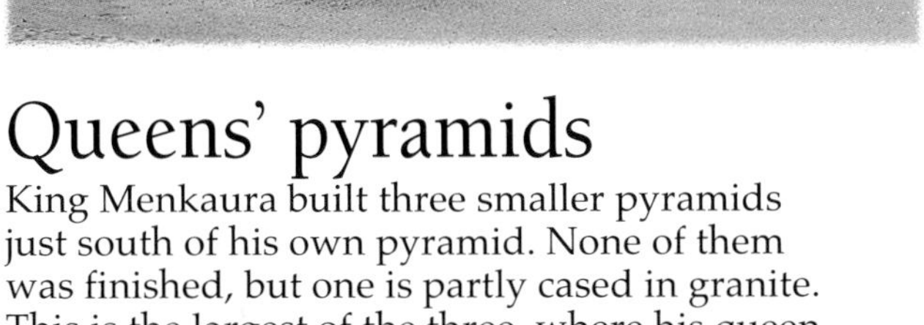

Queens' pyramids

King Menkaura built three smaller pyramids just south of his own pyramid. None of them was finished, but one is partly cased in granite. This is the largest of the three, where his queen Khamerernebty was probably buried. Many other pyramid complexes include smaller "queens' pyramids." But not all of them were built as tombs for the king's wives. Some were tombs for his daughters, and others seem to have had different, more symbolic purposes.

The Great Pyramid

THE LARGEST AND MOST FAMOUS PYRAMID is the Great Pyramid at Giza. It was built or King Khufu beginning around 2550 B.C. Tourists have come to marvel at it for the last 4,500 years. With its original casing of white limestone glittering in the sunlight, it must have been a truly awesome sight. Many people believe it is the greatest monument ever made. The base is bigger than any temple, cathedral, or mosque. Until the Eiffel Tower was finished in 1887, the Great Pyramid was also the tallest structure ever built. The precision of its construction is astonishing. The four sides, each slightly more than 755 ft (230 m) long, are aligned almost exactly with true north, south, east, and west. The difference between the longest and shortest sides is only 7.9 in (20 cm). This mountain of stone contains approximately 2,300,000 blocks, weighing a total of about 6,500,000 tons. Inside is a fascinating network of passages, shafts, galleries, and hidden chambers (pp. 50–51).

CLIMBING THE MOUNTAIN
The Arabs used to call the Great Pyramid "the Mountain of Pharaoh." In the 19th century, European tourists paid local guides to carry them to the top. This was very dangerous – people who slipped and fell were often killed. Writing in 1875, the American author Mark Twain said it was "a lively, exhilarating, lacerating, muscle-straining, bone-wrenching and perfectly excruciating and exhausting pastime." Nowadays climbing the pyramids is against the law.

ANCIENT AND MODERN
Giza is now a suburb of the huge modern city of Cairo. This photo shows a Muslim cemetery built next to the Great Pyramid. Khufu's boat museum (p. 94) can be seen against the pyramid. Pollution from cars and factories is damaging the ancient stones. The foundations of the Great Pyramid are shaken every day by the constant flow of buses carrying thousandsand thousands of tourists.

The pyramid's sides rise at an angle of 51.5 degrees to the peak, which was originally 481 ft (147 m) above the desert sands

HUNDREDS AND THOUSANDS
The Great Pyramid is the largest stone structure ever built. It is impossible to count all the blocks, so the total number can only be guessed at. At the core is an outcrop of rock that was incorporated in the base. The outer casing blocks were so skillfully laid that a knife blade will not slip between them.

AND ON THE INSIDE...
Khufu was probably buried in the King's Chamber, in the heart of his pyramid. This room, lined with shiny red granite, was robbed long ago. But it still contains a sarcophagus, slightly larger than the door. It must have been put there as the pyramid was being built.

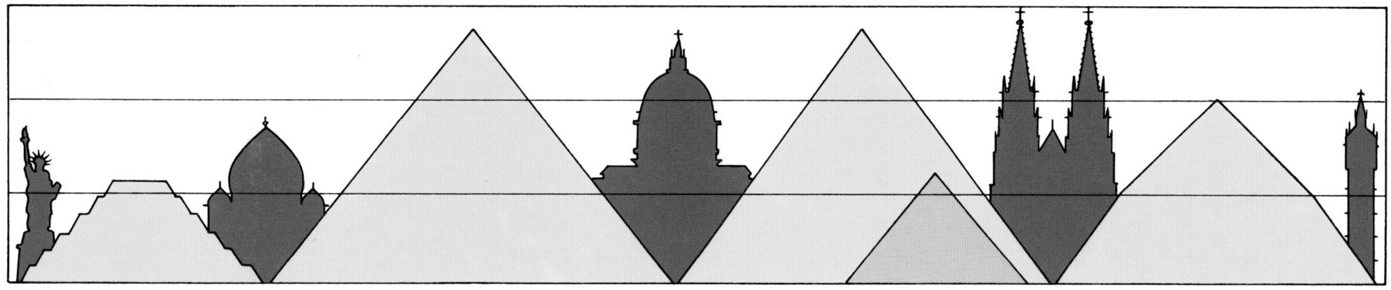

HOW HIGH?
The Great Pyramid is 481 ft (147 m) high, slightly higher than Khafra's pyramid. This is still taller than most world-famous monuments. But it is much smaller than recent wonders like the CN Tower in Toronto, Canada (1,815 ft/553 m) or skyscrapers like the Sears Building in Chicago (1,454 ft/443 m).

CAIRO CITADEL
Huge quantities of stone were needed to build Cairo's many grand buildings and mosques. Some of this stone was taken right off the Great Pyramid.

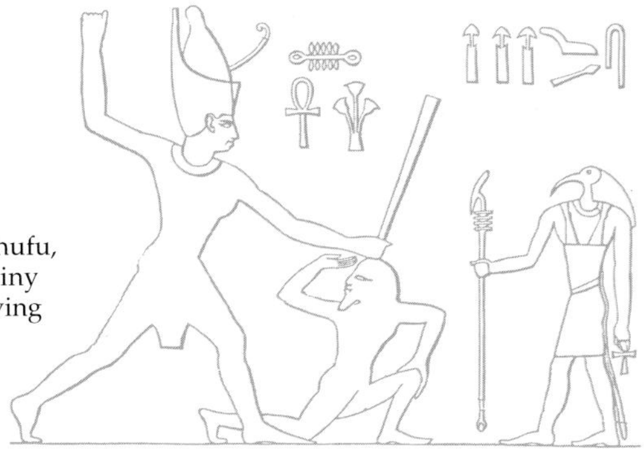

STRIKING DOWN THE ENEMY
There are only two known images of Khufu, builder of the Great Pyramid. One is a tiny ivory statue (p. 46). The other is this carving cut into a cliff in the Sinai Peninsula. It shows Khufu killing a Bedouin chieftain with a club. Thoth, the ibis-headed god of scribes, is looking on.

THE LAST WONDER
The three Giza pyramids were the oldest of the Seven Wonders of the Ancient World. But they are the only one left. The other six – the Lighthouse of Alexandria (right), the Colossus of Rhodes, the Hanging Gardens of Babylon, the Temple of Artemis, the Mausoleum at Halicarnassus, and the Statue of Zeus – are all vanished or in ruins.

One of three small queens' pyramids

Inside the pyramid

FORCED ENTRY
The original entrance to the Great Pyramid was concealed by polished casing blocks. Today visitors enter by a lower hole cut by the Arab leader Caliph Ma'mun in the 9th century.

WHAT WONDERS ARE HIDDEN inside the pyramids? This question has fascinated people throughout history. The early Christians thought the pharaoh used them to store grain, as the biblical story of Joseph relates. But the pyramids were really royal tombs. Somewhere inside or beneath the huge mass of stone was a burial chamber where the dead king was laid to rest. Since the earliest times, there have been fantastic rumors about the glittering treasures buried with the dead pharaohs. To stop robbers, the pyramid builders hid the entrances and sealed the internal passages with huge plugs of stone. The Middle Kingdom kings created extra passages and false shafts to try and fool robbers. Despite all these efforts, every known pyramid had been looted by 1000 B.C. The few fragments that have been found were overlooked by hasty thieves. The only intact king's burial ever found belonged to Tutankhamun, who had been buried in an underground tomb in the Valley of the Kings. He was lying in three stunning coffins, one made of solid gold, surrounded by priceless treasures. We can only imagine what marvels were buried inside the pyramids.

Two views of French explorers in the Grand Gallery of the Great Pyramid, from the *Description of Egypt*, 1809–1822.

EXPLORING WITHIN
In 1818, the famous Italian adventurer Giovanni Belzoni became the first European to enter Khafra's pyramid at Giza. He was disappointed to find that the burial chamber had been thoroughly robbed. The massive granite sarcophagus was still set into the floor. But there was no trace of the king's body or any treasures.

STARS ON THE CEILING
The burial chamber was at the very heart of the pyramid. The sarcophagus often sat at the far end. The roof followed the angle of the pyramid. Unas's pyramid is decorated with stars and hieroglyphs.

Texts from Unas's pyramid

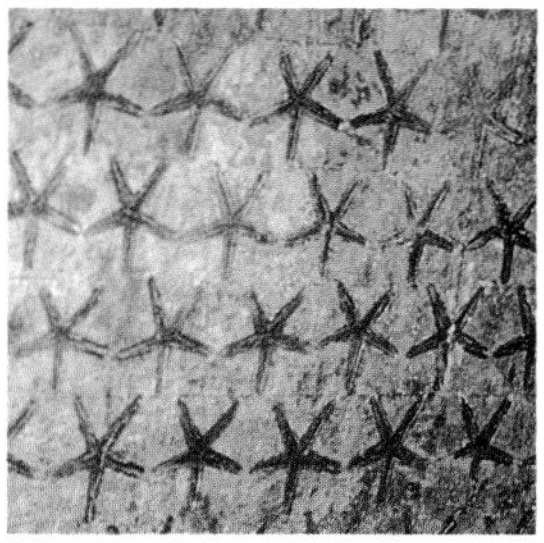

Stars from roof

Painted decoration

The Pyramid Texts

On the inner walls of King Unas's pyramid are the earliest known religious hieroglyphs. These are the Pyramid Texts. Once brightly colored, these magical spells, prayers, and hymns are about the rebirth of the king and his reunion with the gods in the afterlife. They date from about 2340 B.C., which makes them the oldest known religious writings. Later versions of the texts were painted on Middle Kingdom coffins, and on New Kingdom papyruses, in the famous Book of the Dead.

STRIKE A LIGHT
Napoleon's men explored the Great Pyramid in the early 1800s. These engravings show them scaling the Grand Gallery, which leads to the King's Chamber. In scale and design, there is nothing like this gallery in any other pyramid. The huge blocks that sealed the passages were stored inside. Over the centuries, the soot from countless torches has blackened the perfectly polished limestone.

KHUFU'S FINAL RESTING PLACE
The King's Chamber is made of granite. The roof includes nine slabs that weigh 50 tons each. It also contains five compartments, probably to reduce the pressure from the colossal weight of the stone above.

KHUFU WAS HERE
Some of the rough stones over the roof of the King's Chamber are scrawled with graffiti left by workers. These red hieroglyphs are the only place on the pyramid where Khufu's name appears.

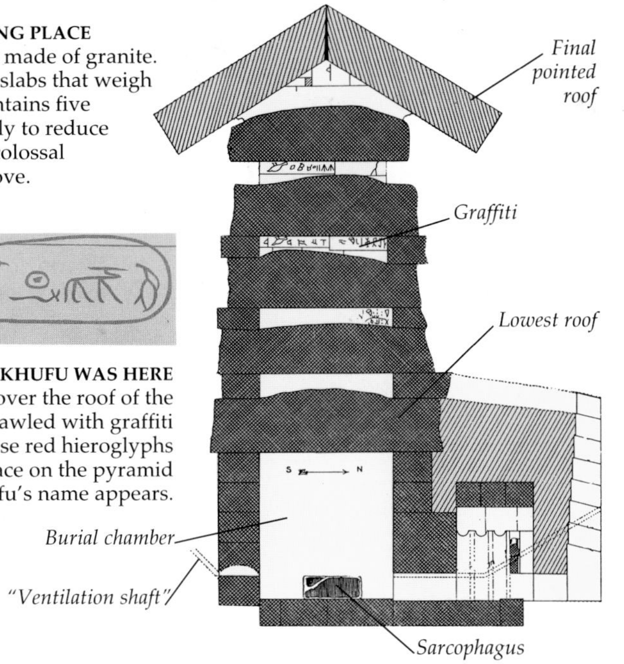

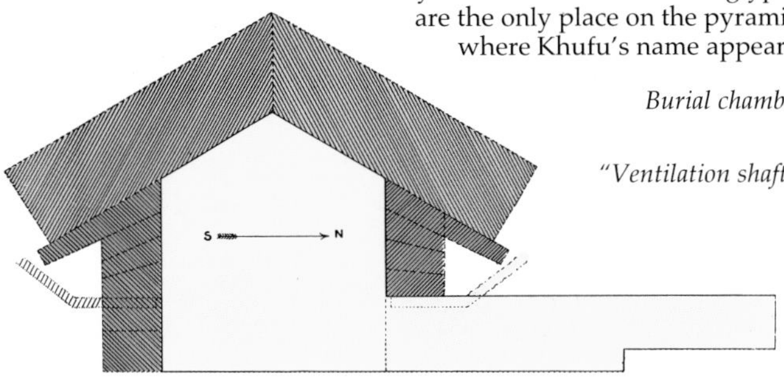

EMPTY CHAMBER
Early explorers called it the Queen's Chamber. But this smaller room has nothing to do with any queen. Experts now think it was meant for Khufu but was abandoned when the plans were changed.

CHANGE OF PLAN
The internal layout of the Great Pyramid was changed several times during construction. The entrance leads to a descending corridor that runs underground to an unfinished chamber. A second, ascending corridor leads through the Grand Gallery to the King's Chamber. Thin passages called "ventilation shafts" run from both main chambers toward the surface (p. 48).

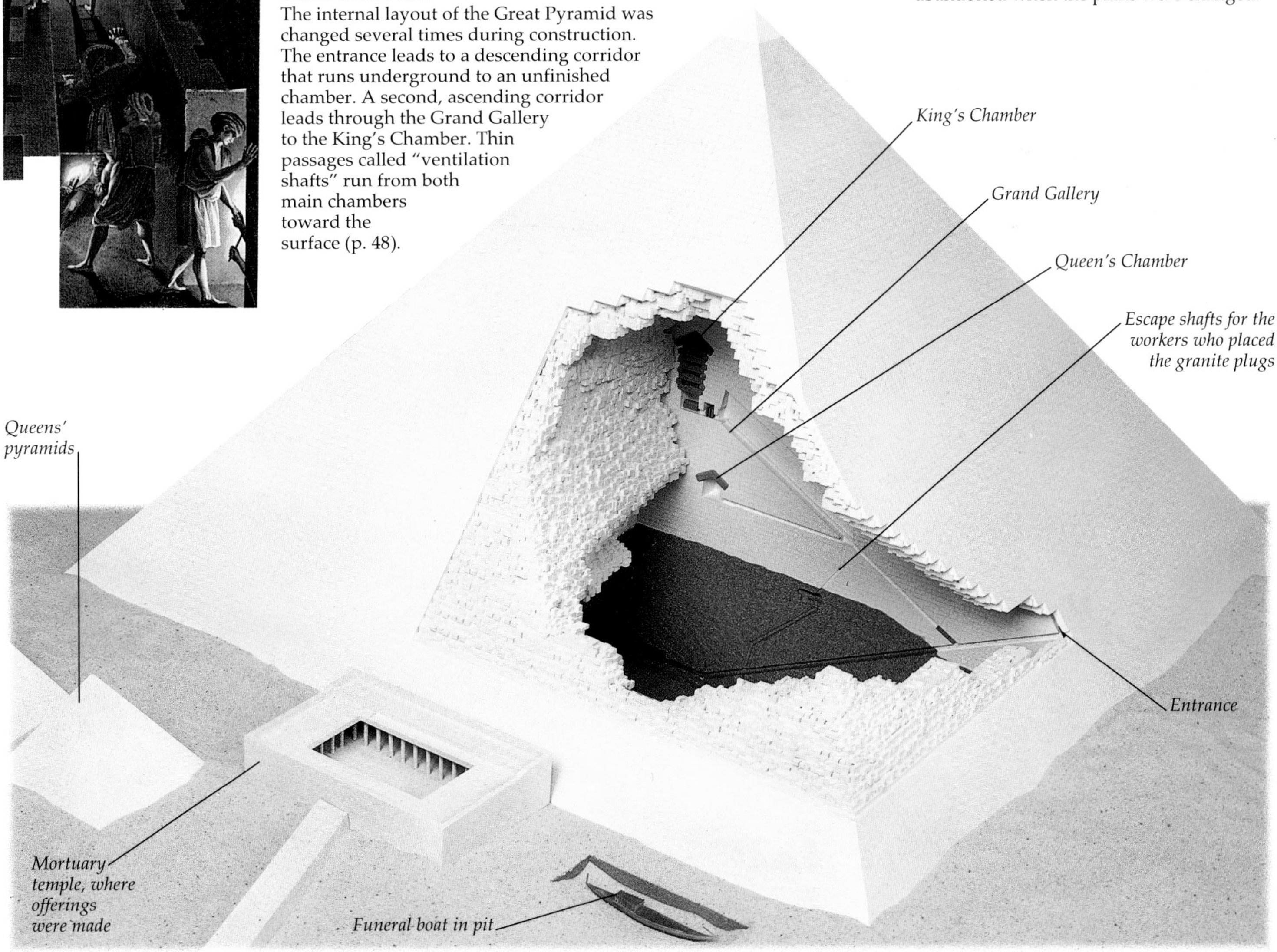

PEEK-A-BOO
This is a statue of Ti, an important official in charge of worship at the pyramid temples of Abusir. It was meant as a substitute body that Ti's spirit could inhabit after his death. The statue was placed in a special dark chamber in his tomb called a *serdab*, from the Arabic word for cellar. Ti's face could peer out of a spy hole cut into the tomb wall.

Temples and offerings

A TYPICAL PYRAMID COMPLEX included two temples connected by a long causeway. After the king died, his body was rowed across the Nile to the river or valley temple. Here it was mummified – embalmed, anointed with oils, and wrapped in linen bandages. Seventy days later, when the body was ready, the funeral began. Priests led the procession; women wailed and threw sand into the air. The dead king was carried up the causeway to the mortuary or offering temple. Here the priests performed sacred rites on the mummy before it was laid to rest in the pyramid. After the burial, the pharaoh's spirit would need regular supplies of food and drink. Every day, meals were placed on an altar in the mortuary temple. Before he died, the king would have set aside lands for the maintenance of a community of priests. Their duty was to maintain the temple and provide offerings for the dead king long into the future.

IN THE SHADOW OF THE GREAT PYRAMID
The Great Pyramid was surrounded by a mass of smaller buildings. Khufu's mortuary temple was built on the east side, where the sun was reborn (rose) every day. The dead king hoped to be reborn in the same way. The temple centered around an oblong court with 50 red granite columns. The contrast of white limestone walls, a black basalt floor, and red columns must have been very beautiful. Unfortunately the temple was destroyed long ago. This picture shows the tomb of the nobleman Seshemnufer. Like many important Egyptians, he chose to be buried in the shadow of Khufu's monstrous tomb.

LAND OF PLENTY
The spirits of the dead depended upon the living for their survival in the next world. Tomb pictures often show heaps of bread, beer, fruit, vegetables, and geese piled high on a table. By reciting the formula written beside the picture, the dead person could have a fantastic banquet in the afterlife.

MAGIC DOORWAY
Colorful images of food and drink decorate the false door of Prince Merib. If no offerings were left, these magic pictures would come to life.

ESTATE MANAGER
The dead person's family was often pictured on the walls of the tomb. These two young women holding ointment jars are the daughters of Sennedjsui, a treasurer to the king around 2150 B.C. He ran an estate where food for offerings was grown. His titles included "Sole Friend of the King."

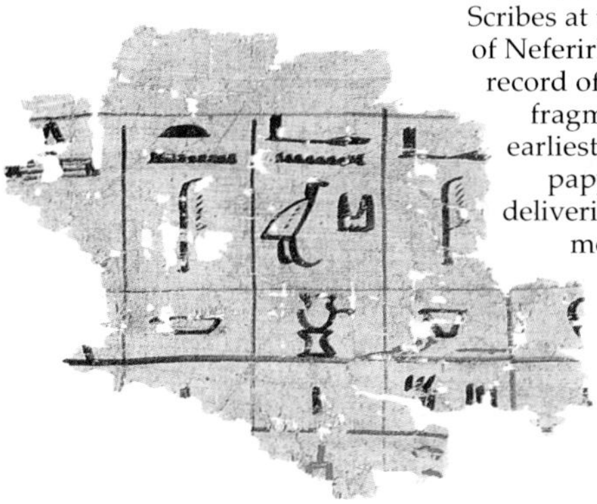

ANCIENT BOOKKEEPING
Scribes at the pyramid temple of Neferirkara kept a detailed record of all offerings. These fragments are among the earliest known writings on papyrus. They list daily deliveries of food including meat, bread, and beer.

False doors and stelae

Worshipers came to pray and lay offerings before a stela or false door in the mortuary temple. The stela was a slab of stone inscribed with the dead person's name and titles. In the Old Kingdom, it often took the form of a false door connecting the world of the living with the world of the dead. The door did not open. But the dead person's *ka* (spirit) was thought to pass through it, so he or she could leave the tomb and enjoy a meal in the temple.

DAILY BREAD
Princess Nefertiabet was buried in a tomb at Giza. She was probably a daughter of one of the pharaohs who built their pyramids there. Her stela shows the princess wearing the leopard-skin robe of a priest. She is seated at a table piled high with loaves of sacred bread. A leg of meat and a headless goose hover above the table. On the right is a list of precious linen to clothe the princess in the afterlife.

The Sphinx

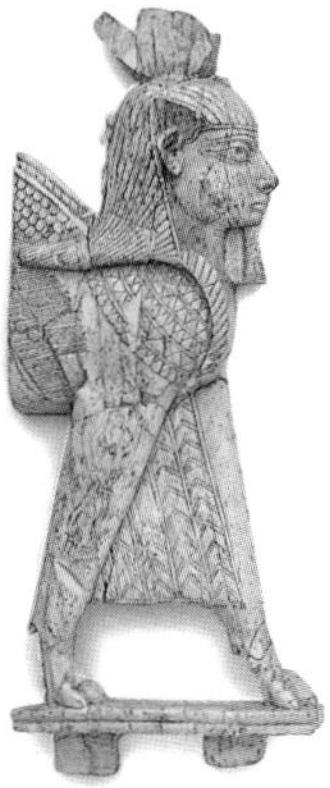

Winged sphinx made of ivory

For more than 4,500 years, the Sphinx has guarded Khafra's pyramid at Giza. Carved from a huge outcrop of limestone, it is the largest freestanding sculpture to survive from ancient times. It has the body of a lion and the head of a king. The drifting sands have buried it up to the neck for most of its history. Attempts were made to clear it as early as 1400 B.C., by Thutmose IV. When he was a prince, Thutmose fell asleep under the Sphinx's head after a tiring hunt in the desert. In the prince's dream, the Sphinx promised to make him king if he freed it from the suffocating sand. After he had dug the Sphinx out, the prince recorded his dream on a stone tablet between its huge paws.

THE SPHINX'S BEARD
This fragment of the Sphinx's beard was found in the sand beneath its head. The beard was probably added a thousand years after the Sphinx was built. Its surface still has traces of its original red coloring. It seems to have been held in place by a column of stone that included a colossal statue of a pharaoh.

HEADS LIKE RAMS
In later times, the sphinx became popular as an image of Amun, the most important state god. A long avenue lined with ram-headed sphinxes once linked the great temples of Karnak and Luxor. This pair of bronze sphinxes comes from Nubia (pp. 74–77).

BATTERED AND WORN
The Sphinx was carved from an outcrop of rock that was too crumbly to be cut into building blocks for Khafra's pyramid. Its shape probably suggested the form of a lion, onto which Khafra's stonemasons carved an image of their king. The sculpture is about 187 ft (57 m) long and 66 ft (20 m) high. The limestone has been badly weathered over the centuries. The paws were protected with stone facings in Roman times. These were redone recently.

Stone facings added to protect paws

GUARDING THE PYRAMID

Statues of lions often guard the entrances to Egyptian temples. The Sphinx was probably meant to protect the pyramid complex of Khafra in the same way. There is no evidence that it was worshiped in its own right when the pyramids were built. But in later times the Sphinx was identified with Horemakhet, or "Horus in the horizon," a form of the sun god.

The Sphinx stands next to the causeway of Khafra's pyramid, looking east toward the rising sun

The sculpture is wearing the nemes *headcloth, a symbol of royalty*

In the 15th century A.D.*, Muslim troops broke off the Sphinx's nose because their religion forbids images of a god*

Crumbling limestone, eroded by blowing sand and pollution

Stone stela (tablet) erected by Thutmose IV to record his dream

BURIED IN THE DRIFTING SANDS

In 1818, an Italian sea captain, Giovanni Caviglia, tried to find a way into the Sphinx. He cleared the sand off its chest anduncovered a chapel. This was one of many modern attempts to free the Sphinx from the desert sands. It was finally dug out in 1925. Many conservationists are worried about the effects of pollution on its crumbling body. Some even suggest it may be safer buried in the sand again!

Planning the pyramid

THE PYRAMIDS REQUIRED careful planning. First a site had to be chosen. For religious reasons, this was always on the west bank of the Nile, where the sun set. It had to be close to the river, because the stone would arrive by boat, but well above flood level. The pyramid also required a solid base of rock that would not crack under its enormous weight. Then the site was leveled and true north was calculated, so the sides could be lined up with the four compass points. The Egyptians probably did this by using the stars, since they did not have magnetic compasses. They had set squares and special tools like the *merkhet* to help in their calculations.

Pegging the foundations

DIVINE PROPORTIONS
Like sculpture and painting, pyramid building followed a fixed system of proportion. Artists' models like this one show that the Egyptians drew a grid of horizontal and vertical lines to calculate what they called "divine proportions." They used small models or sketches to plan large works. Two small limestone models of pyramids have been found. But there is no way of knowing if these were made before or after the pyramids.

Wooden peg

Cord made from the flax plant

LEVEL PEGGING
This ancient cord on a peg is probably one of a pair used to mark out the foundations of a building. The southeast corner of the Great Pyramid is only 0.5 in (1.3 cm) higher than the northwest corner. This incredible accuracy was achieved by digging trenches, filling them with water, and marking the level. Then all the rock above the line was hacked away until the foundation was perfectly flat.

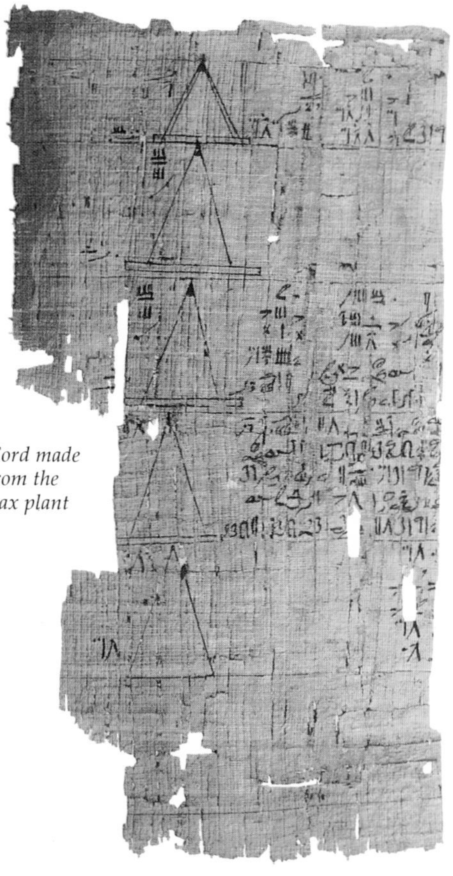

PYRAMID CALCULATIONS
This is part of the Rhind Papyrus, written about 1550 B.C. It shows a series of problems about the relationship between the angle of a pyramid and its overall dimensions. The angle of the sloping sides is called the *seked*. It is equal to half the width of the base, divided by the pyramid's height and multiplied by seven.

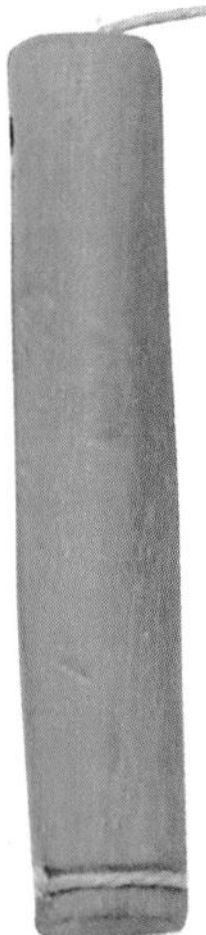

GUARANTEEING A TIGHT FIT
Egyptian masons (stonecutters) had tools called boning rods to make the stone blocks perfectly smooth. This scene from the tomb of the official Rekhmire (c. 1450 B.C.) shows how these were used. The masons are holding the rods at right angles to the stone so the string is stretched tight. Any bumps are chiseled smooth.

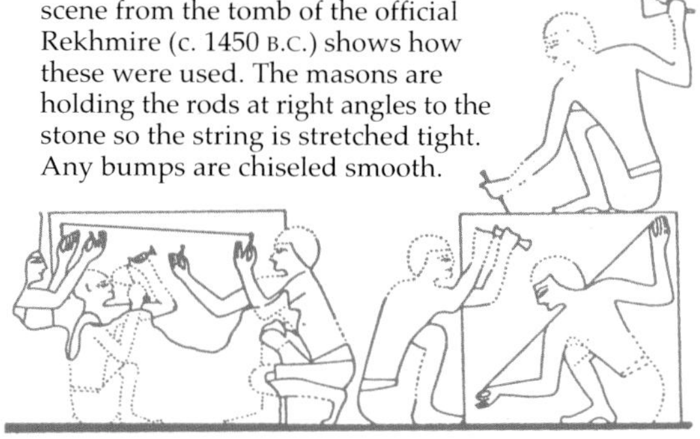

Pair of boning rods

BREAKING THE RULES
The basic unit of measurement was the cubit, the length from the elbow to the tip of the thumb. This was equal to 20.62 in (52.4 cm). The wooden rod below is marked in cubits, palms, and digits. There were four digits in a palm, and seven palms in a cubit. The Egyptians also buried ritual cubit rods during foundation ceremonies.

Fragment from a ritual cubit rod made of schist

Cutting the earth

Pouring seed or incense

Molding the first mud brick

BLESSING THE FOUNDATIONS
Building foundations had magical significance to the Egyptians. These drawings show a pharaoh performing sacred rites at a foundation ceremony for Edfu Temple. This is like the modern custom of getting a famous person to lay the first brick.

CHIEF OF SCRIBES
Hesire's titles included "chief of scribes" and "chief dentist." This picture of him dates from 2700 B.C., around the time the Step Pyramid at Saqqara was built (pp. 38–41). He is shown with ink wells, a palette, and a pen case over his shoulder. He holds a staff and scepter, symbols of authority, and is seated at a table piled high with loaves of bread.

The scribe is wearing a double wig – his head may have been shaved underneath

This statue made of brown quartzite dates from about 700 B.C.

Ink wells and palette slung over shoulder

WRITING IT DOWN
Scribes recorded the planning stages of the pyramid. On the building site, they kept notes of how much stone was used, and which tools each team was given. If a worker called in sick, the scribe wrote down his excuse.

Scribe is holding an unrolled papyrus scroll with his name, Pes-shu-per, written on it in hieroglyphs

Scribes are usually shown sitting cross-legged

Hieroglyphic text to secure offerings to the gods for eternity

Building in brick and stone

IT TOOK HUNDREDS OF THOUSANDS of pieces of stone to build a pyramid. The Great Pyramid is made of about 2,300,000 blocks, each weighing an average of 2.5 tons. The largest slabs, in the roof of the King's Chamber, weigh 50 tons. Quarrying all this stone and moving it to the site was an awesome task. The core of the pyramid was made from local limestone, a fairly soft rock. But the high-quality limestone used for the outer casing came from Tura, across the Nile. Some internal chambers and passages were made of granite, a harder stone that came from Aswan, 500 miles (800 km) upriver. All year round, gangs of workers at the quarries cut rough stone blocks out of the ground. When the river flooded and rose closer to the quarries, the stone blocks were loaded onto boats and carried to the pyramid site. The teams even wrote their names on the stones – some blocks in the Meidum Pyramid (p. 42) are labeled "Enduring Gang," "Vigorous Gang," or "Boat Gang."

BASALT
This hard black stone could be highly polished. This quality made it popular for sarcophagi, sculpture, and monumental inscriptions like the Rosetta Stone.

Both cartouches (hieroglyphic names) of Ramses II, who ruled from 1279 to 1213 B.C.

SANDSTONE
Harder than limestone but softer than granite, sandstone was used for building and sculpture. This is a foundation deposit (p. 57) from the temple of Ptah at Memphis.

GRANITE
This hard, heavy stone was used for sculpture and sarcophagi (stone coffins) and sometimes for lining passages and chambers inside pyramids. It was very difficult to quarry. An unfinished obelisk (stone pillar) is still lying in the Aswan quarry. It weighs over 1,000 tons and would have stood about 100 ft (30 m) tall.

ROWING STONES
Quarries and pyramids were close to the Nile, so the stone could be transported by boat. This carving from the tomb of the official Ipi shows a cargo boat carrying a huge block of stone. The sail is rolled up, so the boat is probably cruising downstream (northward) with the current.

LIMESTONE
Old Kingdom pyramids were mostly made of limestone. Because papyrus – the ancient Egyptians' paper – was so expensive, sketches and rough notes were often done on fragments of pottery or limestone. These are called ostraca. This ostracon has a sketch of the god Osiris.

RESTORATION PROJECT
The best Tura limestone was saved for the pyramid's outer casing. Most of these "casing blocks" were stripped away by later builders who were too lazy to quarry their own. This block shows the original angle of the pyramid of Unas at Saqqara, c. 2340 B.C., which has collapsed into a heap of rubble. More than a thousand years after it was built, Khaemwaset, Ramses II's son, tried to restore it by refitting the fallen casing blocks.

BROKEN SURFACE
Seen from the side, the pyramids of Giza appear to be stepped. This is the pyramid of Menkaura. The original Tura limestone had a flat, polished surface that would have shone brilliantly in the Egyptian sun.

BRICKMAKERS AT WORK
This painting from the tomb of Rekhmire at Thebes, c. 1450 B.C., shows workers mixing and molding mud bricks.

Straw and sand keep the brick from cracking when it dries

Cartouche

Mud brick from Thebes, c. 1000 B.C.

ROYAL STAMP
Mud bricks were often stamped with the name of the pharaoh. This wooden stamp has the cartouche of King Amenhotep II, c. 1400 B.C.

Mud bricks

These were the most common building material in ancient Egypt. Middle Kingdom pyramids were made of mud bricks with only an outer facing of limestone. Today mud bricks are still made by the same process used by the ancients. Wet Nile mud is mixed with straw and sand and pushed into a wooden mold. Then the soft bricks are set out to dry in the burning sun. The Egyptian word for brick, *tobe*, is the origin of the modern word *adobe*, a kind of brick architecture.

A worker leaves rows of bricks to dry in the sun, in this picture from the tomb of Rekhmire

Tools for building

ROCK DRILL
This curved flake of flint is an Egyptian tool from the Pyramid Age. It looks too fragile to work stone. But attached to a wooden pole and spun vigorously with a bow, it became a powerful drill. For a smoother cut, the drill would be used with sand or crushed quartz, mixed with water or a little olive oil.

ALL AROUND THE GREAT temples, tombs, and pyramids, Egyptologists have found tools left by builders and sculptors. Some of these were lost or broken on the site. But others were left there for religious reasons. The Egyptians believed that a sacred building, such as a temple or pyramid, had a spirit that would have to be repaired in the next world. So the workers left tools for their spirits to use after they died. The design of these tools has changed little over the centuries. It is amazing what wonders the builders created with such simple implements.

FOREMAN AND SON
Tools were precious. They were often issued each morning by a foreman, who organized his team of workers and locked the tools away at night. This painting shows Anherkhau, a foreman who worked in the Valley of the Kings, with his son. It dates from 1150 B.C.

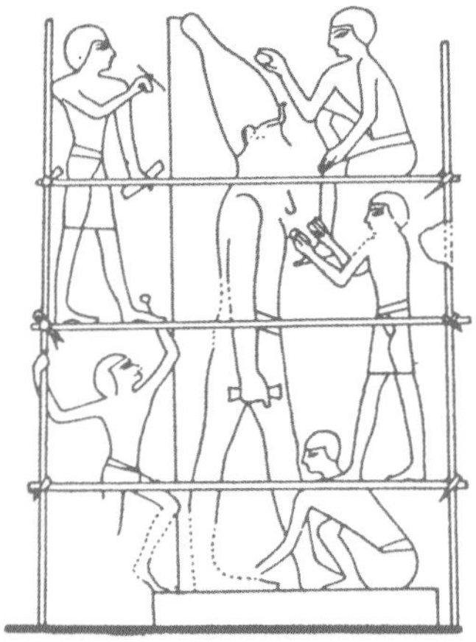

HIGHER AND HIGHER
Ancient paintings show that the Egyptians built scaffolding. This detail from the tomb of Rekhmire, c. 1450 B.C., shows workers putting the final touches on a statue of the pharaoh. They are standing on a network of light poles lashed together with knots of plant rope.

POLISHING IT UP
After a block of stone had been roughly cut and shaped, it might be burnished (rubbed down with a smooth stone) to give it a polished surface.

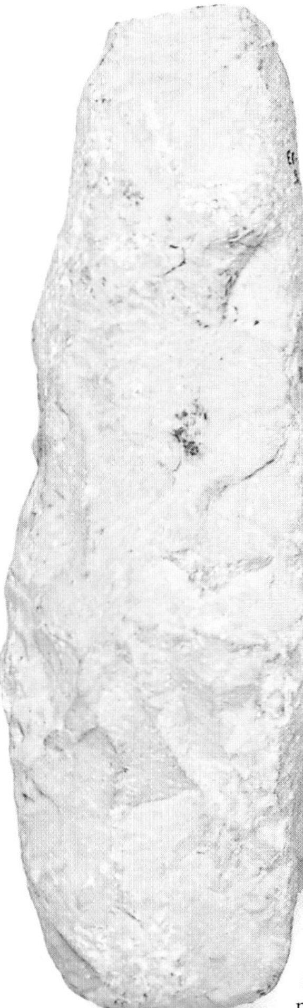

HARD ROCK
Most stones are too hard to be worked with copper tools. Instead they were quarried with pieces of dolerite, a very hard rock. This pounder is made of softer granite.

MASON'S MALLET
For thousands of years, masons all over the world have hit their chisels with mallets (wooden hammers). This one is made of very hard wood.

CHISELS
Masons work stone with chisels. These bronze and copper chisels were used to create fine details. The tips could be heated to make them cut better.

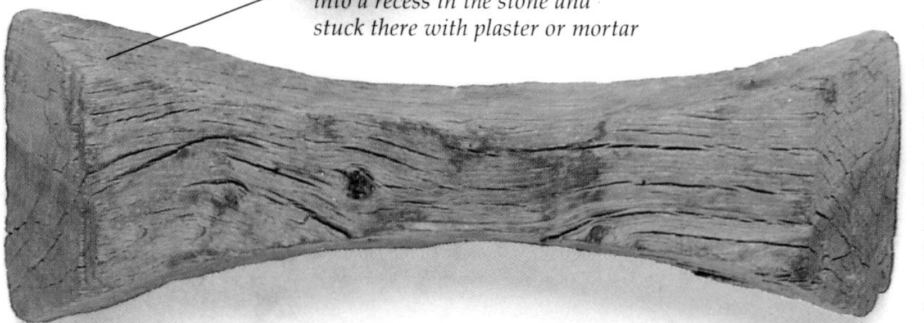

BUTTERFLY CLAMP
Clamps were used to hold blocks of stone together. The wide ends were plastered into holes in the two stones. Many clamps are inscribed with the cartouche (name) of the royal builder.

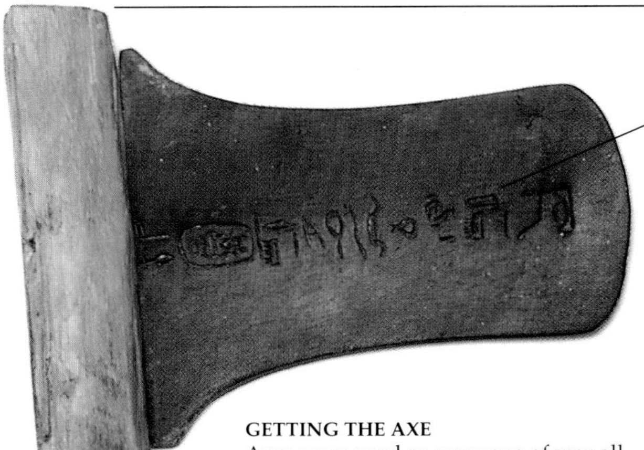

Hieroglyphs with cartouche of the pharaoh Thutmose III, who ruled from 1479 to 1425 B.C.

GETTING THE AXE
Axes were used as weapons of war all over the ancient world. They were also good for chopping wood, or to show the owner's power. This ceremonial axe was found in the foundations of a temple.

Wood was very rare in the desert and often had to be imported from Lebanon

Furniture maker hitting a chisel with a wooden mallet

Model saw with wooden handle and copper blade

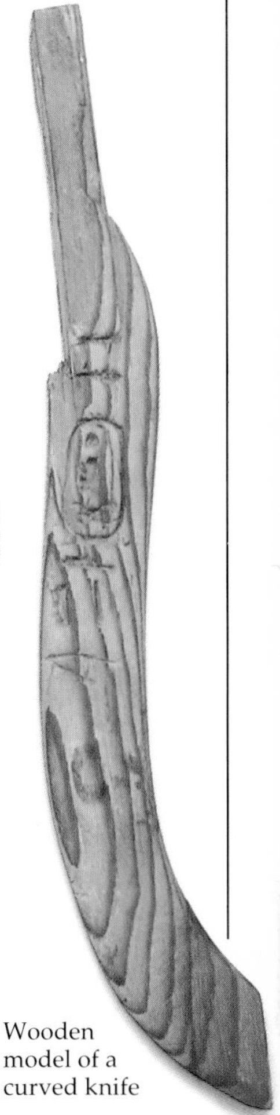

Wooden model of a curved knife

FOR CUTTING (NOT SHAVING)
The adze was an ancient carpenter's favorite tool. Many paintings show workers chopping and planing wood with adzes. This one from c. 1400 B.C. is unusual because the carpenter is unshaven with scruffy hair. Egyptians are almost always shown with perfect hair and makeup.

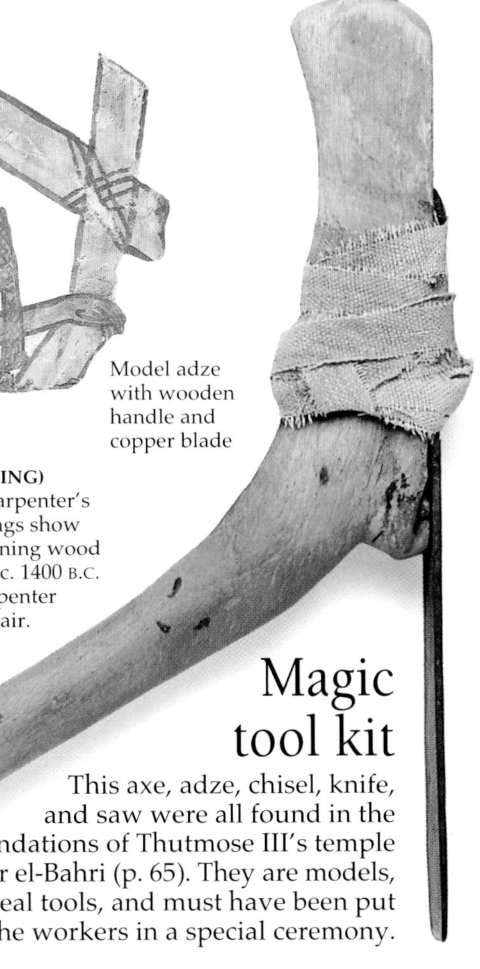

Model adze with wooden handle and copper blade

Model chisel

Magic tool kit

This axe, adze, chisel, knife, and saw were all found in the foundations of Thutmose III's temple at Deir el-Bahri (p. 65). They are models, not real tools, and must have been put there by the workers in a special ceremony.

Worker cutting with knife-like saw, from tomb of Rekhmire, c. 1450 B.C.

Tang, a projection that fitted into the wooden handle

Tip is curved up so it will not catch

Cutting edge

Blunt edge that rubbed against wood but did not cut

PULL (DON'T PUSH)
Unlike a modern saw, this ancient tool was designed to cut as the worker pulled it toward his or her body. Its wooden handle has long since rotted away.

The pyramid rises

NO RECORDS SURVIVE to tell us how the pyramids were built. The only ancient account, by the Greek historian Herodotus, was written 2,000 years later and cannot be trusted. He claimed that gangs of 100,000 workmen toiled for 20 years to build the Great Pyramid. We now believe that about 4,000 skilled laborers worked all year round. During *Akhet*, the yearly flood, thousands of peasants left their flooded fields and came to help on the site. There are many theories about how the heavy blocks of stone were lifted into place. Herodotus said they used lifting machines, but there is no evidence for this. It seems more likely that the stones were dragged up a ramp that grew as the pyramid rose. Once the capstone was in place, the ramp was dismantled.

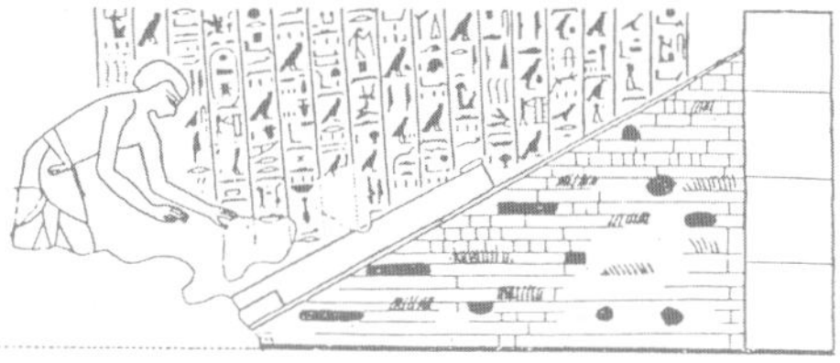

MUD-BRICK RAMP
Remains of ramps have been found near several pyramids. This detailed drawing is from the tomb of Rekhmire, made 1,000 years after the Great Pyramid. It shows a building block lying on a ramp.

Polished casing was probably white

TWO-WAY TRAFFIC
The ramp was probably strictly organized into up and down lanes. One lane – in this model, the far left lane – is being raised, and is closed to traffic.

Side of ramp being raised

Stones going up

Empty sleds coming down

Stacks of blocks ready to be hauled up ramp

BUILDING A TRUE PYRAMID
This model shows the most popular theory – the use of one long supply ramp. As the pyramid grew higher, the ramp was increased in height and length. The top of the pyramid was a great square platform ready to receive the next layer of stones. In the model, the fine outer casing stones are being added as each layer is finished. But some experts argue that the whole pyramid was cased from the top down as the last stage of construction. The boat is delivering logs for use in ramps, rollers, and scaffolding.

The ramp was narrow, and was always kept at a gentle angle

Teams of men, at least 30 per sled, pull stones up ramp

BIG DRAG

Wooden sleds with runners were the best way of moving heavy loads. Sleds are quite common in Egyptian art, and several real sleds have been found. This papyrus painting (c. 1000 B.C.) shows a funeral procession. Men are dragging the coffin, which is covered by a canopy and mounted on a sled. When moving stones, the workers probably laid logs across the ramp to stop the heavy sleds from getting bogged down in the mud.

UPWARD SPIRAL

Some experts have proposed that the stones were dragged up a system of spiral ramps winding around the pyramid. The ramps could have stood either on the casing blocks, or on separate foundations in front of the pyramid. But it would have been virtually impossible to turn the stones around the corners. Spiral ramps would also obscure the whole pyramid, which would make measurements difficult. Making sure the four sides came to a perfect point would have required constant measuring.

CRACK THE WHIP

Drawings and films about ancient Egypt often show sweating slaves being driven on by bosses with whips. This is totally untrue. The hard labor was done by peasant-farmers. They believed their pharaoh was a god and were probably happy to help him achieve everlasting life.

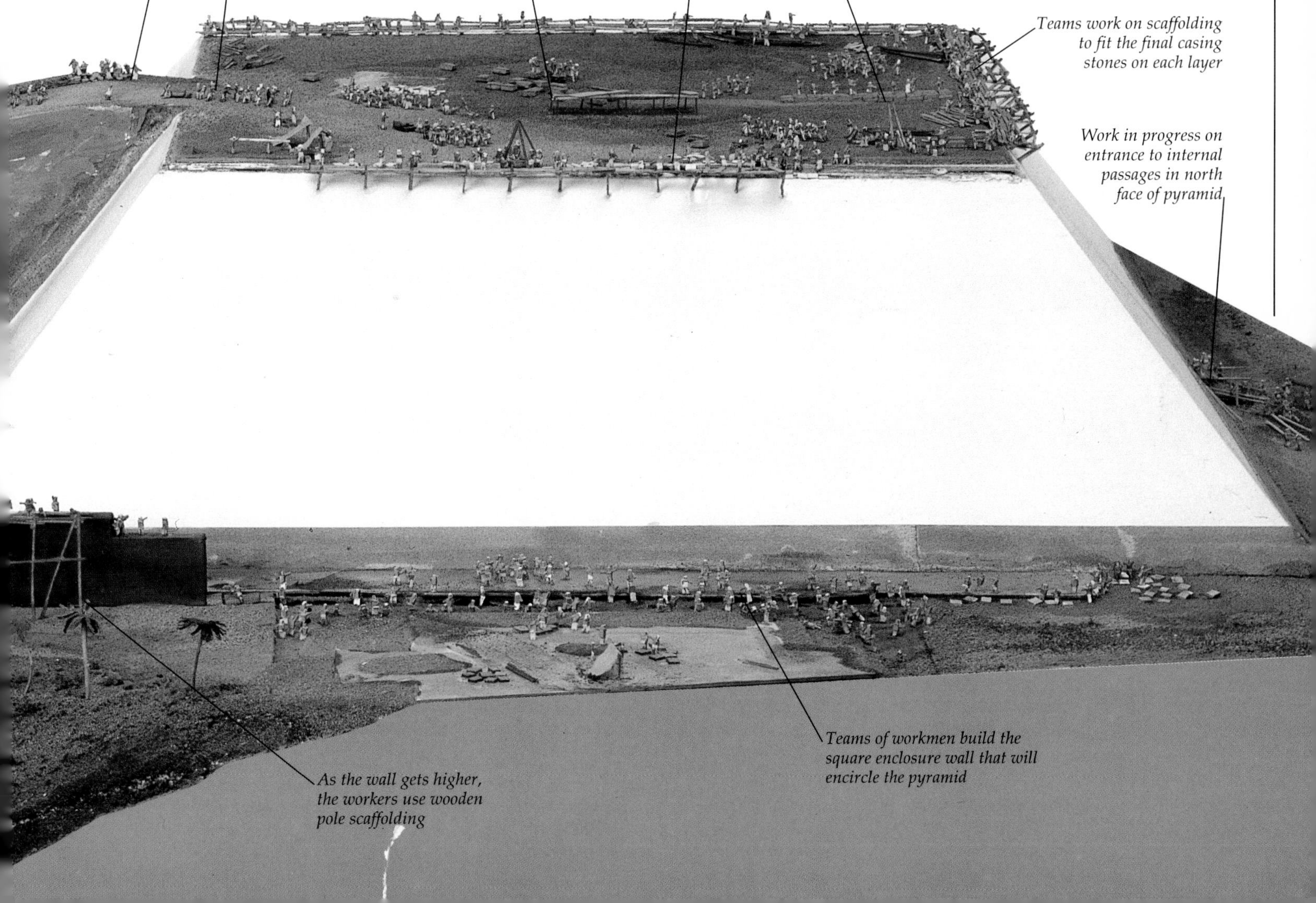

Workers add to height of ramp

A team dragging a block of stone arrives at the top

Awnings to shelter foremen and supplies of food and water

Fine white Tura limestone for outer casing

Stockpile of local limestone for core

Teams work on scaffolding to fit the final casing stones on each layer

Work in progress on entrance to internal passages in north face of pyramid

Teams of workmen build the square enclosure wall that will encircle the pyramid

As the wall gets higher, the workers use wooden pole scaffolding

The Middle Kingdom revival

AFTER A LONG PERIOD OF DISORDER and civil war, Egypt was reunited around 2040 B.C. The period that followed is known as the Middle Kingdom. Strong kings expanded the empire and revived the tradition of pyramid building. They were inspired by the great pyramids of the Old Kingdom and often built their tombs near the old sites. But the Middle Kingdom pyramids do not have the same grandeur. They were usually based around a core of mud bricks, many of which slowly collapsed over the years. Middle Kingdom pharaohs were preoccupied with creating complicated devices and false passages to keep thieves from finding their burial chambers. But the kings were buried with priceless treasures, and the robbers stopped at nothing. Despite the elaborate precautions, all the pyramids were robbed in the period of unrest that followed the end of the Middle Kingdom, around 1750 B.C.

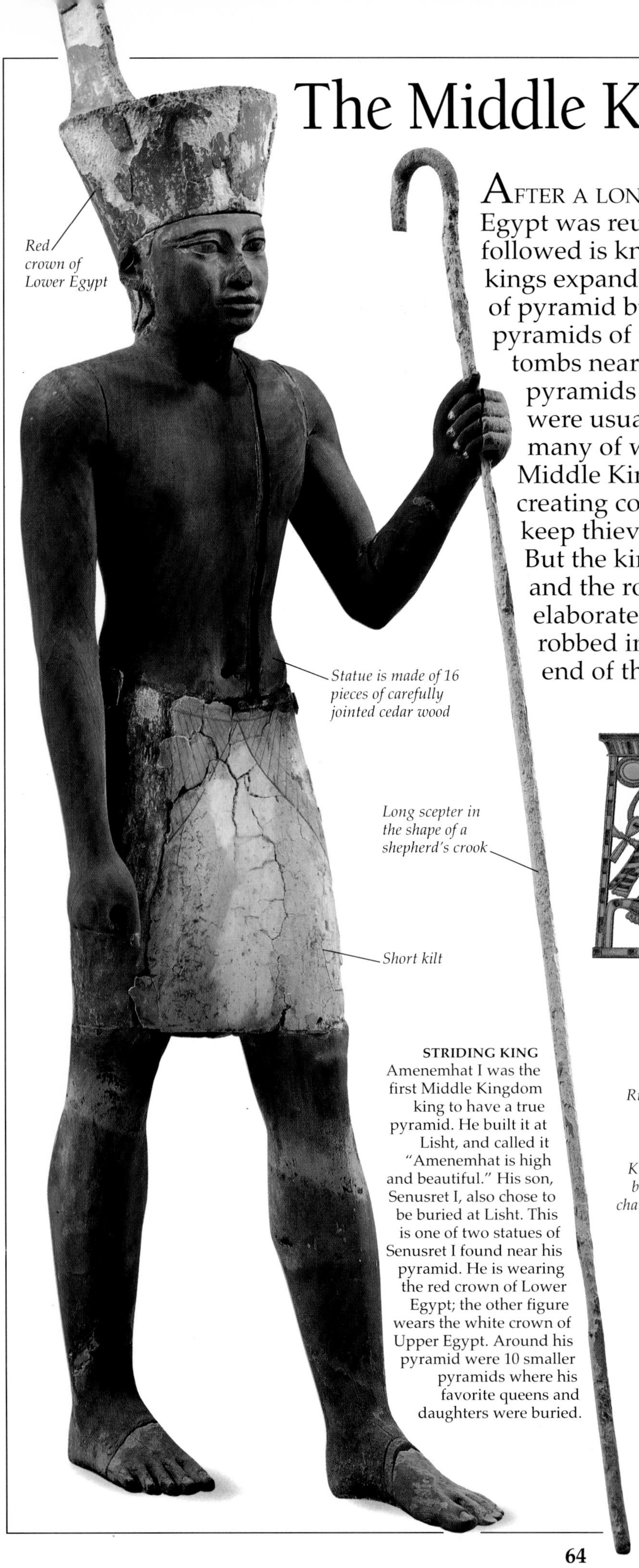

STRIDING KING
Amenemhat I was the first Middle Kingdom king to have a true pyramid. He built it at Lisht, and called it "Amenemhat is high and beautiful." His son, Senusret I, also chose to be buried at Lisht. This is one of two statues of Senusret I found near his pyramid. He is wearing the red crown of Lower Egypt; the other figure wears the white crown of Upper Egypt. Around his pyramid were 10 smaller pyramids where his favorite queens and daughters were buried.

SENUSRET II
The cartouche (hieroglyphic name) of Senusret II can be seen on this colorful piece of gold jewelry. It was part of a treasure found in the tomb of the princess Sat-Hathor III at Dahshur. Senusret II built his pyramid at El Lahun, near the Faiyum oasis.

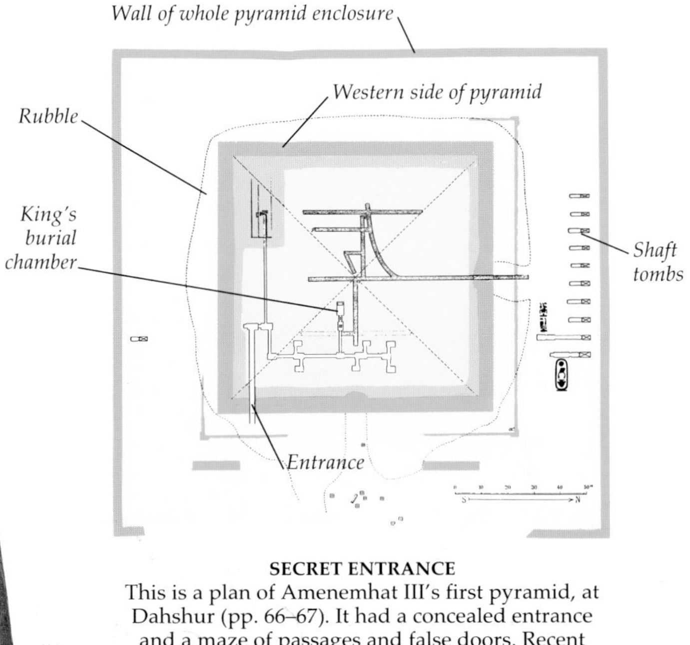

SECRET ENTRANCE
This is a plan of Amenemhat III's first pyramid, at Dahshur (pp. 66–67). It had a concealed entrance and a maze of passages and false doors. Recent excavations have revealed even more inner rooms.

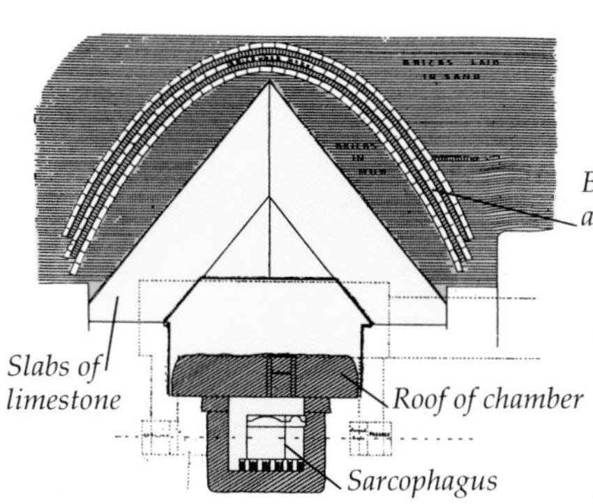

THE SECOND PYRAMID
Amenemhat III built his second pyramid at Hawara. His architects built an amazing series of devices to baffle robbers – deep wells, blind corridors, secret trapdoors, and passages sealed with mighty stone slabs. This is his burial chamber, which is covered by limestone blocks weighing 50 tons each. Thieves still broke in, stealing all the king's treasures and burning his body.

MIGHTY HEAD
The eyes have been gouged out of this massive head of Amenemhat III. Carved in black granite, it was once part of a full-length statue.

Reconstruction painting of Amenemhat III, by Winifred Brunton, done in the 1920s

Amenemhat III

The grandson of Senusret III, Amenemhat III was one of the most powerful pharaohs ever to rule Egypt. He built two pyramids and a famous labyrinth (maze) said to contain 3,000 rooms. He is also credited with building an impressive irrigation network. It was an ancient forerunner of the Aswan Dam, with massive dikes and sluices to control the water level of the Nile.

CAPSTONE
In the rubble around the Dahshur pyramid, a granite capstone was found. It is carved with Amenemhat III's royal titles and prayers to the sun god. The hieroglyphs on this detail read "Seeing the beauty of Re." Why wasn't Amenemhat buried in the Dahshur pyramid? He may have built it as a cenotaph, a symbolic place for his spirit to dwell. Or he may have decided that the layout wasn't complex enough to fool robbers.

LORD OF ALL LANDS
Another piece of gold jewelry from Princess Mereret's tomb. Near Amenemhat III's name are hieroglyphs that read, "The good god, lord of all lands and foreign countries."

The Valley of the Kings

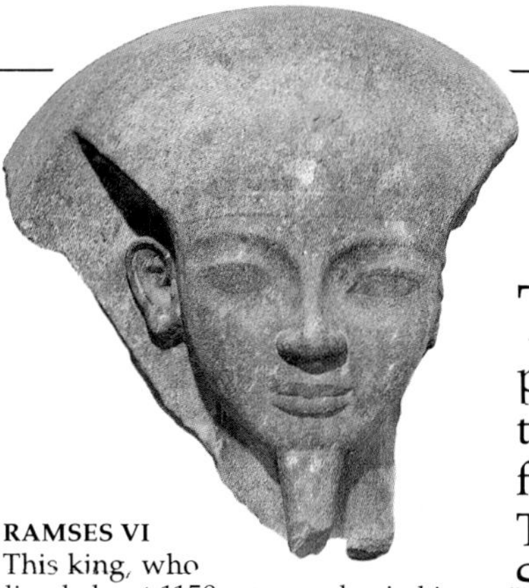

RAMSES VI
This king, who lived about 1150 B.C., was buried in a granite coffin that weighed many tons. This is part of the lid.

THE PYRAMID AGE drew to a close around 2150 B.C. Nearly all the pharoahs from Tuthmosis I (1540 B.C.) to Ramses XI (1070 B.C.) chose to be buried in tombs in the Valley of the Kings. Far away from the flood plain, the valley lay deep in the cliffs to the west of the Nile. There was a ridge in front of the entrance where guards were posted. Some of the tombs were placed high in the cliffside in an attempt to conceal their entrances from robbers; others had elaborate doors and were much more obvious. The usual pattern was for the tomb to have a deep corridor – known as the Way of the Sun God – with a well or shaft near the inner end that was intended to catch rainwater and to deter tomb robbers. Beyond this was the Hall of Gold, where the king was buried. He was surrounded by gilded furniture and jewelry, royal clothing, and regalia (crook, scepter, etc.). The contents of the tomb of Tutankhamun were the only ones to escape the hands of robbers before c. 1000 B.C.

UNDERWORLD DEITY
This hippopotamus-headed god was found in the tomb of Tuthmosis III. It is covered in a black resin. It looks ferocious, but its anger is directed only at the king's enemies. It probably represented one of the guardians of the secret doors of the mansion of the god Osiris.

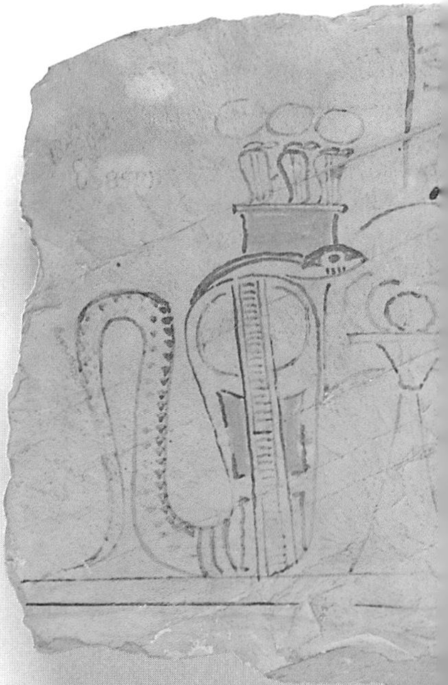

SACRED SERPENT
The valley was thought to be protected by a goddess, called Meretseger, who was portrayed as a cobra. The tomb workers thought she would blind or poison criminals and those who swore false oaths.

VALLEY VIEW
This view of the Valley of the Kings by the 19th-century artist David Roberts conveys something of the solitude of the place. Today it is much busier, with a modern road, parking lot, and the stalls of souvenir sellers destroying the ancient atmosphere.

FOREMAN AND HIS SON
Foremen like Anherkhau, shown here with his son, were responsible for making sure that the metal tools were distributed to the workers. They also had to organize the crew in the tomb so that the stonecutters would be immediately followed by the plasterers and painters, and the flow of work would not stop. This picture of Anherkhau comes from his own colorfully painted tomb.

UNKNOWN KING
This king's statue was found in the tomb of Tutankhamun, but no one knows why it was buried there. The monarch wears the Red Crown, showing authority over Lower Egypt. His crook stands for kingship, his flail for the fertility of the land.

DEIR EL MEDINA
These stone foundations are all that is left of Deir el Medina, the village where the tomb workers lived. Founded in the 16th century B.C., the village flourished for 500 years – as long as the kings continued to be buried in the valley. Usually about 60 families lived in these houses.

ALL DRESSED UP
The delicate items discovered in Tutankhamun's tomb had to be carefully prepared for transport to the Cairo Museum. Archaeologists Howard Carter and Lord Carnarvon are here wrapping up one of the guardian statues from the tomb.

Tutankhamun's tomb

The resting place of the young king Tutankhamun was the only tomb of a New Kingdom pharaoh (the New Kingdom lasted 1570–1090 B.C.) to escape almost untouched by robbers. It was found by Howard Carter in 1922, the last of the valley tombs to be discovered. Its contents included weapons, clothes, furniture, jewelry, musical instruments, and model boats, as well as the king's famous coffins and mask (p. 11). Many of these items were made of solid gold or were richly decorated with gold leaf. The king was buried with his two stillborn daughters and a lock of hair of his grandmother Queen Tiye.

The royal mummies

INSIDE THE PYRAMIDS
The mummies of the kings who built the Giza pyramids have not survived. Despite their hidden entrances sealed with huge blocks of stone, these tombs were looted in ancient times. Once inside, robbers had to find the burial chamber in the darkness, along narrow passages full of false corridors and traps.

THE FAMOUS PHARAOHS of the New Kingdom were buried at Thebes, in a desolate valley called the Valley of the Kings (p. 34). The tombs were cut deep into the rock. But despite all the precautions, they were robbed again and again in ancient times. Each time the priests had to rewrap the mummies and bury them again. Around 1000 B.C., they decided to group the royal mummies together and hide them in two caches (secret hiding places). The dead pharaohs lay hidden in these caches for nearly 3,000 years. The first cache was found in the early 1870s by three brothers who lived nearby. They kept it a secret and began to sell the treasures bit by bit. But the priceless antiquities were eventually traced to them, and in 1881 archaeologists entered a deep tomb near Deir el-Bahri. They were amazed to find 40 mummies, among them famous pharaohs such as Seti I and Ramses II. The second cache, found in 1898, held another 16 mummies, ten of them royal. When this cache was shipped to Cairo, the customs officers at the city's gate had no idea how to classify it. In the end they decided to tax the dead pharaohs at the same rate as dried fish!

LABELING THE KINGS
To avoid confusion, the priests wrote the pharaohs' names on the outer shrouds. This mummy is inscribed with the name Ramses III.

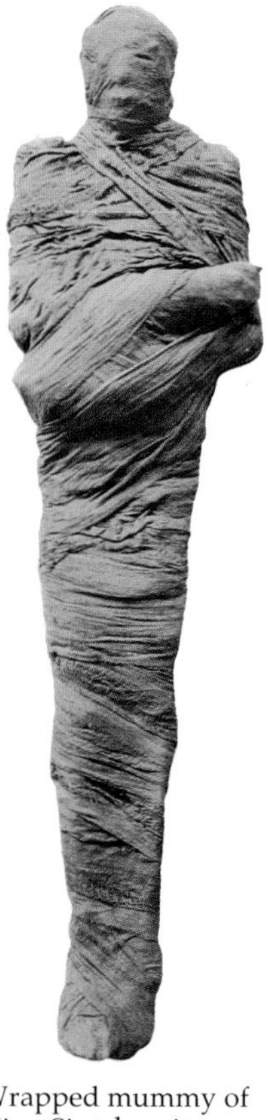

Wrapped mummy of King Siptah as it was found in 1881

Unwrapped mummy of King Siptah

REPAIR JOB
The mummy of King Siptah, who died in 1188 B.C., was badly damaged by tomb robbers searching for precious amulets in his bandages. The priests who moved him around 1000 B.C. put his broken arm in a splint before rewrapping him.

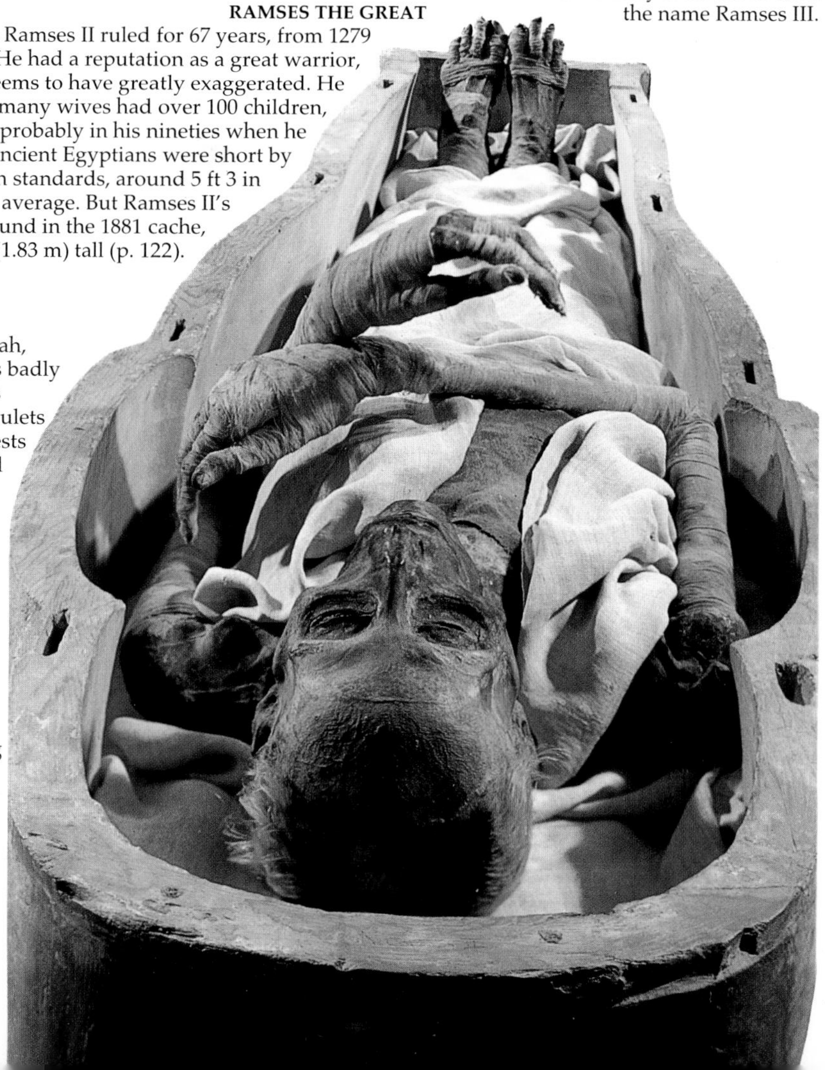

RAMSES THE GREAT
The famous Ramses II ruled for 67 years, from 1279 to 1212 B.C. He had a reputation as a great warrior, which he seems to have greatly exaggerated. He and his many wives had over 100 children, and he was probably in his nineties when he died. Ancient Egyptians were short by modern standards, around 5 ft 3 in (1.60 m) on average. But Ramses II's mummy, found in the 1881 cache, is 6 ft (1.83 m) tall (p. 122).

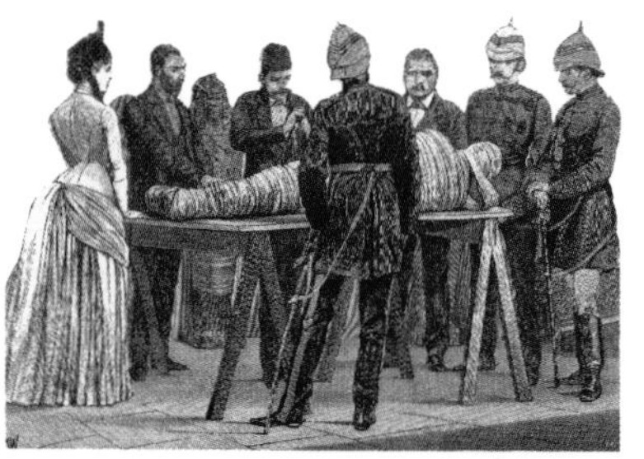

GASTON MASPERO
This French archaeologist (third from right) supervised the unwrapping of the royal mummies in Cairo. "And when I see, and touch, the bodies of so many illustrious persons we never imagined could be more than names to us", he wrote later, "I … find it hard to believe that I am not dreaming."

ROYAL COFFIN
The mummy case of King Intef (c. 1650 B.C.) is made from a hollowed-out tree trunk. This was plastered and covered with gold leaf engraved with a *rishi* feather design (p. 25). Robbers often stripped the gold leaf off royal coffins like this.

MISTAKEN IDENTITY
This well-preserved mummy was found wrapped in a shroud inscribed with the name of Tuthmosis I. But examination of the mummy suggests that it is someone else. Surviving historical records show that this pharaoh lived to about 50 years of age. But the mummy is in excellent health and seems to belong to a much younger man. The mummy's true identity is still a mystery.

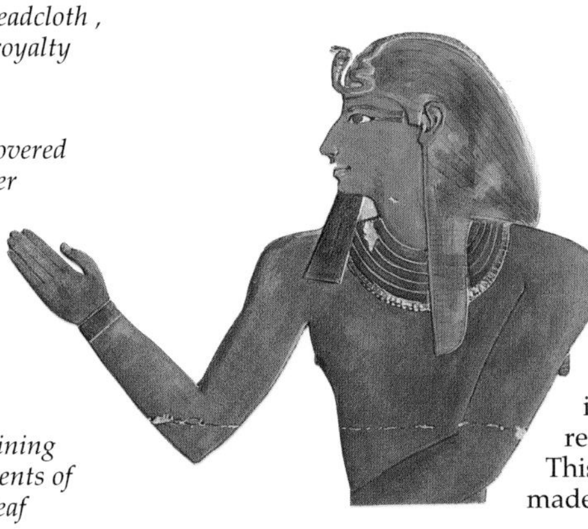

TUTHMOSIS I
A painting in a temple in Thebes shows the real king Tuthmosis I. This accurate copy was made by Howard Carter.

GARLANDS OF FLOWERS
Flower wreaths were placed around a mummy's neck as it was laid in the coffin. When the lid of Amenhotep I's coffin was lifted, the sweet smell of flowers filled the room, 3,000 years after his burial. A wasp that had been attracted by the smell had been trapped in the coffin all those years ago. Its mummified body was found next to the king's.

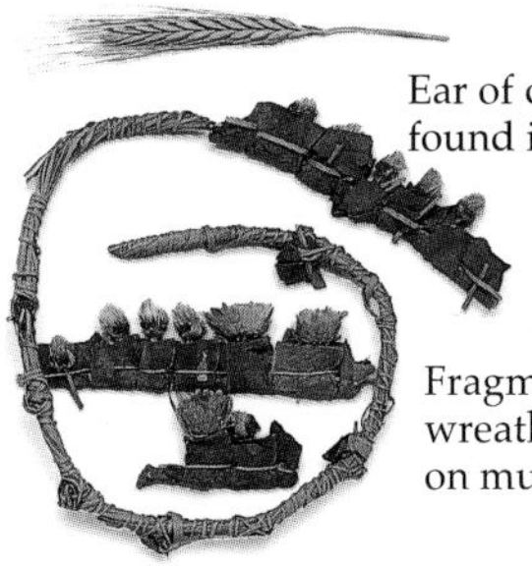

UNKNOWN QUEEN
Egyptologists are still not sure about the identity of this elderly woman with wonderful hair. Her mummy was found in the second royal cache of 1898. Some experts believe she is Hatshepsut, a female pharaoh who is often shown wearing the royal false beard. Others think she is Queen Tiy, one of the wives of Amenhotep III. Tiy is probably the grandmother of Tutankhamun (pp. 11, 73).

CRUEL DEATH
The strangest body found among the royal mummies was this unknown man. His face is distorted with agony, and his mouth is open as if he was screaming. He must have died horribly, perhaps by being poisoned, suffocated, or even buried alive. His body was wrapped in a sheepskin, a material the Egyptians thought was unclean. No one knows what horrible crime he committed to deserve such a cruel death.

A KING AT REST
The second cache of royal mummies was found in the tomb of Amenhotep II in 1898. Most of the mummies were shipped to Cairo, but Amenhotep was left lying in his sarcophagus where he had been found. Shortly after this photo was taken, a band of robbers overcame the armed guards and ripped open his bandages looking for valuable amulets.

The treasures of Tutankhamun

Howard Carter (center) and his team stare in wonder at the sarcophagus through a door in the fourth shrine

ON NOVEMBER 26, 1922, Howard Carter peered through a small hole into a dark tomb in the Valley of the Kings (pp. 34, 68–71). "As my eyes grew accustomed to the light," he wrote later, "... I was struck dumb with amazement." The English archaeologist and his rich supporter Lord Carnarvon, had just discovered the tomb of the pharaoh Tutankhamun, sealed over 3,200 years before. Five years of exploration had led them to the only fully intact royal tomb ever found – and probably the most exciting archaeological discovery ever made. Inside was the king's mummy, wearing a superbly crafted mask of solid gold. The body lay in a nest of three gold mummy cases, each fitting inside the next. The cases rested in turn in a sarcophagus surrounded by four gilded wooden shrines and an amazing array of statues, furniture, and jewelry. As Carter put it, it was a room full of "gold – everywhere the glint of gold."

KING AND QUEEN
The carving on this ebony and ivory box shows Tutankhamun in a garden receiving flowers from his queen. When his father, the powerful pharaoh Akhenaten, died, Tutankhamun was no more than nine years old. He probably never had much real power, and would barely be remembered if his tomb had not survived in such perfect condition.

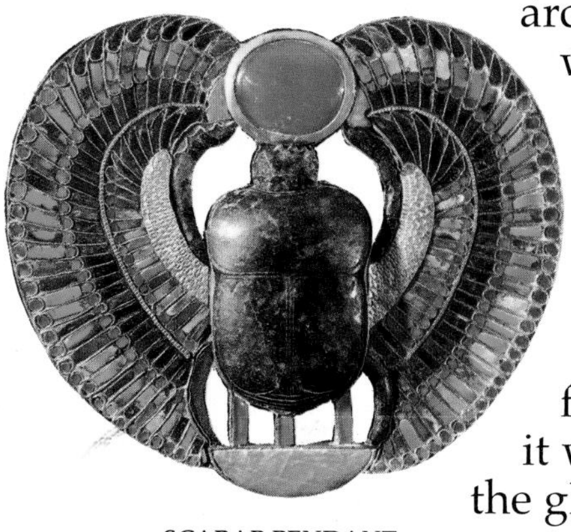

SCARAB PENDANT
This pendant of a winged scarab beetle is made of gold and semi-precious stones. The design spells out the three hieroglyphs – Neb, Kheperu, and Re – of Tutankhamun's name.

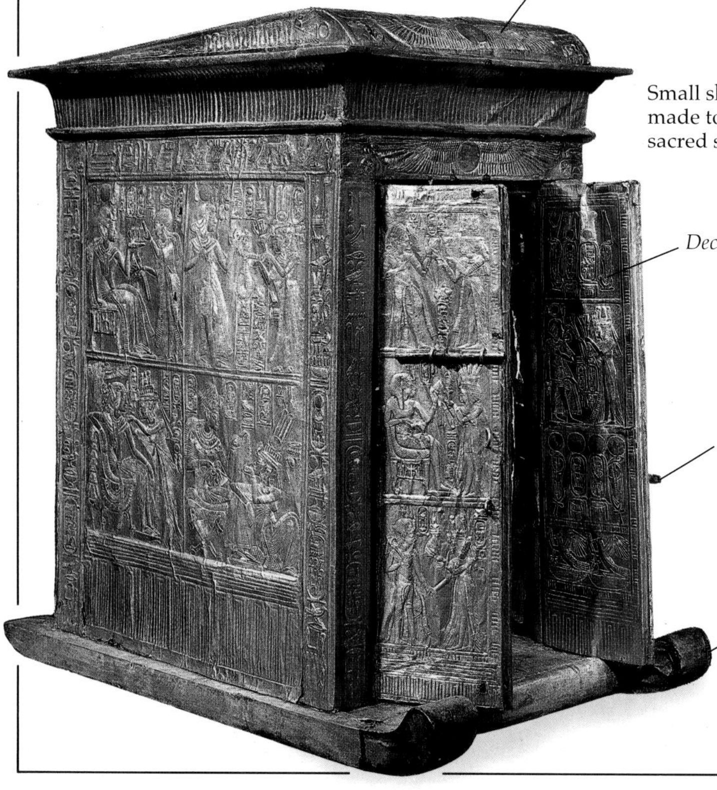

Small shrine made to hold a sacred statue

THE KING'S DUMMY
This painted wooden "dummy" shows the king as he must have looked when he died c. 1324 B.C. It was probably dressed in his clothes and jewelry.

THE MUMMY
The king's mummy was poorly preserved because of chemical reactions with embalming resins. He was slightly built and stood about 5 ft 5 in (1.65 m) tall. Studies of his teeth gave an age of 16 or 17, though he may have been as old as 22. X-rays showed damage to his skull, but his actual cause of death is uncertain. The uneasy political situation during his reign suggests that he may have been murdered.

PAINTED BOX
This wooden box was stuffed with clothes, including the pharaoh's sandals. It is painted with scenes from Tutankhamun's life. On this side, he can be seen leading his army to victory over the Syrians. But it is unlikely that the king ever went to war, and the painting is thought to be a symbolic representation of the pharaoh's supreme power. In two similar scenes on the lid, the young king hunts lions, ostriches, and antelopes in the desert.

GOLD MASK
The king's mummy mask was made of solid gold inlaid with colorful glass and stones, including dark blue lapis lazuli. It weighed over 22.5 lb (10.2 kg). The pharaoh is wearing a *nemes* headdress (p. 33), and a vulture and a cobra sit on his brow.

ILLVSTRAZIONE DEL POPOLO
Supplemento della Gazzetta del Popolo

SLOW GOING
An Italian newspaper from 1924 tells the tale of the amazing discovery. Though Carter and Carnavon found the tomb in November 1922, Carter was so careful and painstaking in his work that he didn't begin to open the coffins until October 1925. It took him almost a decade to examine the entire contents of the tomb.

A NEST OF GOLD AND GEMSTONES
This is Tutankhamun's middle mummy case. Like the outer case, it was made of wood covered in gold and colored stones. It fitted so snugly inside the outer case that Carter had a lot of difficulty lifting it out. Inside it was a third, inner case. This was solid gold and weighed an unbelievable 245 lb (110.4 kg).

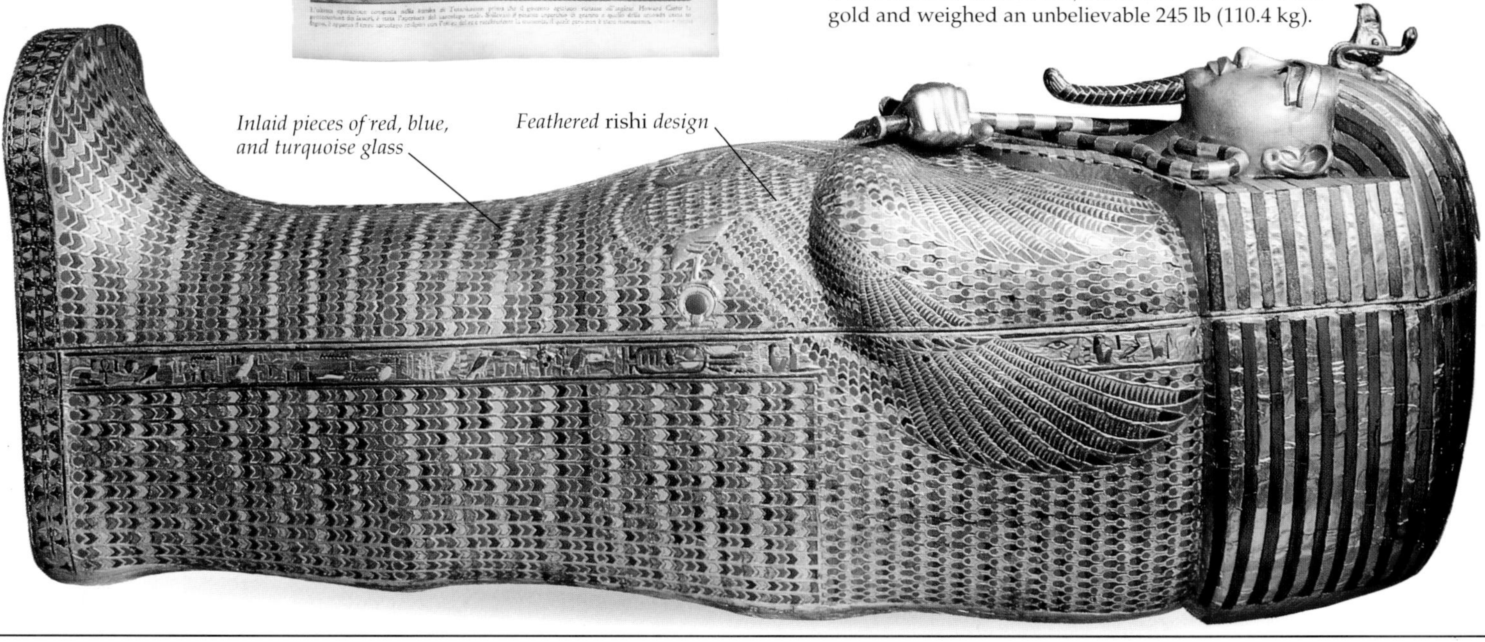

Pyramids of Nubia

STEEP SIDES
Nubian pyramids are smaller than the great Egyptian ones and have much steeper sides. Against the eastern face was a small funerary chapel with a gateway decorated like an Egyptian temple. Priests and pilgrims who came to honor the dead king and queen said prayers and placed offerings within the chapel. This is one of the pyramids at Meroe, in modern Sudan, as it appeared in 1820. Some 14 years later, several pyramids at Meroe were badly damaged by an Italian adventurer searching for treasure (pp. 76–77).

FARTHER UP THE NILE RIVER, to the south of Egypt, lies Nubia. This desert land was one of the areas where African civilization first developed. It was rich in gold and exotic goods. Nubia's position on the Nile gave it great strategic importance, and for centuries Egypt's pharaohs fought to control it. There are more than one hundred pyramids in Nubia. Over the centuries, they were all plundered for their stone, and today most of them are shapeless mounds. Like the Egyptian pyramids, they were also robbed of their treasures long ago. The first Nubian pyramids were built around 700 B.C., during a brief period when the Nubian kings ruled Egypt. They are at Kurru and Nuri, near Napata, the Nubian capital. When the capital was moved south to Meroe, around 300 B.C., pyramids were also built there. The kings and queens were mummified and buried underneath. Servants were often sacrificed and buried in the pyramid too, so that they could wait on their kings and queens in the next world.

STEPPING DOWN
The burial chamber was dug under the pyramid, not built into the structure. It was approached by a long, descending flight of steps, which opened into a series of three connecting chambers cut deep into the bedrock.

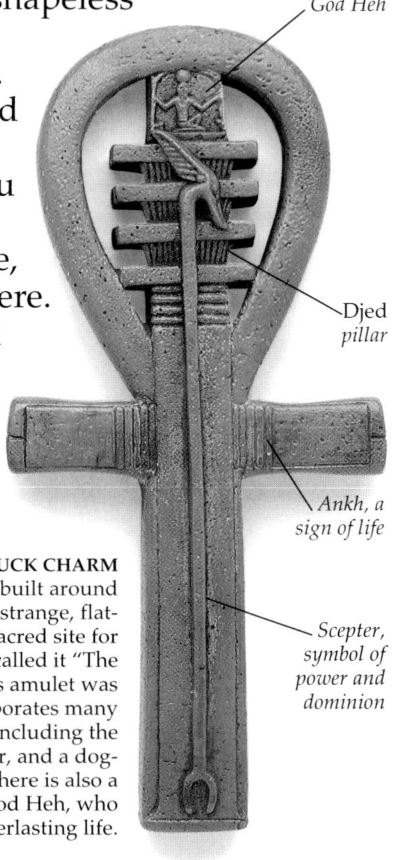

GOOD LUCK CHARM
Some pyramids were built around Gebel Barkal. This strange, flat-topped peak was a sacred site for the Nubians, who called it "The Pure Mountain." This amulet was found there. It incorporates many magical symbols, including the ankh, the *djed* pillar, and a dog-headed scepter. There is also a figure of the god Heh, who represented everlasting life.

A PYRAMID FIELD AT MEROE
These are the pyramids in the northern cemetery at Meroe. They were built between 300 B.C. and about A.D. 350, when Nubia was conquered by the Axumites. By the 1st century A.D., Meroe was the center of one of Africa's great civilizations. At its peak, Nubia was a fascinating mixture of Egyptian, Greek, Roman, and central African culture. As the kingdom declined, the kings built smaller, less impressive pyramids.

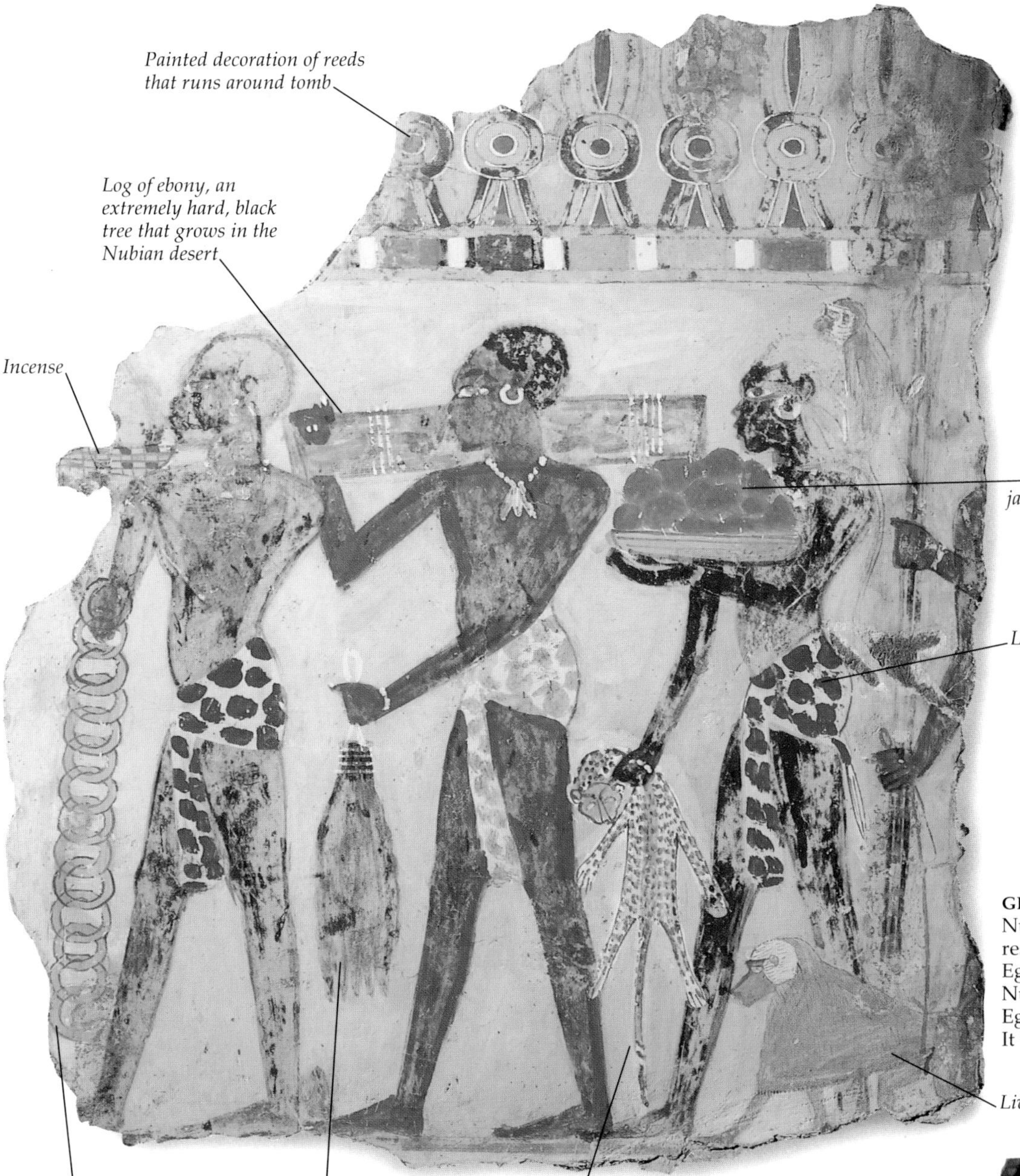

EGYPTIAN STYLE
The Egyptians settled in Nubia, founding new towns and spreading their culture. This slender pot is decorated with lotus leaves in a typical Egyptian style.

GIRAFFE TAILS FOR THE KING
Nubia was rich in natural resources, especially gold. This Egyptian tomb painting shows Nubians giving exotic gifts to the Egyptian pharaoh Thutmose IV. It was painted around 1400 B.C.

A queen's treasure

Of all the hundreds of pyramids in Egypt and Nubia, a hoard of treasure has been found in only one. The pyramid, at Meroe in the Sudan, belonged to Queen Amanishakheto, who ruled Nubia in the first century B.C. In 1834, the Italian adventurer Giuseppe Ferlini found a magnificent collection of jewelry in a secret chamber near the top of the tomb. At that time, the pyramid was one of the best preserved in Nubia. But Ferlini was not an archeologist. He tore the pyramid to pieces in his greedy hunt for more treasure.

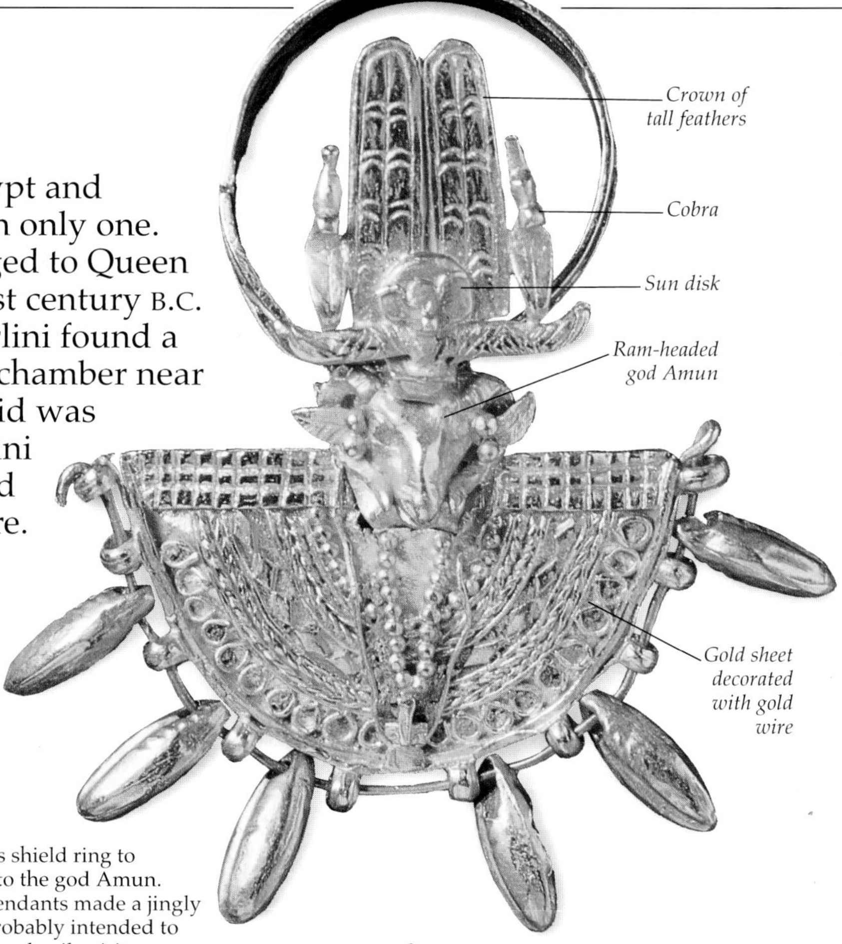

ARMS FULL OF BRACELETS
Ferlini found five pairs of bracelets. Nubian queens were shown wearing many bracelets, and Amanishakheto may have worn all ten at the same time. This is Queen Nawidamak, Amanishakheto's predecessor.

JINGLE BELLS
The queen wore this shield ring to show her devotion to the god Amun. The drop-shaped pendants made a jingly noise, which was probably intended to please Amun and repel evil spirits.

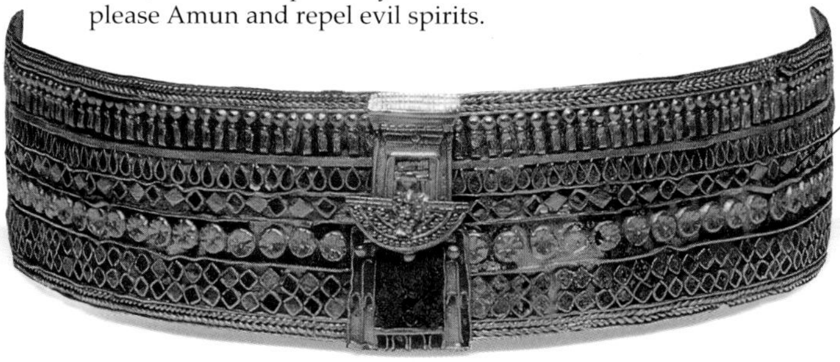

Bracelet with a small image of Amun before a chapel

Engraving published by Richard Lepsius in the 1840s

ALL EYES TOGETHER
The *wadjet* eye was a very popular good luck charm. It was also known as the Eye of Horus. Egyptians and Nubians wore an eye amulet to protect them from evil. These *wadjet* eyes have been linked in a chain, together with a hanging pendant shaped like a lotus flower.

SPREADING HER WINGS
The goddess Mut is the centerpiece of this beautiful gold bracelet. She is holding out her feathered wings in a protective gesture. Nubian queens identified themselves with Mut, believing she was the wife of their most important god, Amun.

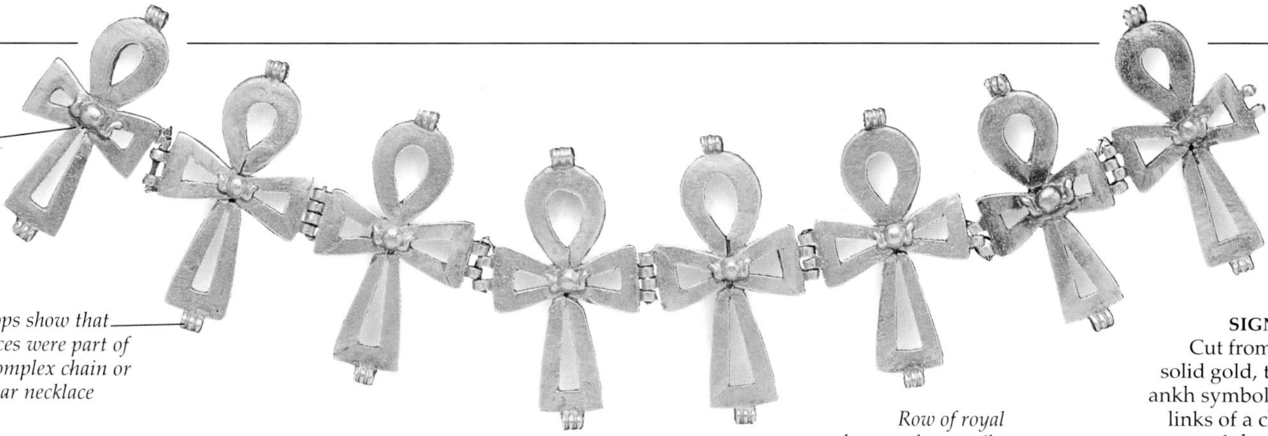

SIGNS OF LIFE
Cut from a sheet of solid gold, these eight ankh symbols form the links of a chain worn around the neck. The ankh was the sacred sign of life and was usually reserved for kings, queens, and gods. Only they had the power to give or take away life. The origin of the looped cross is uncertain, but it may represent the tie straps of a sandal.

EVERYDAY JEWELRY
There were nine shield rings in Amanishakheto's jewelry collection. This one features the lion-headed god Apedemak. It was not worn on the fingers like an ordinary ring. Instead he queen must have attached it to her hair and hung it over her forehead. Scientific examination has revealed traces of wear on the queen's jewelry. This proves that it wasn't made specially for her tomb. She must have worn it in her daily life.

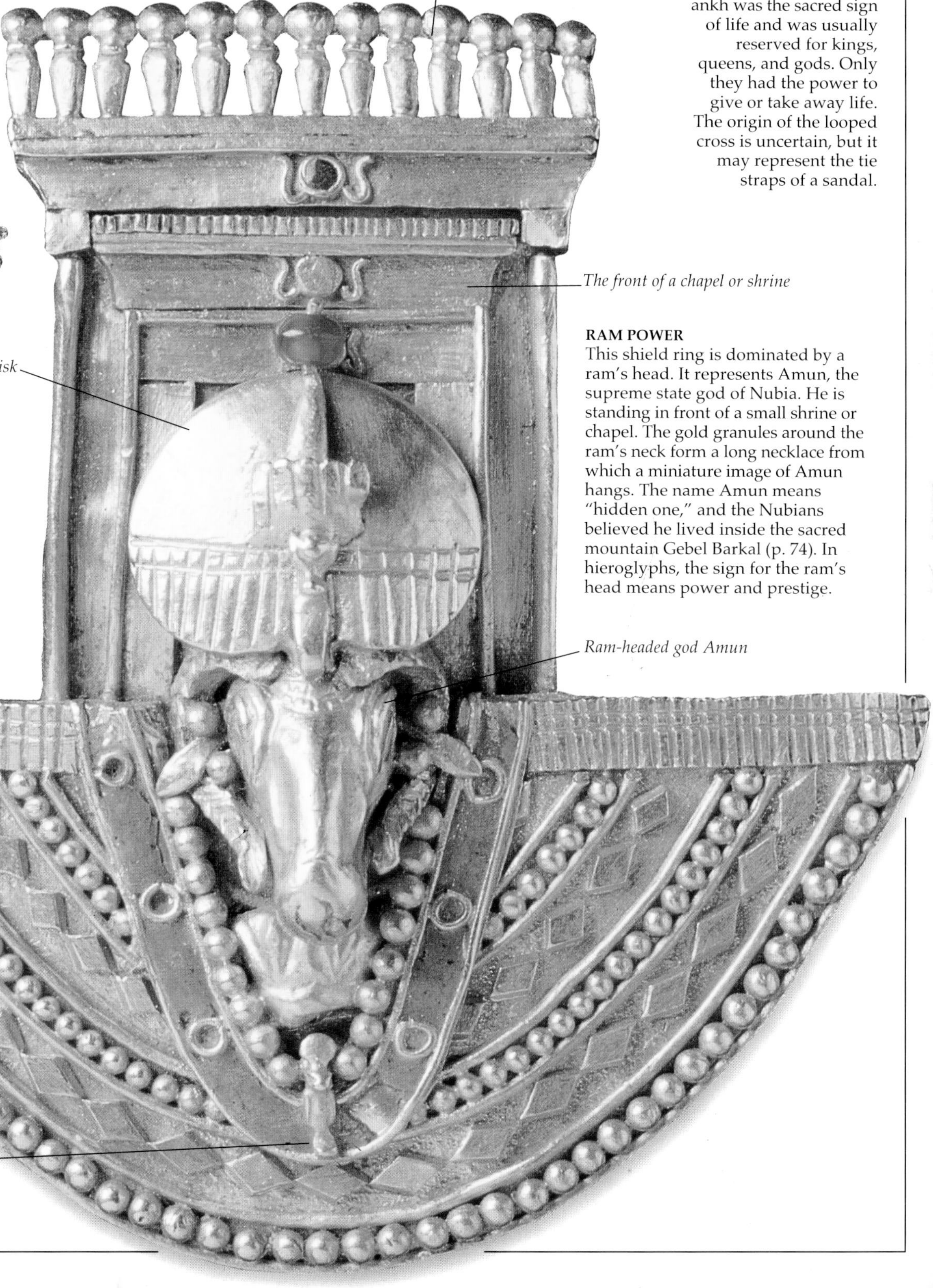

RAM POWER
This shield ring is dominated by a ram's head. It represents Amun, the supreme state god of Nubia. He is standing in front of a small shrine or chapel. The gold granules around the ram's neck form a long necklace from which a miniature image of Amun hangs. The name Amun means "hidden one," and the Nubians believed he lived inside the sacred mountain Gebel Barkal (p. 74). In hieroglyphs, the sign for the ram's head means power and prestige.

Gods and goddesses

THE GODS AND THEIR MAKERS
This detail from a 19th-century painting shows the artist's idea of a workshop in which Egyptian figures of the gods were made. The cat is modeling for an image of Bastet (opposite).

THE EGYPTIANS worshiped hundreds of different gods and goddesses, and sometimes it is difficult to work out who was who. Many of the gods are represented by animals. For example, a baboon might stand for Thoth, god of wisdom, at one temple, and a moon god called Khonsu at another. Each of the 42 different administrative districts, or nomes, had its own god, and there were many others besides. Overall, the sun god was the dominant deity in Egyptian religion, although he could take different forms. At dawn he would be Khepri, the scarab beetle rolling the sun disk above the eastern horizon. He could then become Re-Harakhty, the great hawk soaring in the sky. He was seen as responsible for all creation – people, animals, the fertility of the soil, and the king's journey through the underworld. As Amun-Re he was king of the gods and protector of the pharaoh when he went on military campaigns. The pharaoh Akhenaten saw the sun god as a disk with rays ending in human hands holding the sign of life (p. 13). During his reign all other gods were banished, but his son-in-law Tutankhamun restored them (pp.10-11).

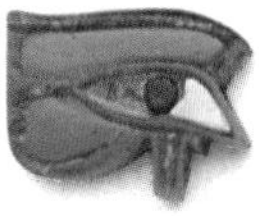

Wadjet eye

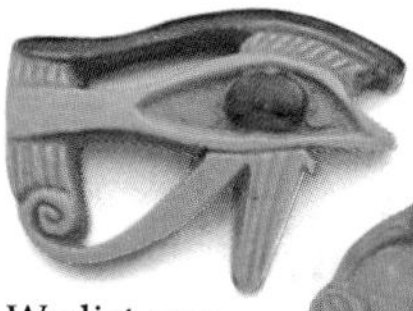

Wadjet eye

Scarab

Ibis

Winged scarab

AMULETS
The wadjet eye symbolizes both the vengeful eye of the sun god and the eye of the god Horus, torn out by Seth (a god of evil) in the struggle for the throne of Egypt, but magically restored. It was said to protect everything behind it. The scarab beetle symbolized the sun god Khepri. The real insect pushes a ball of dung around, and the Egyptians imagined that the sun was propelled in a similar way. The sacred ibis represents Thoth, god of wisdom and healing.

AMUN-RE *right*
Amun-Re became the principal god during the New Kingdom. He handed the scimitar of conquest to great warrior pharaohs like Tuthmosis III. He had a mysterious nature, which even the other gods were unaware of – the word *Amun* means "hidden."

THOTH *below*
The curved beak of the ibis was like the crescent moon, so the bird became the symbol of the moon god Thoth. He was the patron of the scribes, and gave the Egyptians knowledge of writing, medicine, and mathematics.

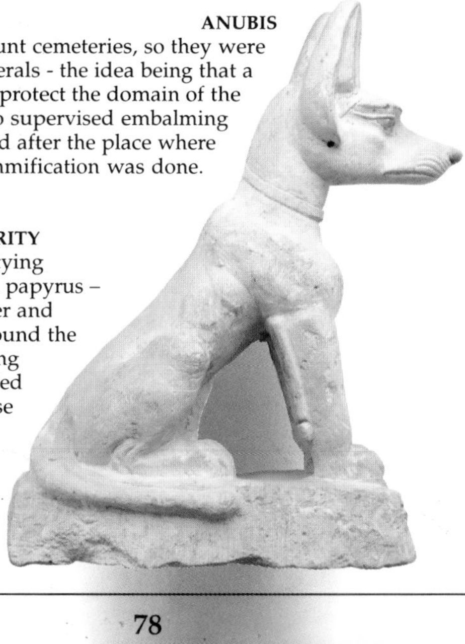

ANUBIS
Jackals used to haunt cemeteries, so they were linked with funerals - the idea being that a jackal god would protect the domain of the dead. Anubis also supervised embalming (p. 14) and looked after the place where mummification was done.

GODS OF PROSPERITY
These figures are tying together lotus and papyrus – the plants of Upper and Lower Egypt – around the hieroglyph meaning "unite." Often called the Nile gods, these figures were symbols of the fertility that came from the river's annual flood.

FACE TO FACE
The king of Egypt was the embodiment of the god Horus and was therefore thought to be divine himself. This relief shows Tuthmosis III before the god. The hawk-headed god was also a solar deity - the hawk high in the sky whose eyes were thought of as the sun and moon. The name Horus in Egyptian meant "he who is far above."

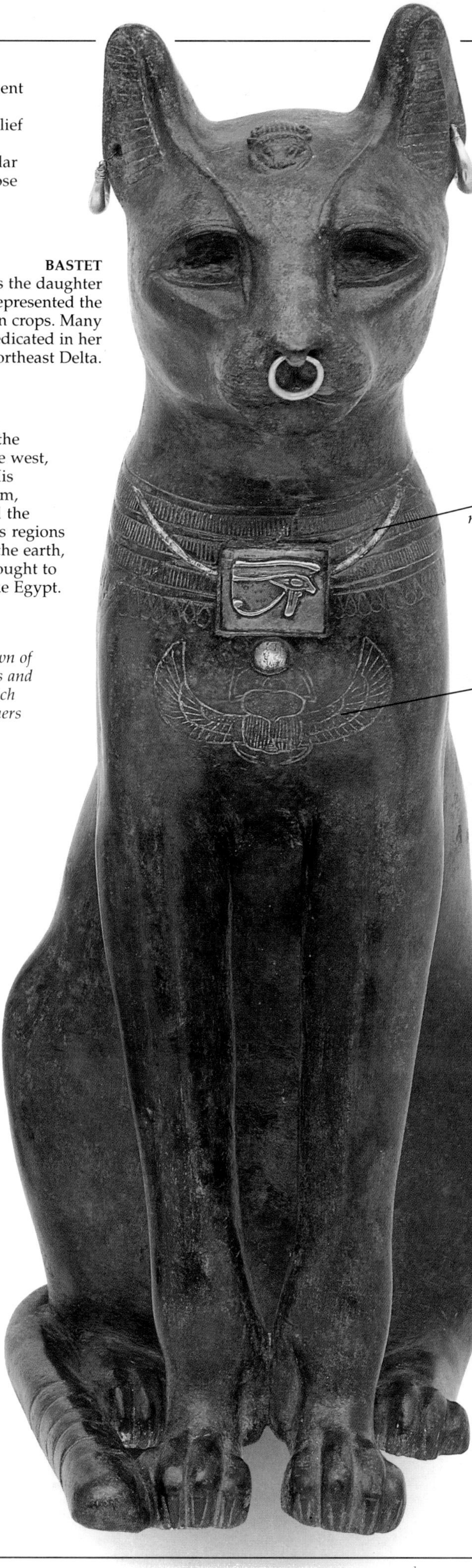

BASTET
The cat goddess Bastet was the daughter of Re, the sun god. She represented the power of the sun to ripen crops. Many bronze cat figures were dedicated in her now ruined temple in the northeast Delta.

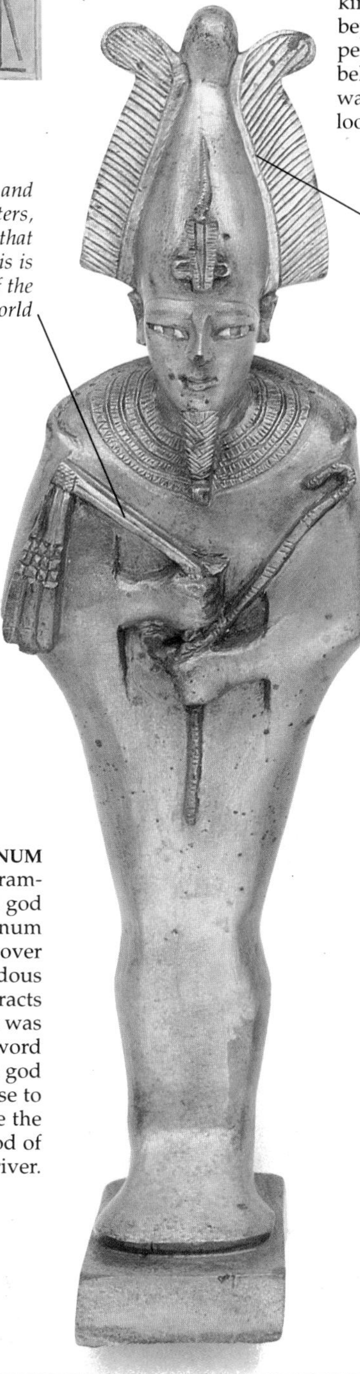

OSIRIS
Osiris, called "foremost of the westerners," because most of the cemeteries were situated in the west, was god of the underworld. His kingdom, beyond the perilous regions below the earth, was thought to look like Egypt.

KHNUM
The ram-headed god Khnum presided over the hazardous Nile cataracts (rapids). It was on his word that the god Hapy rose to cause the yearly flood of the river.

The mummy and the god Osiris

THE GOD OSIRIS was said to have triumphed over death, and every ancient Egyptian wanted to follow his example. Legend told that far back in history, Osiris was a good pharaoh who was murdered by his evil brother, Seth. But his wife, Isis, and son, Horus, brought Osiris back to life. The story of the dead king's miraculous resurrection gave Egyptians hope in everlasting life. So to be reborn, a dead person tried to be identified with Osiris in every possible way. Mummies were prepared in exactly the same way as the body of Osiris had been long ago. If all went well, the mummy would "become an Osiris" and live forever.

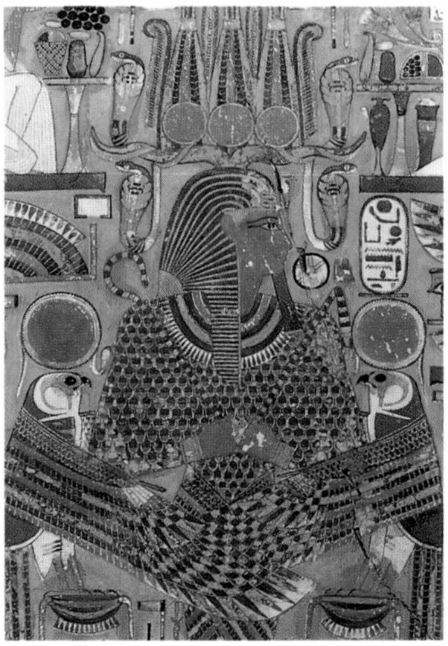

Brightly colored coffin painting of Osiris wearing cobra crown and protected by falcons

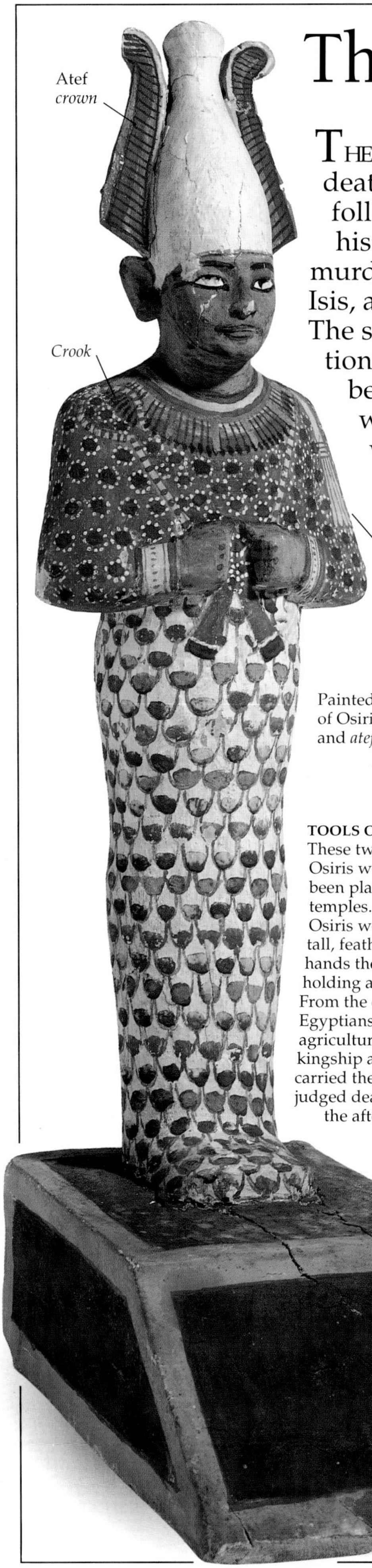

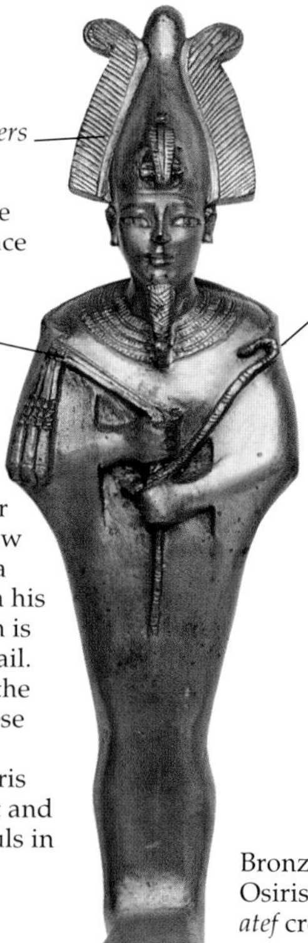

Painted wooden statue of Osiris with green face and *atef* crown

TOOLS OF THE TRADE
These two statues of Osiris would have been placed in tombs or temples. They both show Osiris wearing an *atef*, a tall, feathered crown. In his hands the dead pharaoh is holding a crook and a flail. From the earliest times, the Egyptians associated these agricultural tools with kingship and justice. Osiris carried them when he sat and judged dead people's souls in the afterlife (p. 13).

Bronze statue of Osiris wearing *atef* crown

KEEP A STRAIGHT BACK
The djed pillar is an amulet placed in the wrappings of a mummy (pp. 20–21). It was believed to represent the backbone of Osiris, and was thought to give the mummy strength after death.

MUMMY AND SON
The goddess Isis was the wife of Osiris. In this statue she is holding their son, Horus. The ancient Egyptians respected her as a devoted wife and loving mother.

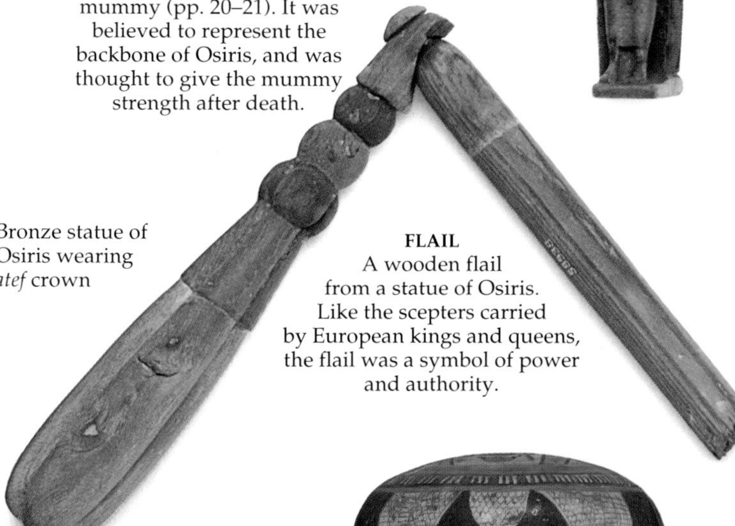

FLAIL
A wooden flail from a statue of Osiris. Like the scepters carried by European kings and queens, the flail was a symbol of power and authority.

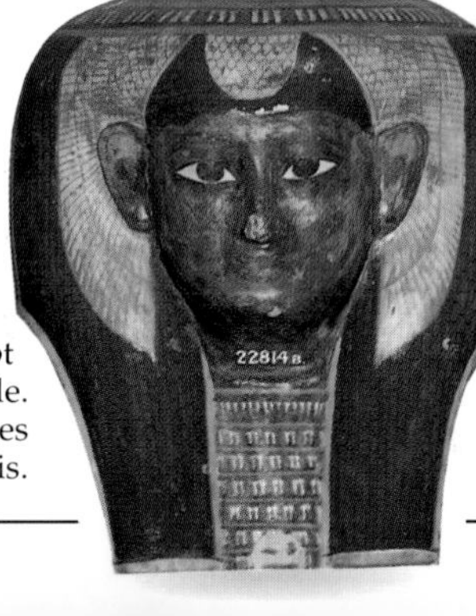

GREEN FACE
Among other things, the all-important Osiris was the god of vegetation and natural rebirth. In this role he was connected to the yearly flood of the Nile, which kept Egypt's lands green and fertile. Mummy cases often have green faces to link them with this aspect of Osiris.

CORN MUMMY

It looks like a real mummy. But inside the linen bandages of this mummy-shaped model are grains of corn, not an embalmed body. The corn "mummy" is wearing a wax mask modeled to look like Osiris. The Egyptians associated the god with the success of the corn harvest. Placed in a tomb, the corn mummy would also help a real mummy to join Osiris in the next world.

GROWING POWER

The power of Osiris was thought to be shown in the sprouting of corn seeds. Figures of the god were even modeled in Nile mud and sown with corn. This one was found in Tutankhamun's tomb (pp. 38–39).

Panel from the tomb of Hesire, the king's dentist in c. 2700 B.C.

Magic and medicine

THE GODS OF THE TEMPLES played little part in the lives of ordinary Egyptians, so many people used magic to ease problems like the dangers of childbirth, infant mortality, and fevers. The Egyptians also had great medical skill. Physicians' papyrus manuals survive which describe how to treat ailments and reveal a detailed knowledge of anatomy. They wrote about the importance of the heart and how it "speaks out" through the back of the head and hands – a reference to the pulse beat. There were remedies for eye disorders, tumors, and some physical complaints. The Egyptians believed that many diseases came from wormlike creatures invading the body. Physicians and magicians worked together, using both medicines and spells for problems like snake bites and scorpion stings. They also used magic to ward off possible injuries from crocodiles or the ghosts of the dead. Letters to the dead could be written on pottery bowls and put in tombs if a person felt that a dead relative's spirit was upset or likely to cause trouble. Dangers were also counteracted by amulets, or magical charms.

Headrest amulet

Pillar amulet

Knot amulet

AMULETS
Magical charms could be worn on necklaces and bracelets while a person was alive, and placed on the person's corpse in the mummy wrappings to give protection in the next life. They were supposed to ward off injury and were sometimes accompanied by spells.

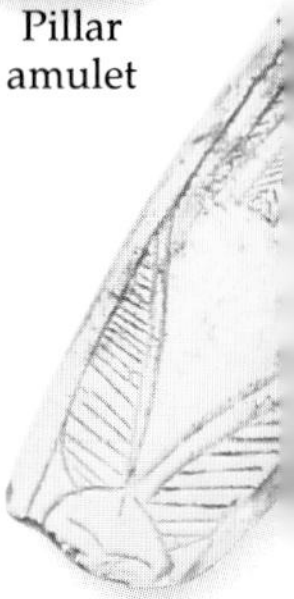

Powerful plants

Plants played an integral part in both magic and medicine. Juniper berries were valued enough to be imported from Lebanon. Garlic was prized for its medicinal properties and was used in magic, too.

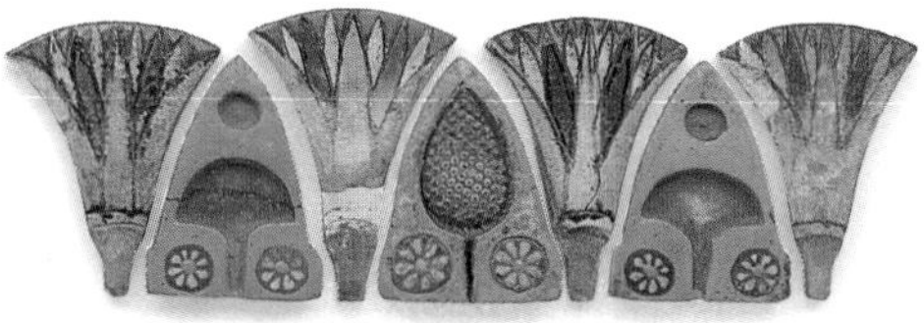

LOTUS
The lotus was very important to the Egyptians – they decorated their temples and many of their belongings with images of the lotus.

Lotus blossom

HEAR OUR PRAYER
On this stela (stone tablet) is a prayer to the god Ptah, and ears to help him hear it.

JUNIPER BERRIES
These were placed in the mummies of royalty and courtiers or were left in baskets in their tombs. The juice was used in the purification rituals performed over the corpse.

GODDESS OF CHILDBIRTH
Prayers to the goddess Taweret were an essential part of giving birth. She was shown as a pregnant hippopotamus and sometimes looked ferocious – this was to keep evil from attacking the woman as she gave birth. Magic liquid could be poured from her breast.

HENNA
Henna, used to color the hair and skin, was supposed to have the power to ward off danger.

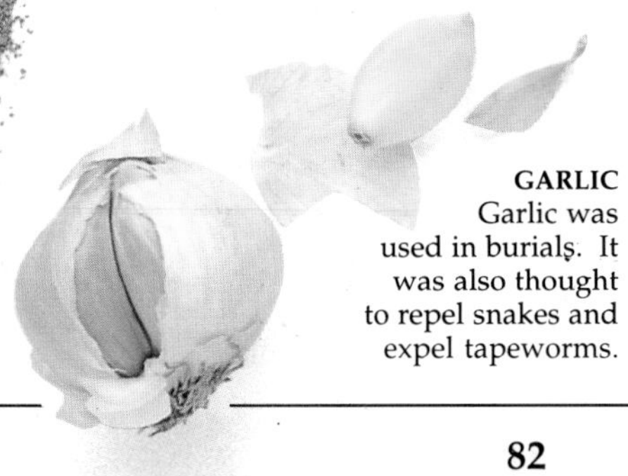

GARLIC
Garlic was used in burials. It was also thought to repel snakes and expel tapeworms.

MAGICAL KNIFE
The designs on these boomerang-shaped objects were thought to have great power. It was the total combination of all the creatures that gave this knife its power. The knife was probably used to draw a magical protective barrier around vulnerable parts of a house.

READY FOR SACRIFICE
This painting of a calf shows it adorned with a garland of flowers, as it would be when taken to be sacrificed. Offerings of food were made to the temple gods (p. 86).

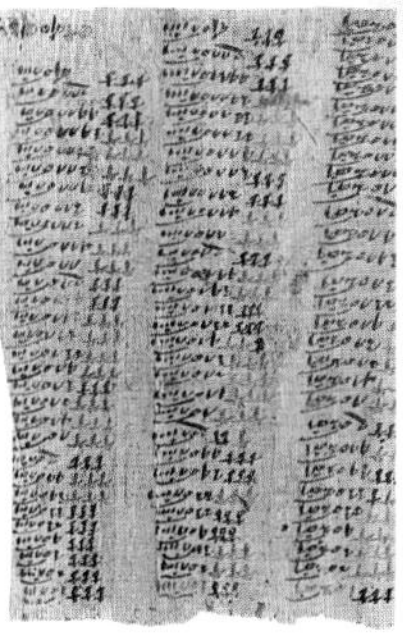

CALENDAR
On this papyrus calendar, most of the days are written in black. The days in red are unlucky ones. The color red reminded the Egyptians of the dry deserts and was often used to represent bad fortune.

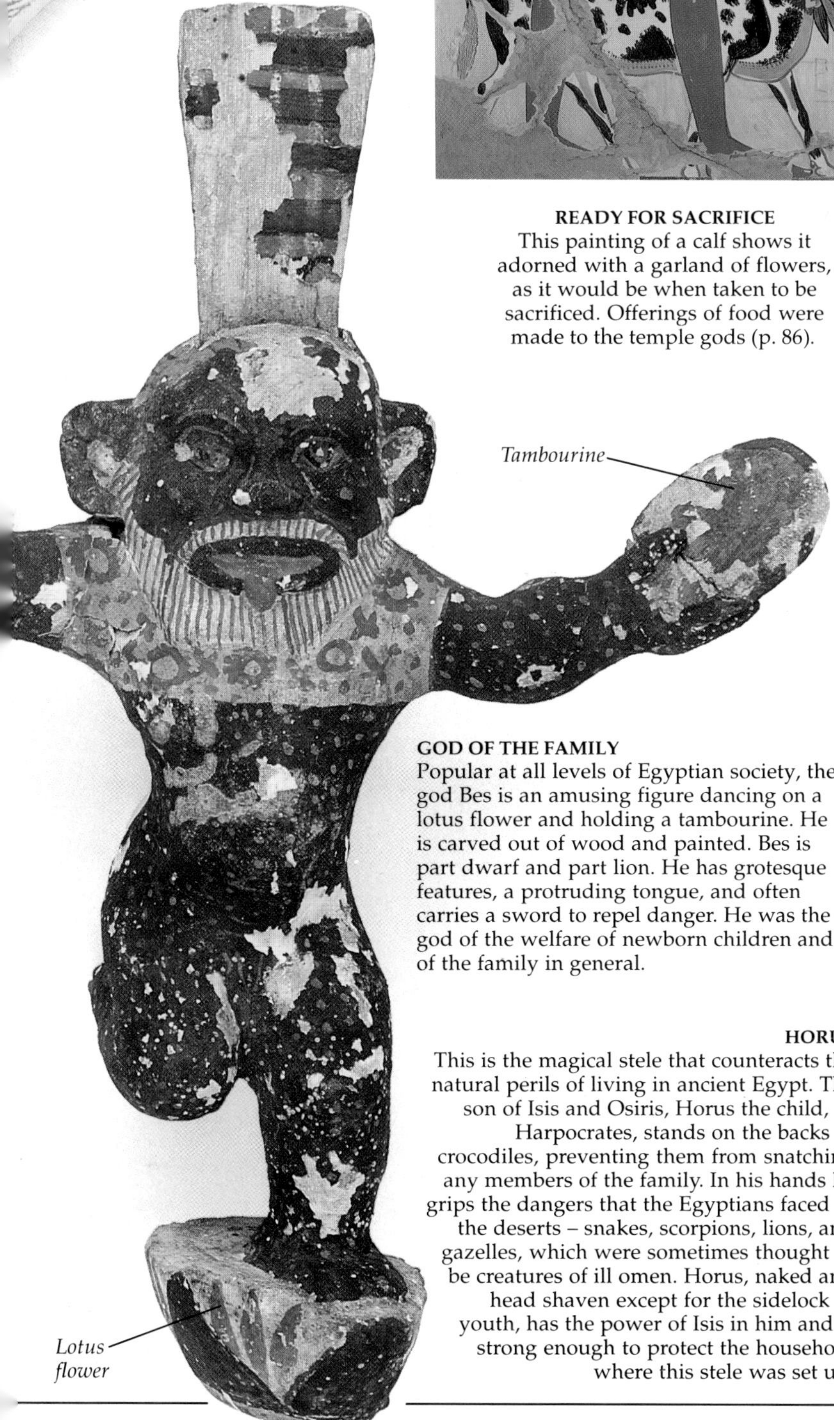

GOD OF THE FAMILY
Popular at all levels of Egyptian society, the god Bes is an amusing figure dancing on a lotus flower and holding a tambourine. He is carved out of wood and painted. Bes is part dwarf and part lion. He has grotesque features, a protruding tongue, and often carries a sword to repel danger. He was the god of the welfare of newborn children and of the family in general.

HORUS
This is the magical stele that counteracts the natural perils of living in ancient Egypt. The son of Isis and Osiris, Horus the child, or Harpocrates, stands on the backs of crocodiles, preventing them from snatching any members of the family. In his hands he grips the dangers that the Egyptians faced in the deserts – snakes, scorpions, lions, and gazelles, which were sometimes thought to be creatures of ill omen. Horus, naked and head shaven except for the sidelock of youth, has the power of Isis in him and is strong enough to protect the household where this stele was set up.

Priests and temples

FEED THE BIRDS
Ibises, sacred to the god Thoth, were revered in Egypt. This detail from a fanciful 19th-century painting shows ibises being fed by a priestess.

IN THEORY, the pharaoh was supposed to act as the high priest in every temple in Egypt, but since that was impractical, his duties were usually carried out by the chief priest. In the great temples such as Karnak at Thebes, sacred to Amun-Re, king of the gods, the chief priest had great power and controlled the vast wealth in the temple treasuries and the great lands of the temple estates. It was possible for the office of chief priest to remain in the hands of one family for generations until the pharaoh broke their hold by making an appointment from outside. The priests had titles to indicate their power – they were called God's Servant, with the addition of First, Second, or Third, to show their position. Priests at lower levels were called Pure Ones or God's Fathers, and had the responsibility of serving on the temple rota system, maintaining the temple's property, and keeping administrative records.

KNEELING PRIEST
This type of priest was called a Yun-mutef priest, meaning "Pillar of his Mother." He symbolizes the divine child Horus (p. 83) wears a leopard skin, and has his hair in a sidelock to represent youth. He kneels at an offering table.

FALSE DOOR
Courtiers had tomb chapels with false doors, which stood for the idea of contact between the tomb and the place where offerings to the gods could be made. "Soul priests" would leave offerings of food and drink at these doors - on this door several bearers are shown bringing meat, poultry, and bread to the tomb.

THE TEMPLE OF DENDERA
The goddess Hathor's temple as it survives today was built during the time when Egypt was ruled by the Greeks and Romans (pp. 124–125) – in fact, Queen Cleopatra is shown on its rear wall. The heads belong to the goddess Hathor.

LAST OF THE TEMPLES
This detail of a painting by David Roberts, who traveled widely in Egypt in the 19th century, shows the temple of Isis on the island of Philae. This was the last Egyptian temple to fall to the Christians. The Roman emperor Justinian closed it in the 6th century A.D., and ordered it to be turned into a church.

COLOSSAL CARVINGS
Near the second cataract (rapids) of the Nile at Abu Simbel in Nubia, Ramses II ordered two temples to be carved out of the sandstone cliffs. This one was carved for himself and three major Egyptian gods – Amun, Re-Harakhty, and Ptah. Huge statues of Ramses flank the entrance.

Obelisks

The Egyptians carved stone obelisks with the titles of their kings and dedications to the gods. The pointed tip of the obelisk represents the ground on which the sun god stood to create the universe.

GATEPOST
This obelisk was one of two that stood at the entrance to the temple at Luxor. The other obelisk was given to the king of France and is now in the Place de la Concorde, Paris.

THINKER
This priest seems to have a worried expression. In fact, the lines on his forehead, bags under his eyes, and furrows around his mouth are meant to indicate a life of serious contemplation. He is bald because most priests had to remove their hair.

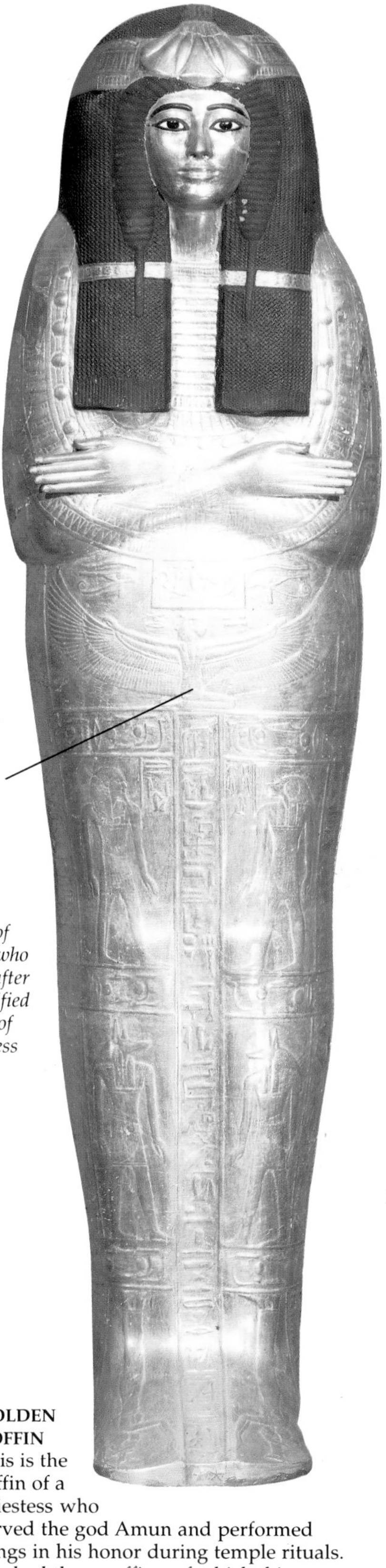

GOLDEN COFFIN
This is the coffin of a priestess who served the god Amun and performed songs in his honor during temple rituals. She had three coffins, of which this one, of gilded wood, is the most impressive. Her face is portrayed as she would have wanted to look for eternity.

Sacred rituals

A SELECT FEW PRIESTS were involved in the ceremonies that took place in the temple's sanctuary. Accompanied by burning incense and lamps, and scattering purified water from the temple's sacred lake, the high priest approached the shrine, saying "I am a pure one." He would break the clay seal on the door of the shrine, and open it to reveal the gold statue of the god. This he would decorate before making an offering of food. The priests then left the sanctuary with someone sweeping the floor as they went out, so as not to leave any trace of their presence.

SACRED BUCKET
This bronze container, called a situla, held holy water from the sacred lake of the temple. It was used in ceremonies involving the sprinkling of holy water. It is decorated with images of various gods and ancestral rulers of Egypt.

Crescent and full moons worshiped by baboons

Tapered base allowing situla to rest on a stand

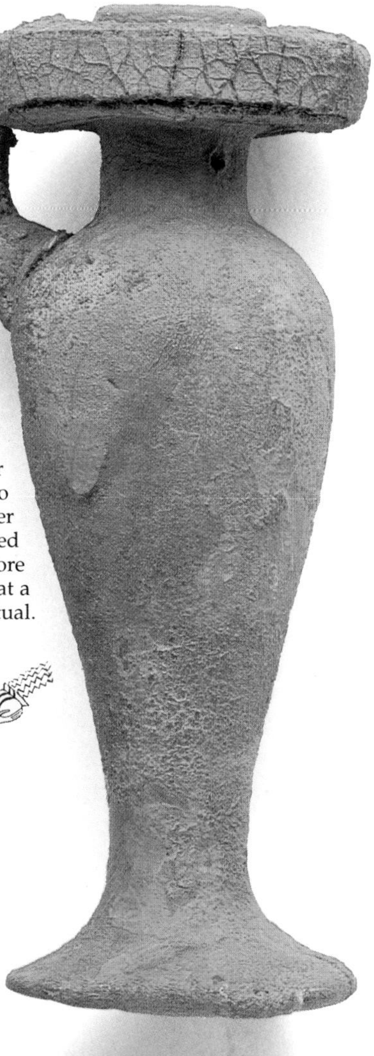

VERDIGRIS VASE
Metal vases were used to pour sacred water over offering tables, to show the purity of the offerings made to the god or goddess. They also held a mixture of water and natron (p. 15), used for ritual washing before and after eating at a temple festival or ritual.

WORSHIPER
This priestess, a woman called Deniu-en-Khons, is making offerings to the god Re-Harakhty. The falcon-headed god is carrying the ankh, the Egyptian sign of life, as well as the royal symbols of crook and flail.

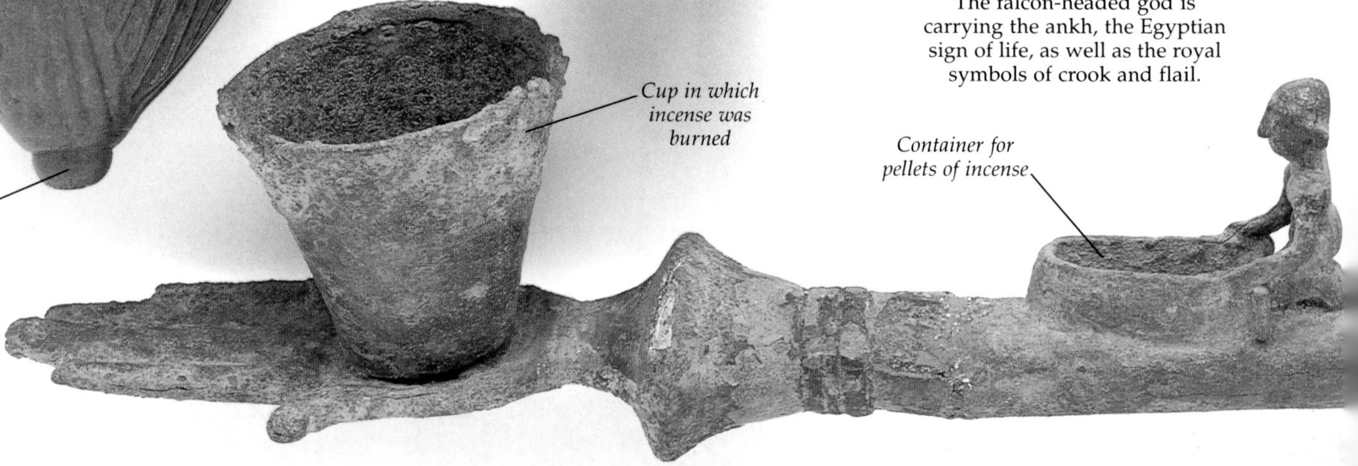

Cup in which incense was burned

Container for pellets of incense

PRIESTLY PROCESSION
This group of priests is bald – priests shaved off their hair to ensure cleanliness. Their leader is carrying an incense burner and scattering sacred water.

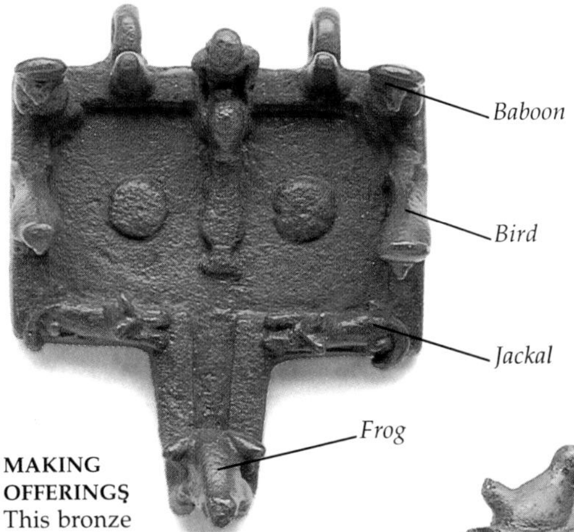

MAKING OFFERINGS
This bronze plaque shows a priest pouring sacred water over some offerings. Round loaves of bread and a vase of liquid are being offered to the god. At the front is a channel through which the holy water could drain away.

STANDARD ORNAMENT
Priests carried standards in their processions through the temples. All that has survived of these are the emblems on top of the supporting poles. This one shows a bundle of papyrus plants and is topped by the falcon god Horus, who is identified with the king of Egypt. Horus wears the combined crowns of Upper and Lower Egypt.

One of many temple paintings showing incense burners in use

AIR FRESHENER
Incense burns with an aroma that rises with the smoke. It was used in temples to attract the attention of the god with a pleasant fragrance, and to purify the atmosphere in the temple. This bronze incense burner has the head of the hawk god at one end.

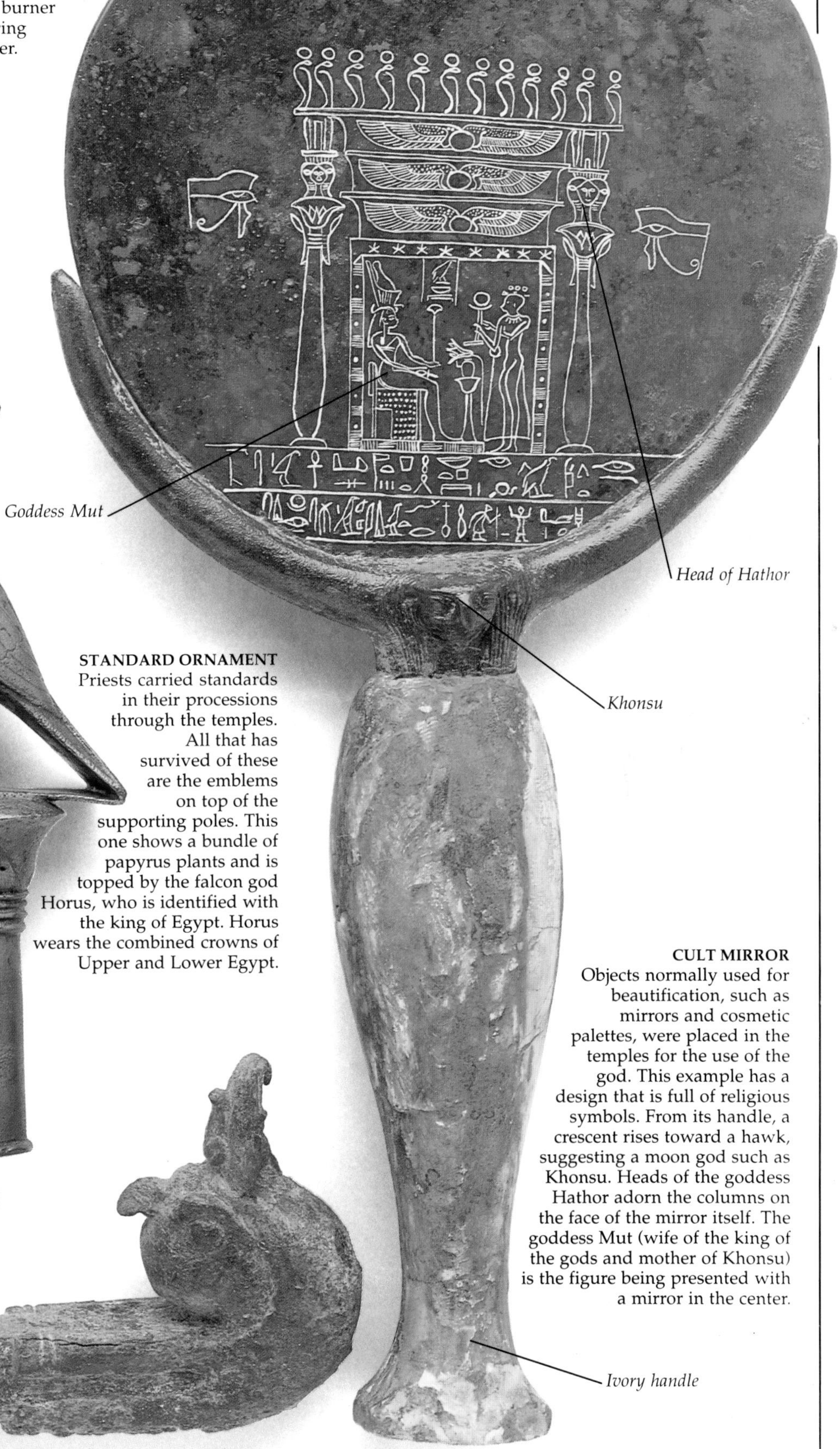

CULT MIRROR
Objects normally used for beautification, such as mirrors and cosmetic palettes, were placed in the temples for the use of the god. This example has a design that is full of religious symbols. From its handle, a crescent rises toward a hawk, suggesting a moon god such as Khonsu. Heads of the goddess Hathor adorn the columns on the face of the mirror itself. The goddess Mut (wife of the king of the gods and mother of Khonsu) is the figure being presented with a mirror in the center.

Scribes and scholars

READY FOR WORK
This young scribe is shown sitting cross-legged with his papyrus scroll on his knees. Scribes are usually shown seated like this in Egyptian art.

SCRIBES WERE NEAR THE TOP of Egyptian society, and capable scribes could do very well – one, Horemheb, even became king. Students were trained rigorously for about five years, beginning at the age of nine. This was often a problem because the young pupils could see children of their own age playing in the fields. Papyri have been discovered containing reprimands from senior to junior scribes about neglecting lessons; sometimes physical punishment was recommended. One form of encouragement offered to pupils was a list of the drawbacks of other professions – exaggerated, of course. For example, jewelers and metalworkers were said to choke in the heat of their furnaces; weavers had to put up with cramped conditions. But the scribe could look forward to authority, freedom from taxes and national service during times of flood, and immortality through his writings.

GOOSE CENSUS
This scribe is counting geese on a nobleman's estate. He will enter the total on his scroll, for taxation records. His basket-work "briefcase" is in front of him, and his palettes and brushes are under his arm.

PAPYRUS
This triangular-stemmed reed, which grew about 13 ft (4 m) tall, flourished along the banks of the Nile, but vanished due to overharvesting for boats, baskets, sandals, rope, and writing material. Attempts are now being made to reintroduce it into Egypt.

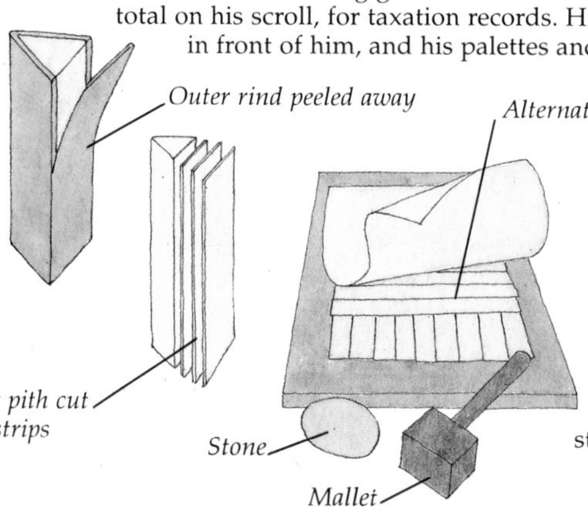

MAKING A PAPYRUS SHEET
The strips of pith were arranged in two layers, one set horizontal, the next vertical, on top of each other. They were covered with linen, and heavy pressure was applied with stones or a mallet. Eventually the strips would weld together in their own sap.

Draughtsmen

Egyptian artists were professional scribes who specialized in draftsmanship for royal or funerary monuments. From unfinished tombs like that of King Horemheb it is possible to see all the stages involved in painting. First junior draftsmen drew the scenes in red ocher on the dry plaster. Next senior artists made corrections in black outline. The painters would then fill in the outlines with color, or sculptors would cut away the background plaster to form a relief for painting.

Grinder for crushing pigments

BASALT PALETTE
This palette is inscribed with a royal name, indicating that the scribe who used it was in the service of the palace. The pigments could be made from charcoal or soot to produce black, or from red ocher, or blue or green minerals.

SKETCH PAD
A red ocher grid allowed the artist to divide the human body into squares to ensure the right proportions in this practice drawing of King Tuthmosis III.

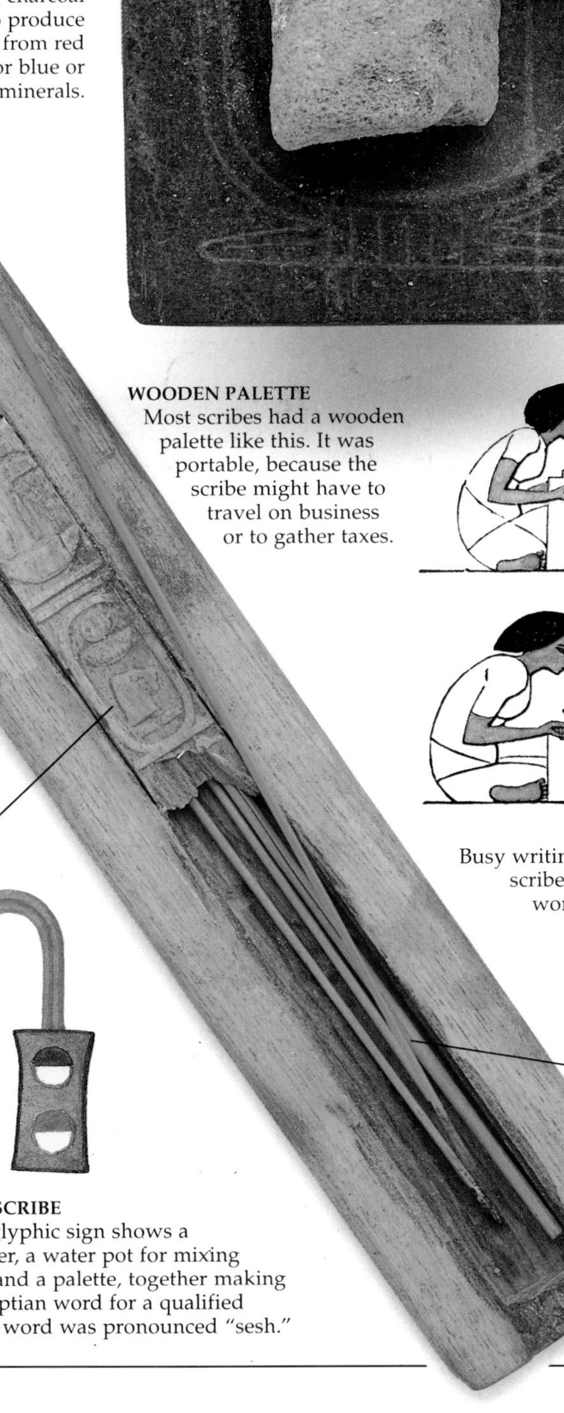

WOODEN PALETTE
Most scribes had a wooden palette like this. It was portable, because the scribe might have to travel on business or to gather taxes.

Name of Ramses I

Reed brushes for precision writing

SCRIBES AND SUPERVISOR
Busy writing on their scrolls, these two scribes appear to be recording the words of the standing overseer. Notice the "briefcase" and document container in front of them.

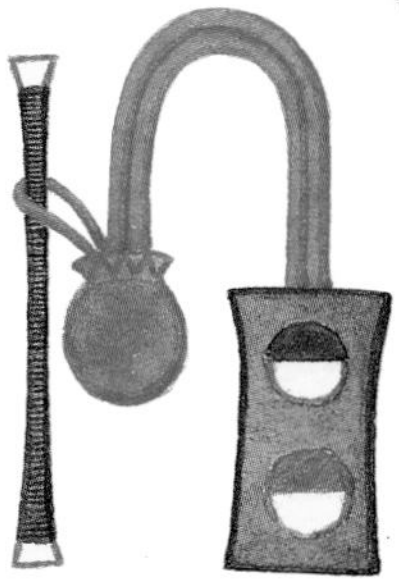

SIGN FOR SCRIBE
This hieroglyphic sign shows a brush holder, a water pot for mixing pigments, and a palette, together making up the Egyptian word for a qualified scribe. The word was pronounced "sesh."

BRUSHES
The thick rope brush made of papyrus twine was used by painters covering large wall surfaces in tombs or temples. The other is also a painter's brush, perhaps used to paint thick hieroglyphs on huge statues.

Writing

SCRIBES HAD TO BE EXPERTS in writing hieroglyphs, an elaborate form of picture-writing using about 700 different signs. It was deliberately kept complicated so that not many people could master it and scribes could keep their special position. Hieroglyphs were used on state monuments, temples, tombs, and religious papyri. They could be written from left to right, right to left, or top to bottom. For business contracts, letters, and stories, scribes used a different form of writing (script), called hieratic, which was a fast-written version of hieroglyphs, always running from right to left. Later on an even more rapid script evolved, called demotic. Demotic was often used for legal documents. At the end of the Egyptian civilization, scribes also had to be able to write Greek, the language of their overlords.

LABEL
Scribes used tags like this to label their scrolls. This one tells us that its papyrus was written in the reign of Amenhotep III and told a story about a fig tree.

ROYAL DOOR PLATE
The hieroglyphs on this metal plate read: "There shall always exist the Son of Re whom he loves, Amenhotep the god, ruler of Thebes."

King's name contained in oval border called a cartouche

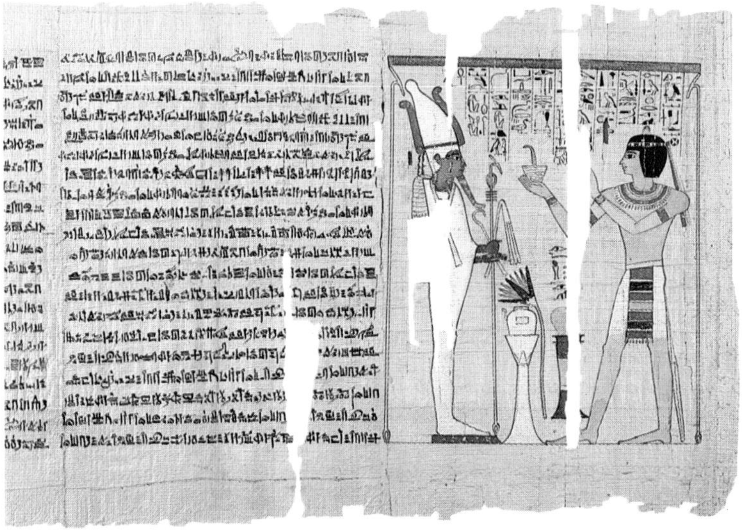

TWO SCRIPTS
On papyrus, scribes usually used the fast form of writing called hieratic. On this example, hieroglyphs appear above the picture of a high priest making an offering to the god Osiris. To the left is the script in hieratic.

IMHOTEP
This talented scribe lived 4,500 years ago. He was High Priest of the sun god as well as the designer of the first pyramid, at Saqqara. After his death he became accredited with limitless wisdom and was eventually turned into a god. Here he is unrolling a papyrus scroll.

Cartouche bearing name of King Meryre

Name of Meryre's official

CYLINDER SEAL
Seals like this were an early way of proving ownership or authority. This one bears the name of King Meryre, and also the name of one of his officials, who was obviously the owner of the seal. To the right is an impression showing the complete surface of the seal.

The Rosetta Stone

When the last temple was closed, in the 6th century A.D., the skill of reading hieroglyphs was lost until the discovery of this stone in 1799. On the stone are three scripts. The bottom section is in Greek, the center in demotic, and the top in hieroglyphs. The stone was first set up in a temple. It was an elaborate "thank you" to the Greek ruler of Egypt, Ptolemy V, who reigned in the 2nd century B.C., for favors that he had given to the priests. The three scripts contained the same text, allowing the hieroglyphs to be translated.

Top

Underside

SCARABS
The beetle, symbolizing the sun god (p. 78), was often carved on the tops of stamp seals. The underside could include names, titles, or information that the owner could stamp on clay or papyrus. The large scarab tells us that Amenhotep III killed 102 lions during his reign.

Small scarab

JEAN-FRANÇOIS CHAMPOLLION
French archeologist, Jean-François Champollion spent many years deciphering the symbols on a slab of basalt found at Rosetta in the western Delta. His work on the Rosetta stone, as it is now called, was an important breakthrough in the translation of ancient hieroglyphics.

HIEROGLYPHS AND THEIR ORIGINS
Scribes chose pictures of their script from the world around them. The barn owl represented the consonant "m"; on the carving in the picture it forms part of the royal name "Amen em hat."

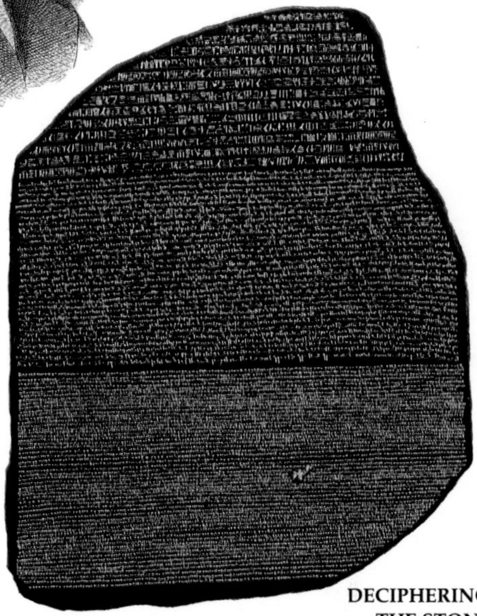

DECIPHERING THE STONE
When it was known that the stone contained royal names such as Ptolemy, their equivalents in hieroglyphs could be found at the top of the stone. From this information, the hieroglyphs for other words were worked out and the text was gradually deciphered.

NOTEBOOK
Some hieroglyphic signs required a lot of practice by pupil scribes. Here a scribe has got carried away drawing the duckling hieroglyph, which was used in writing the word for "prime minister." The scribe has also practiced drawing the head of a lion, which is used in one of the scenes in the Book of the Dead.

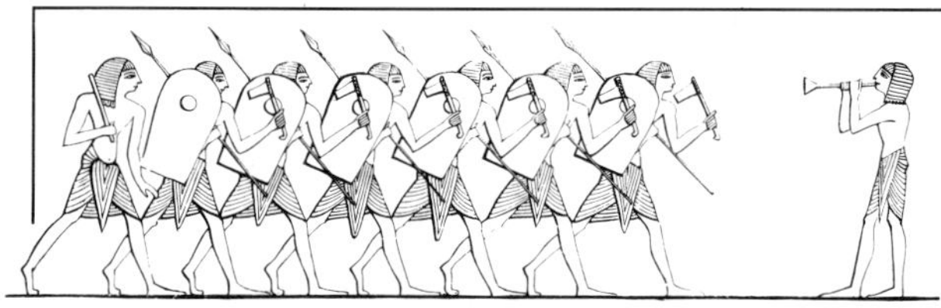

Soldiers carrying spears, shields, and battle-axes

Weapons of war

SOLDIERS FIRST PLAYED an important role in Egypt around 3000 B.C. Later, the pharaohs undertook military campaigns abroad in Palestine, Syria, and Nubia. The Egyptian army was well organized. It had a hierarchy of officers, from the pharaoh himself down to officers in charge of groups of 50 soldiers, and army scribes who wrote dispatches and records of the campaigns. There were both infantry and chariot troops. Egyptian chariots, each manned by two soldiers and pulled by two horses, were made of wood. They acted as mobile firing platforms from which archers could attack the enemy. In peacetime, soldiers would take part in civil tasks such as digging irrigation canals or transporting stone from the desert for the king's tomb.

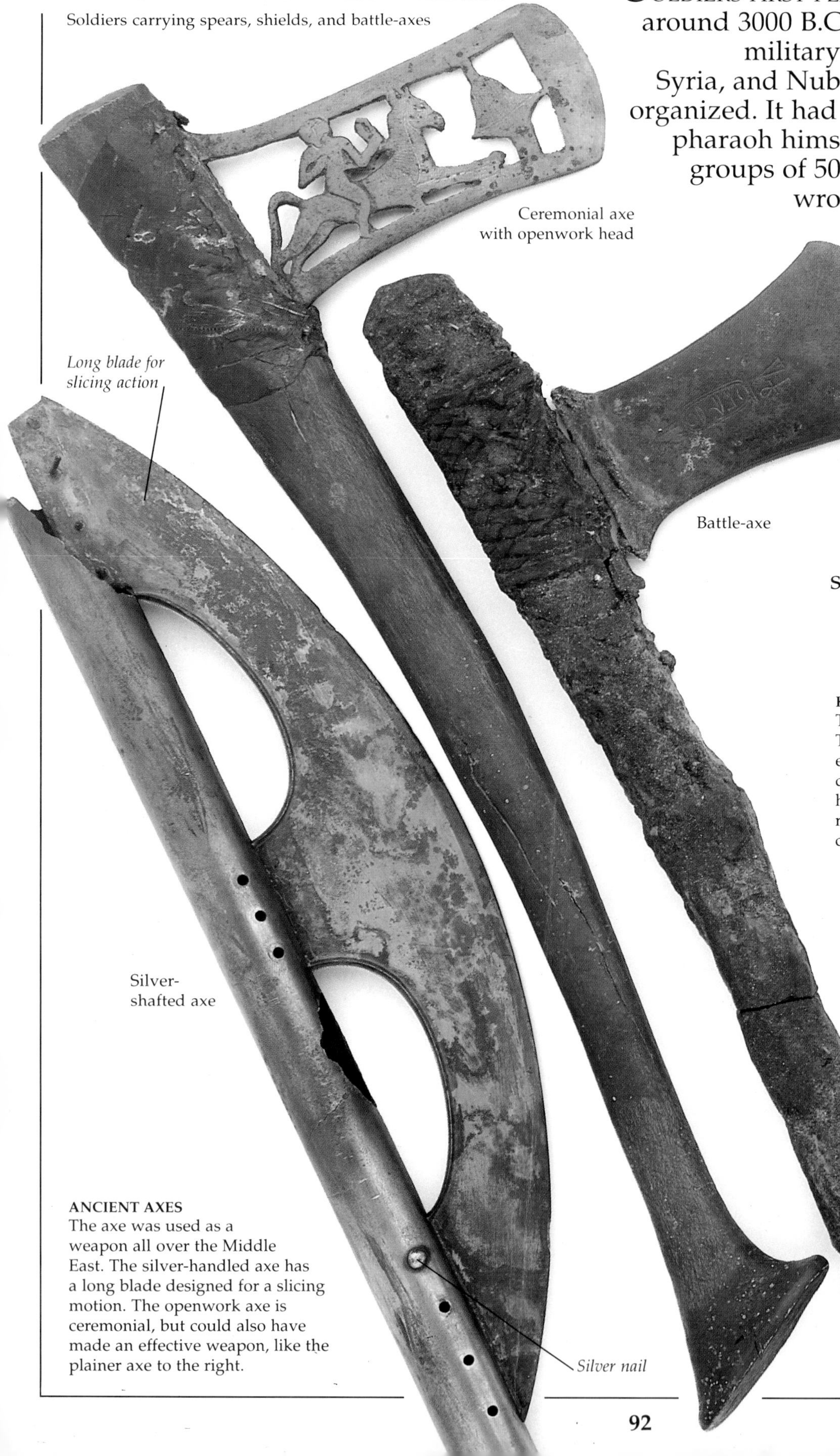

Ceremonial axe with openwork head

Long blade for slicing action

Battle-axe

Silver-shafted axe

Silver nail

ANCIENT AXES
The axe was used as a weapon all over the Middle East. The silver-handled axe has a long blade designed for a slicing motion. The openwork axe is ceremonial, but could also have made an effective weapon, like the plainer axe to the right.

KING AT WAR
This scene from the side of a box discovered in Tutankhamun's tomb shows the king attacking enemies from Nubia. His foes are falling in disarray. He rides in a chariot drawn by two horses, followed by fan bearers. In real life the king had a charioteer to drive for him.

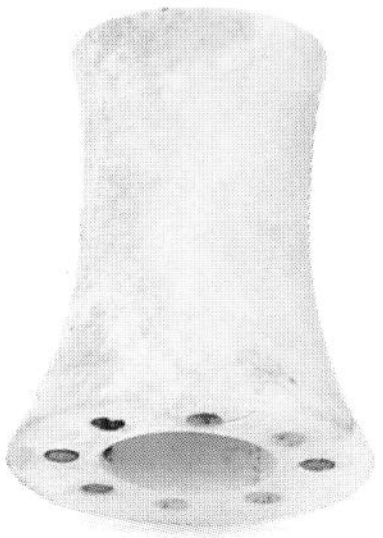

FINGER GUARD
Archers would sometimes draw their bow strings into a triangular shape, pulling them back to their ears. This bone guard protected the archer's finger from pain caused by the taut string (made of animal gut) as he drew his bow.

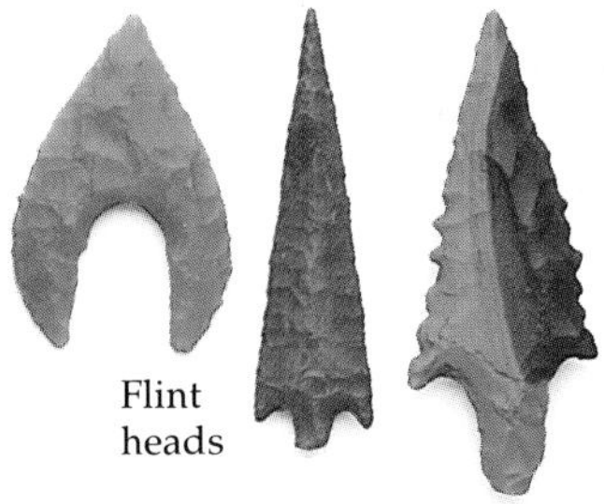

Flint heads

SMALL BUT DEADLY
The first arrowheads were made of flint or a hard wood like ebony. Later bronze was used. The horseshoe shapes were designed to wound, and the sharp triangular arrowheads were meant to kill the victim outright.

ARROW
With its blunt tip and reed shaft, this arrow may have been a hunter's weapon, though it is the size of a soldier's arrow.

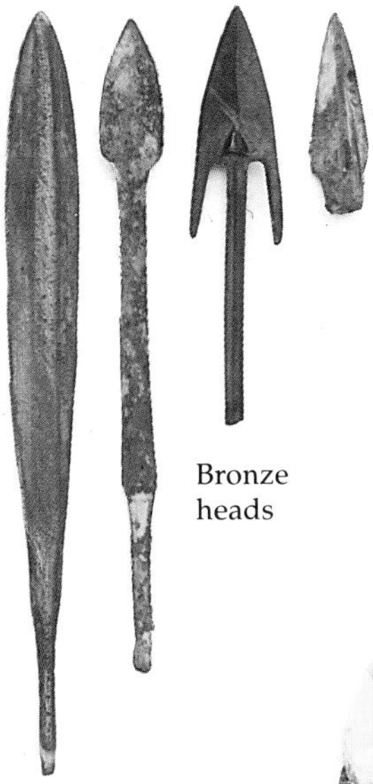

Bronze heads

ON THE MARCH
Protected by large shields made of wood rather than heavy armor, these infantry soldiers are armed with battle-axes and spears.

Tutankhamun wears a wrist protector

TRUSTY BLADES
Inspired by a Middle Eastern design, swords had smoother handles than daggers. They had the advantage that they could be gripped tightly; they could also have a longer blade, attached with rivets.

Dagger

Short sword

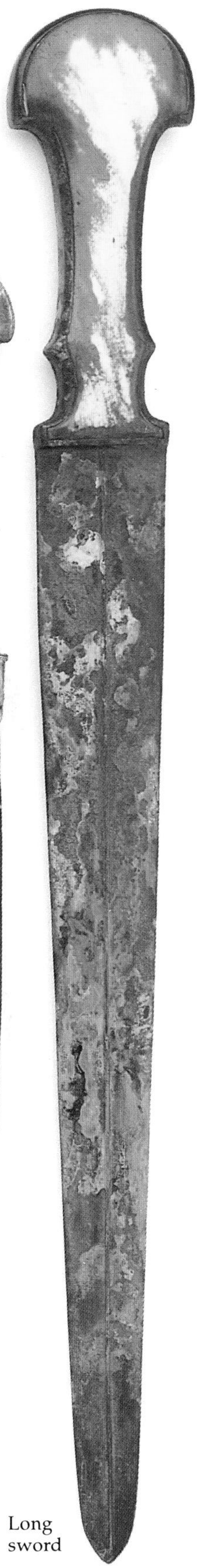

Long sword

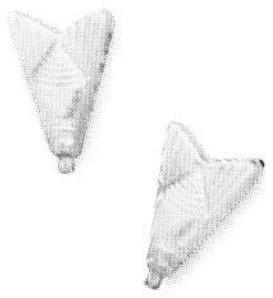

MEDALS
Gold flies were given to a soldier who had done well in combat, persistently "stinging" the enemy.

DEADLY DAGGER
Traditional Egyptian daggers have fine, tapered copper blades decorated with stripes. The wide top of the blade is riveted to the handle. The pommel of ivory or bone on top of the handle fitted into the palm of the hand. Daggers could be carried openly in the belt of a kilt or in wooden sheaths overlaid with gold.

WRIST PROTECTOR
An archer wore this guard on his left wrist to protect himself from the whip of the bowstring when firing an arrow. The tongue-shaped section extended into the palm.

Sailing on the Nile

THE NILE was the main highway of Egypt. The earliest boats were made of papyrus, but dockyards along the Nile were soon busy making boats out of timber. The best example of the skill of the Egyptian shipbuilder is a boat over 130 ft (40 m) long built for King Khufu around 4,500 years ago and discovered in a pit next to the Great Pyramid (pp. 38–39). It was a keel-less ceremonial barge with a cabin for the king and was probably intended for Khufu's journey with the sun-god in the afterlife. Temple reliefs show other large boats transporting huge columns and obelisks of granite from the quarries of Aswan. The Egyptians had a full range of boats for transportation on the Nile, from small cargo boats for carrying grain to state ships for kings and high officials. The Egyptians gave ships names like we do today. For example, one commander started off in a ship called *Northern* and got promoted to the ship *Rising in Memphis*.

THE RA EXPEDITION
The first Egyptian boats were made of papyrus stalks bunched together. If they got waterlogged they could easily be replaced using the plentiful reeds. Explorer Thor Heyerdahl sailed his papyrus boat *Ra* from Egypt to America. He did not prove that the Egyptians made this journey, but he showed that it was possible.

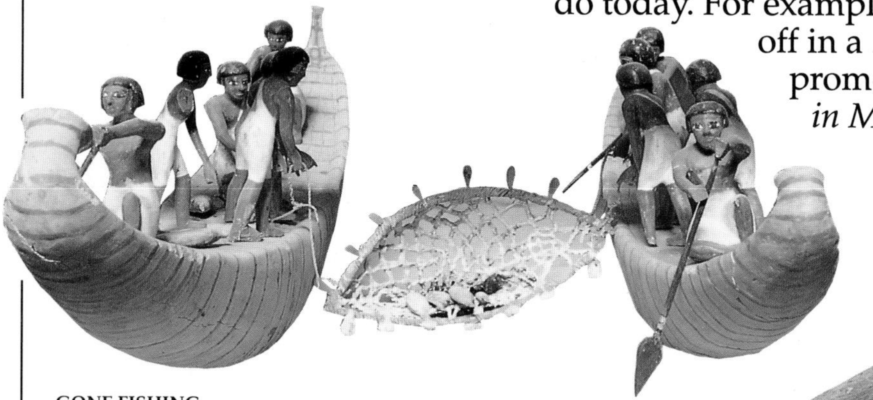

GONE FISHING
These skiffs are made of bundles of papyrus reeds tied together with twine. They are each propelled by two oarsmen and are linked to each other by the dragnet. You can see some of the fish trapped in the net as well as the floats around the edges of it. The fishermen are about to pull the net in with the catch.

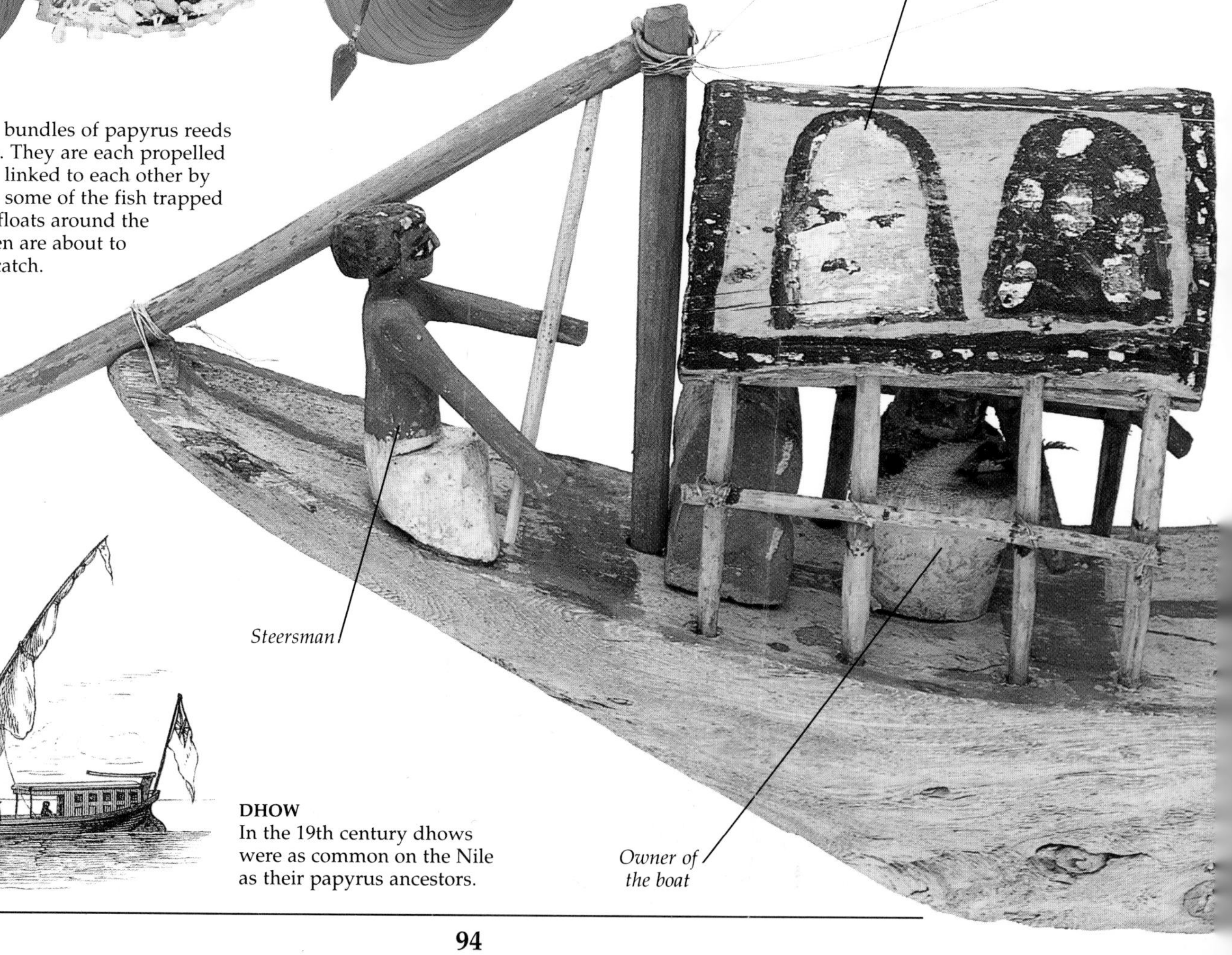

DHOW
In the 19th century dhows were as common on the Nile as their papyrus ancestors.

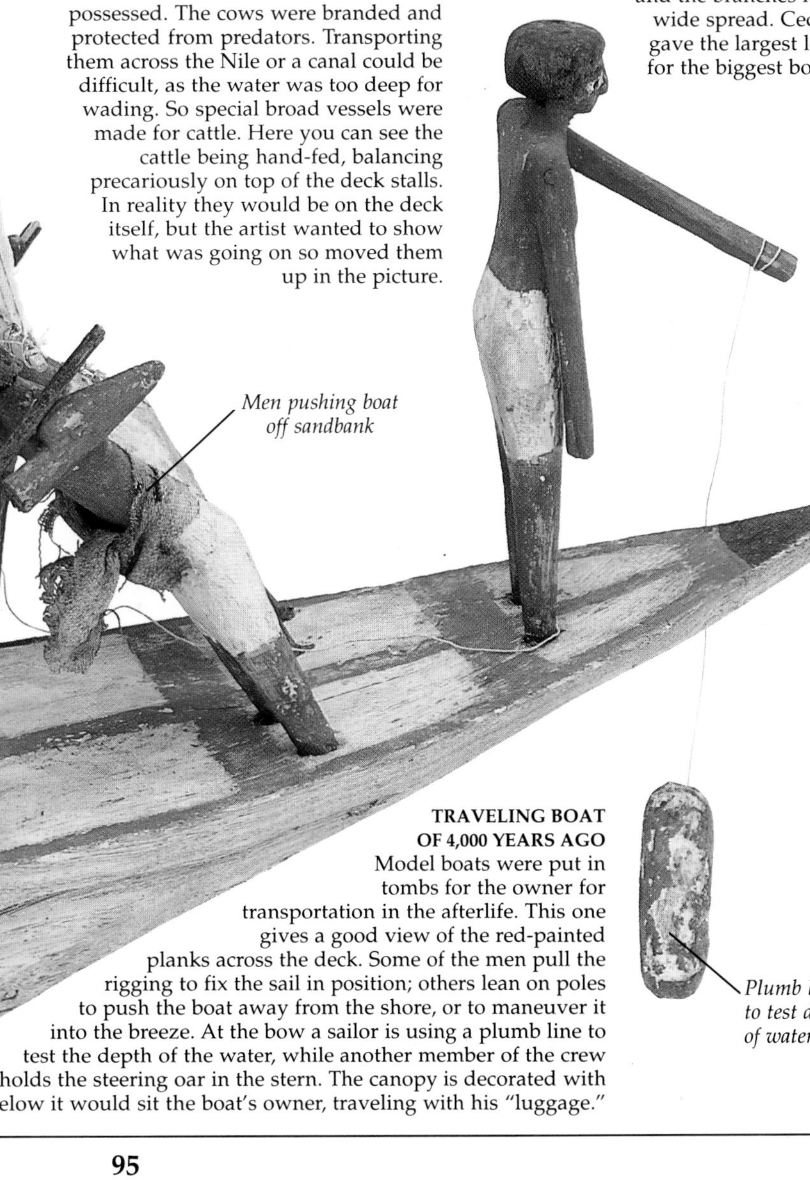

WORK IN PROGRESS
A small boat is propped up with logs while the shipwrights bend the planks that form the deck in a curve to match the hull. By twisting the ropes with sticks, the men gradually get the planks to curve. Other workers are hammering nails into holes and planing the support for the steering oar.

CEDAR OF LEBANON
On the hillsides of Lebanon and Syria grew cedars and junipers, highly prized for building ceremonial boats - King Snefru sent 40 boats to Byblos (in Lebanon) to collect cedar wood. The height of a cedar tree could range from 60 to 100 ft (20 to 33 m) and the branches had a wide spread. Cedar gave the largest logs for the biggest boats.

ALL ABOARD
The real measure of wealth for an Egyptian landowner was the number of cattle he possessed. The cows were branded and protected from predators. Transporting them across the Nile or a canal could be difficult, as the water was too deep for wading. So special broad vessels were made for cattle. Here you can see the cattle being hand-fed, balancing precariously on top of the deck stalls. In reality they would be on the deck itself, but the artist wanted to show what was going on so moved them up in the picture.

TRAVELING BOAT OF 4,000 YEARS AGO
Model boats were put in tombs for the owner for transportation in the afterlife. This one gives a good view of the red-painted planks across the deck. Some of the men pull the rigging to fix the sail in position; others lean on poles to push the boat away from the shore, or to maneuver it into the breeze. At the bow a sailor is using a plumb line to test the depth of the water, while another member of the crew holds the steering oar in the stern. The canopy is decorated with shields; below it would sit the boat's owner, traveling with his "luggage."

BARTERING
This was a common way of exchanging goods. You might exchange a pair of sandals for a fine walking stick, or a linen garment for a large quantity of food. These men are carrying exchangeable items such as ducks and a jar of wine in a rope basket.

Buying and selling

EGYPT WAS THE WEALTHIEST COUNTRY of the ancient world. Some of the gold from the mines of the eastern desert and Nubia was sent abroad in the form of gifts to foreign rulers like the king of Babylon. Manufactured goods and even princesses were sent in exchange to the pharaoh. Although the pharaohs at times controlled long stretches of the Nile beyond the southern frontier at Aswan, produce from deep equatorial Africa was obtained through trade with the princes of Nubia, the area south of the first cataract (rapids) of the Nile. One exchange post was at Kerma, near the third cataract of the Nile. Egyptian merchants brought back a variety of goods like panther skins, greyhounds, giraffe tails for fly whisks, elephant tusks, and animals such as lions and baboons for the temples or palace.

RATES OF EXCHANGE
The writing on this limestone flake shows details of a deal struck when an Egyptian called Amenwau sold some of his possessions. The value of the goods is given in terms of their equivalent in a weight of copper called a "deben." A goat was valued at 1 deben; a bed was worth 2.5 deben.

4 deben

5 kite

2 kite

1 kite

WEIGHING IT UP
The copper "deben" that Egyptian traders used to measure saleable items originally had an accepted weight of around 0.5 oz. Later the deben was revalued at 3.2 oz, divided into 10 "kite."

Large balance for weighing produce

HOARD OF SILVER
Buried in a pot at El-Amarna, these pieces of silver were part of a large hoard. Because the value of the metal was assessed by its weight, the different shapes of the pieces were unimportant. Records exist of gold and copper being weighed out and used as payments in a similar way.

Unloading pottery wine jars from a Nile boat belonging to a high official

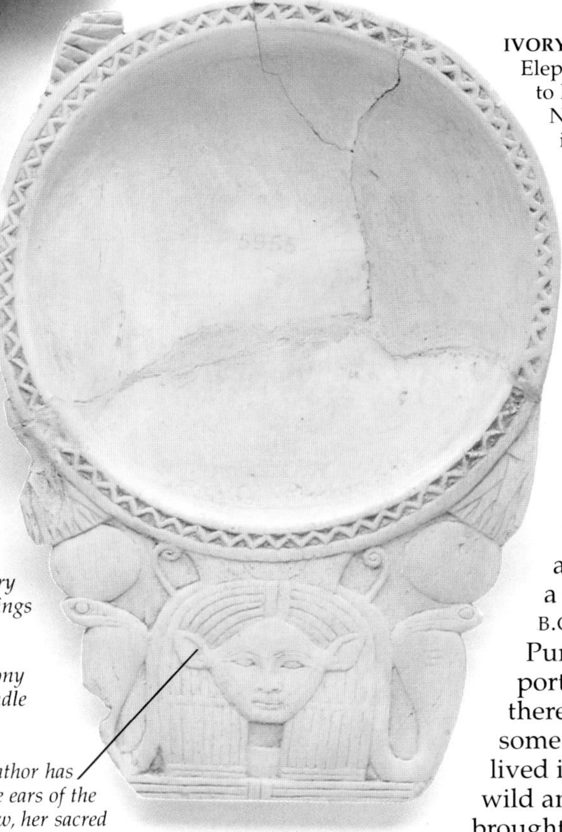

IVORY DISH
Elephant tusks came to Egypt via trade with Nubia and were carved into luxury items like this cosmetic spoon. If the supply of ivory from Nubia fell short, the teeth of hippos could be used instead. The design of this cosmetic spoon includes the head of Hathor, goddess of beauty and foreign countries.

CASSIA
Cassia, the dried bark of a type of laurel tree, was brought from India. The Egyptians used it for perfume and incense.

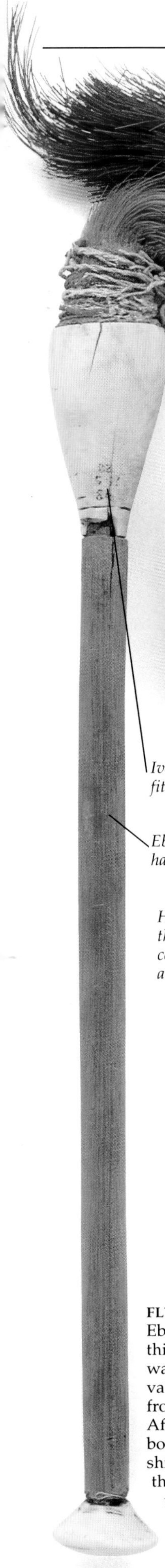

Ivory fittings

Ebony handle

Hathor has the ears of the cow, her sacred animal

The land of Punt

The Egyptians thought of the land of Punt as a remote and exotic place. We do not know exactly where it was, but the most frequent route to it seems to have been along the coast of the Red Sea and then inland toward the Atbara River, a tributary of the Nile. In the 15th century B.C., Queen Hatshepsut sent five boats to Punt. Eventually the boats pulled in at a port on the coast of eastern Sudan. From there the queen's representatives were taken some way inland, where they saw people who lived in houses on stilts to protect them from wild animals. Incense was the main cargo they brought back.

FRANKINCENSE
In Sudan, Ethiopia, Somalia, and Yemen grew trees that yielded frankincense, a fragrant gum resin.

GIFTS FROM SYRIA
These Syrian princes are bringing tribute to the pharaoh. They offer gold vases decorated with lotus flowers, and perfume containers in gold, lapis lazuli, or ivory. One Syrian prince brings his daughter to be raised at court.

FLY WHISK
Ebony, used in this fly whisk, was a highly valued import from central Africa. It was bought with shipments of logs from the Nubians. Courtiers used to carry fly whisks, and these became signs of their status.

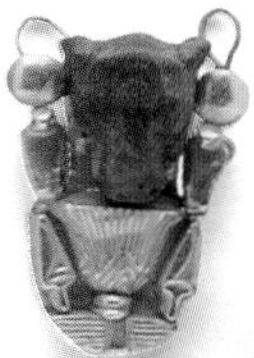

Lapis lazuli bull set in gold

LAPIS LAZULI
Merchants from Afghanistan brought this valuable stone to trading centers like Byblos in Lebanon. The Egyptians prized this gem, and thought that the hair of the sun god was made of lapis lazuli.

Unworked lapis lazuli

THE INCENSE TRADE
The myrrh and frankincense carried back from Punt probably originated even farther south. The Egyptians brought back not only the gum resin for incense but also whole trees to plant in front of the queen's temple.

An Egyptian carpenter

MANY OF THE PRODUCTS and tools of the ancient Egyptian carpenter have survived, including a variety of objects made from the various trees that grew in the Nile valley or delta. For roofing beams the carpenter could use either the date palm or the doom palm. Pegs and dowels for coffins and furniture could be made from acacia; walking sticks were cut from tamarisk trees. One of the best local woods was the sycamore fig, out of which coffins, tables, cosmetic chests, and statues were made. In the upper classes of Egyptian society there was a demand for imported timber. From Lebanon and Syria came cedar, cypress, and juniper. From Africa the dark wood ebony was highly prized for furniture, harps, gaming boards, and statues. Because of the quality of their products, carpenters were valued workers and often held well-paid jobs on estates, in temples, and in the palace.

KINGLY CARVING
This miniature carving of Tutankhamun lying on the bed of mummification shows the carver's skill and attention to detail. The king wears his royal head cloth, and beside him are the hawk god and a human-headed bird that represents the king's soul. This statue was dedicated to the king by his chief treasurer, Maya.

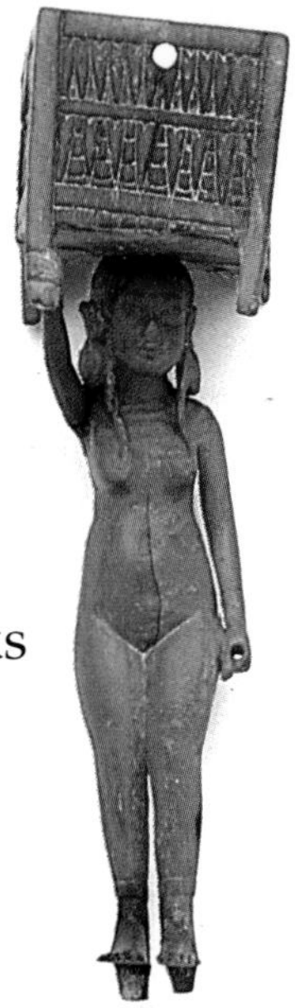

FIGURINE
Much of the carpenter's talents were used in carving elaborate cosmetic containers for Egyptian noblewomen. This one is delicately carved in the shape of a Nubian servant girl.

SAW
The carpenter held the wooden handle and pulled the saw through the timber - opposite to the action of a modern saw, which is pushed. Tomb scenes show a carpenter sawing a plank that he has lashed to a pole fixed in the ground.

CHOPPER
The axe appears in the hieroglyph for the word for carpenter, "medjeh." Its main use was for cutting down trees and hacking the wood roughly into shape for items like boat planks and coffin panels.

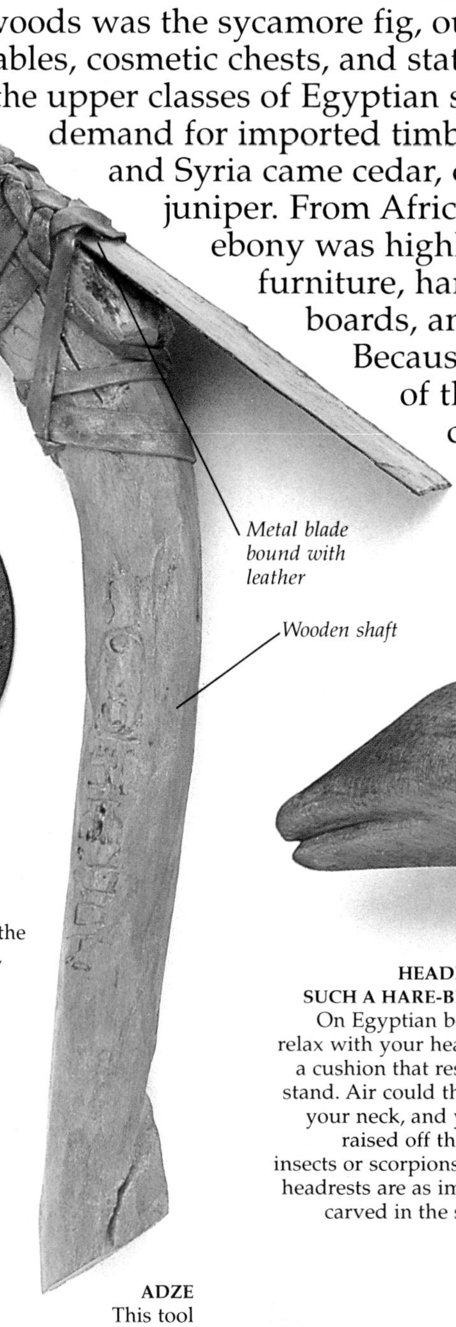

ADZE
This tool was used widely for planing surfaces to a smooth finish. Dockyard scenes show carpenters using adzes on boat hulls; they were also used to carve large funerary chests.

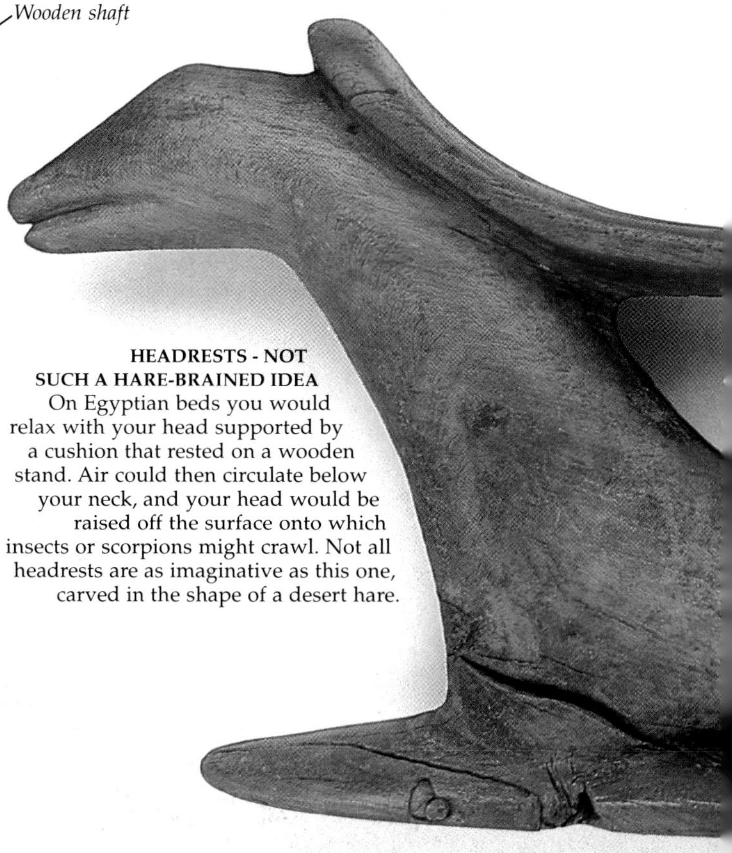

HEADRESTS - NOT SUCH A HARE-BRAINED IDEA
On Egyptian beds you would relax with your head supported by a cushion that rested on a wooden stand. Air could then circulate below your neck, and your head would be raised off the surface onto which insects or scorpions might crawl. Not all headrests are as imaginative as this one, carved in the shape of a desert hare.

GOAT'S HEAD
Chairs, boxes, and chests were often decorated with animal features. A chair could have legs shaped like lion's paws; a throne could have arms topped by winged snakes or vultures. This small fragment has been exquisitely carved to show the horn, curly fleece, and beard of a goat. It probably came from the decoration of a chest.

BORING JOB
To bore a hole in a plank of wood the carpenter used a drill consisting of a metal or flint point in a shaft of wood. He placed it over the spot in the plank where he wanted the hole and rotated the cutting point using a bow. Sometimes an assistant would hold a heavy stone over the shaft of the drill to create more pressure.

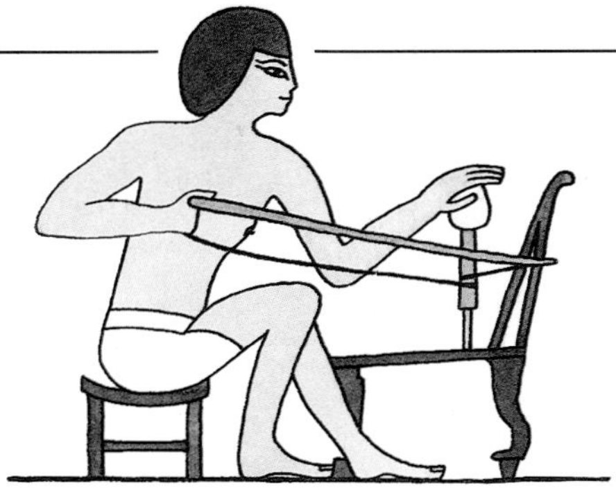

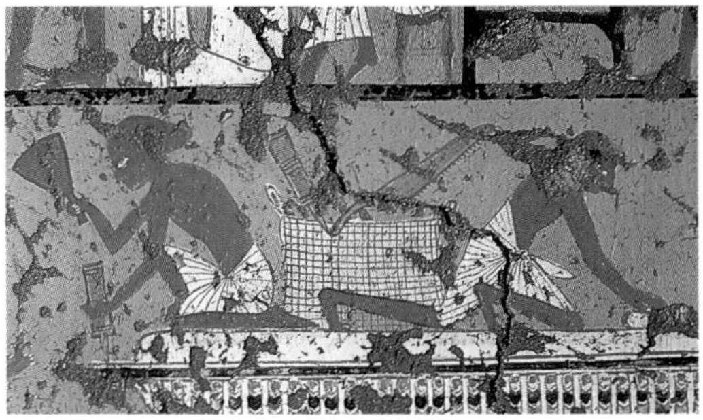

MEN AT WORK
These two carpenters are putting the finishing touches to a large wooden casket that has been inlaid with colorful materials. One uses a mallet to hammer out a hole for a peg while the other is polishing the lid.

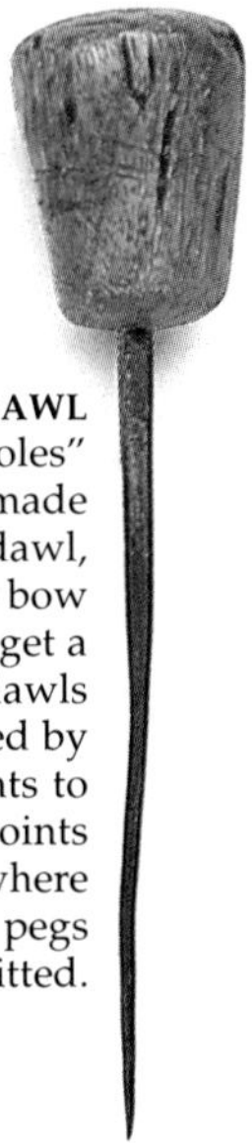

BRADAWL
"Starter holes" could be made with a bradawl, so that the bow drill could get a grip. Bradawls were also used by shipwrights to mark the points on planks where wooden pegs were to be fitted.

CHISEL
A carpenter would need a chisel like this for intricate carving and for cutting hieroglyphs into the surfaces of large rectangular wooden coffins.

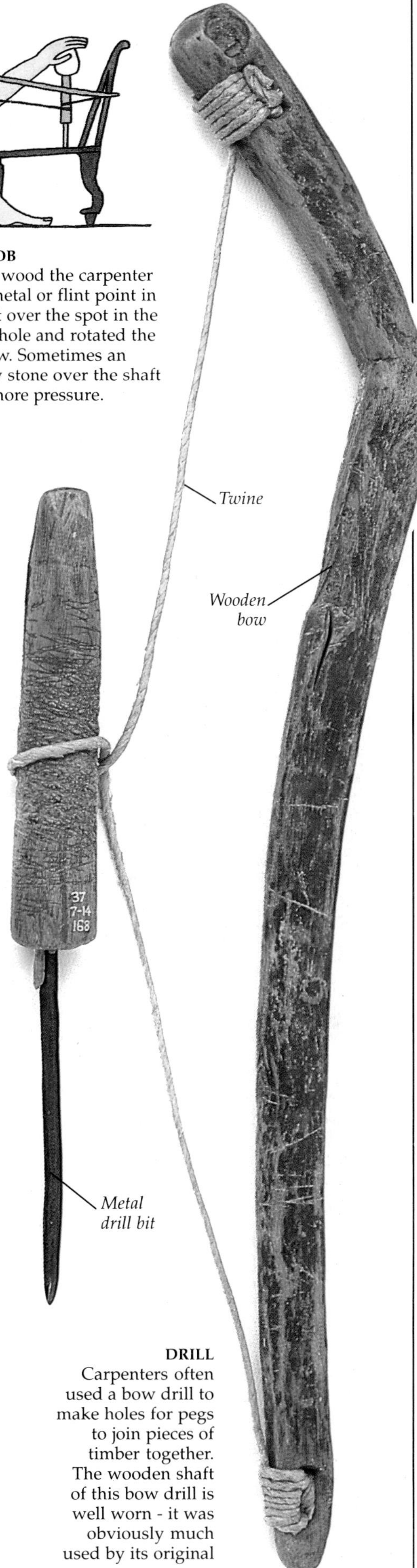

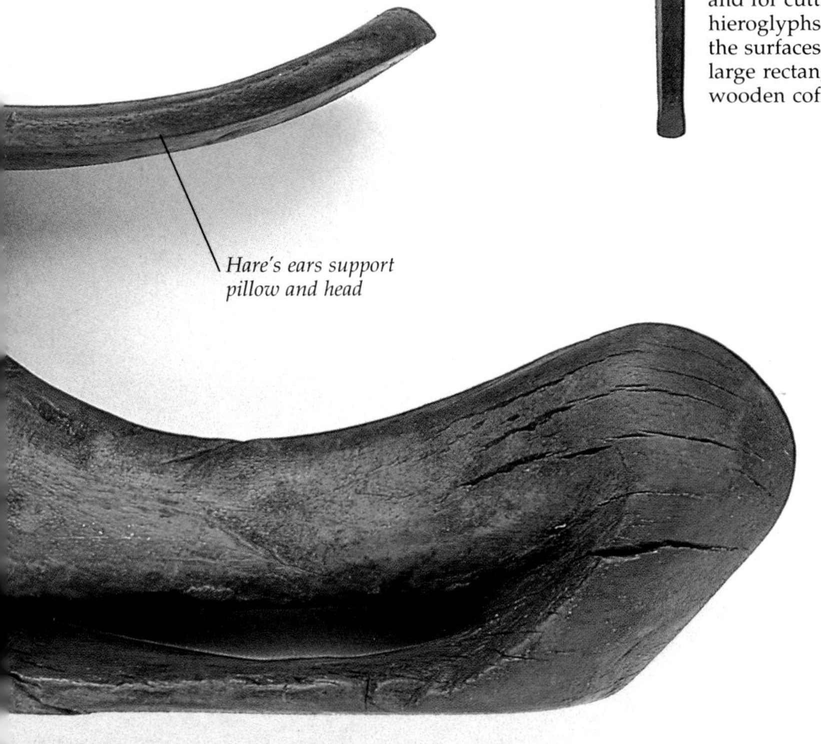

SMOOTHING STONE
The rough surfaces left after carving could be smoothed down using a stone. The highly polished finish of furniture was often achieved in this way.

DRILL
Carpenters often used a bow drill to make holes for pegs to join pieces of timber together. The wooden shaft of this bow drill is well worn - it was obviously much used by its original owner.

Hunting, fishing, and fowling

AT THE TIME of the pharaohs farming produced an abundance of food, so hunting was mainly a recreation for kings and courtiers. In the Egyptian deserts they hunted wild bulls, gazelles, oryx, antelopes, and lions. King Amenhotep III was proud of killing over 100 fierce lions in ten years; he also killed over 90 wild bulls on one hunting expedition. Often there was no danger to the monarch at all if he went hunting - the bulls would be herded into an enclosure in the marshes and picked off one by one by the pharaoh in his chariot. In the beginning, the courtiers hunted on foot, their followers fencing off areas to hem the animals in; later the courtiers too used chariots. The Nile was also plentiful in fish, which could be caught with hooks or nets. The papyrus thickets sheltered a variety of birds and geese. Here the technique was to hurl a throw stick as the wildfowl flew up from the thickets.

FAMILY OUTING
This nobleman is hunting birds in the papyrus marshes. He is using a snake-shaped throw stick, and the three herons he holds disguise his approach. He has brought his cat, which has caught three birds. With him are his daughter, sitting in the boat, and his elegant wife - who is hardly dressed for the hunt!

Flat tips to weaken animal by piercing hide

Sharp tip to kill outright

Cleft end for bowstring

ARROWS
Bows and arrows appear on some of the earliest sculptures from ancient Egypt. The arrows were made of reeds and tipped with ivory, bone, flint, or metal.

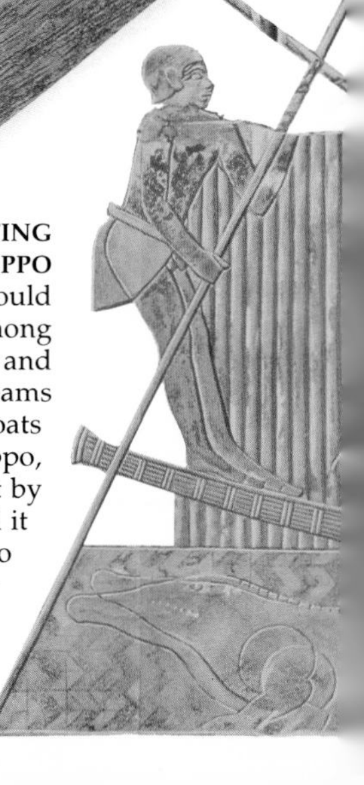

HUNTING THE HIPPO
This animal could cause havoc among reed boats on the Nile and to crops on land. So teams of men in papyrus boats would hunt the hippo, gradually weakening it by repeated spearing until it collapsed. They also used lassoes to hamper the creature's movements.

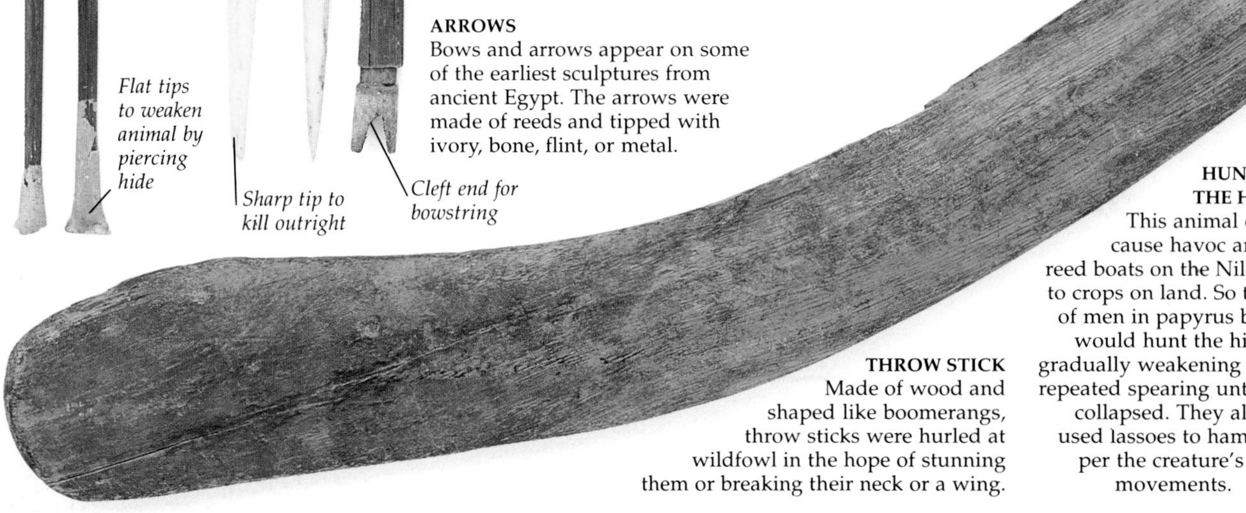

THROW STICK
Made of wood and shaped like boomerangs, throw sticks were hurled at wildfowl in the hope of stunning them or breaking their neck or a wing.

SPOILS OF THE DESERT
Desert hares are often shown in Egyptian hunting scenes. Sometimes a hare pierced with an arrow will still be trying to scramble to safety. Antelopes and gazelles were also found in the desert, and ostrich eggs were a desert delicacy.

HOOKS
Copper or bronze hooks were used for fishing. The fish were pulled from the water, then gutted and dried in the sun.

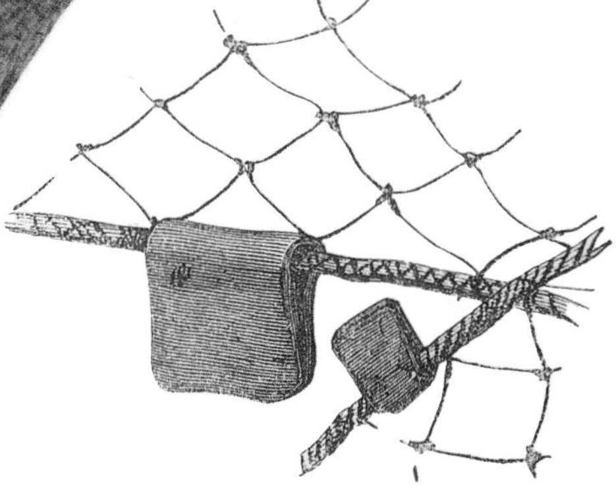

WEIGHING THEM DOWN
Like fishermen today, the Egyptians used lead weights to keep their fishing nets under the water.

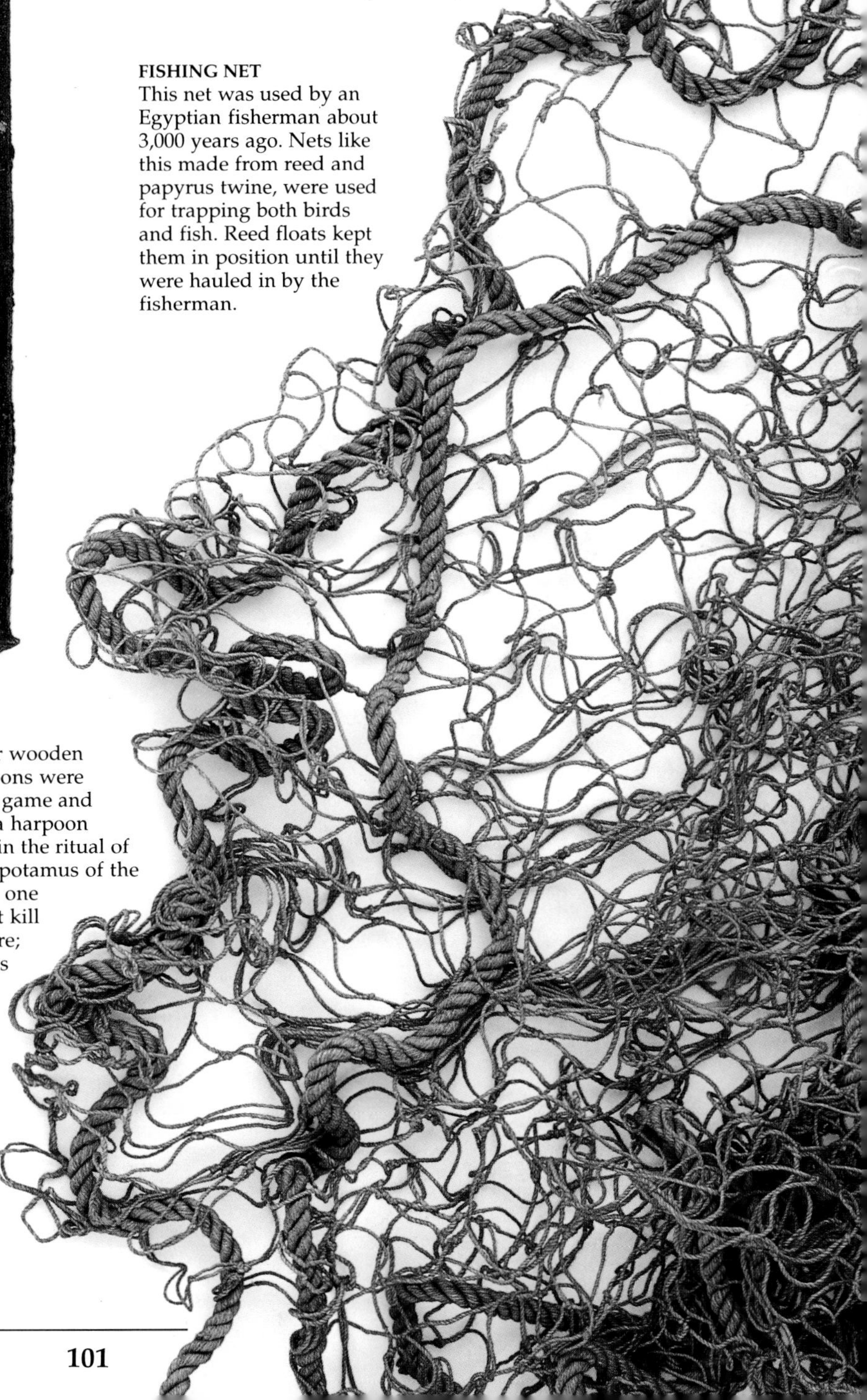

FISHING NET
This net was used by an Egyptian fisherman about 3,000 years ago. Nets like this made from reed and papyrus twine, were used for trapping both birds and fish. Reed floats kept them in position until they were hauled in by the fisherman.

Courtiers used this type of harpoon to test their skill

Prong to attach rope

HARPOONS
Attached to reed or wooden shafts, metal harpoons were used to catch large game and fish. Symbolically a harpoon was held by kings in the ritual of spearing the hippopotamus of the god Seth. In reality one harpoon would not kill such a large creature; a series of harpoons was required.

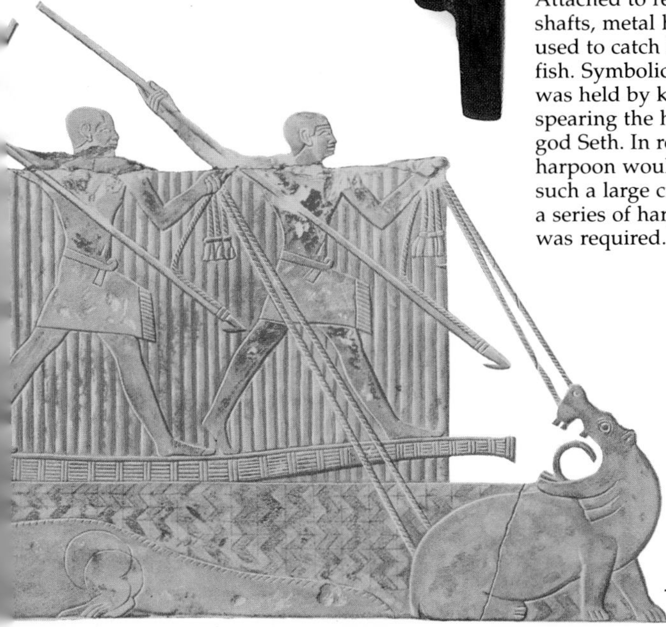

The Egyptians at home

HOUSES IN ANCIENT EGYPT were built from bricks made from the Nile mud. The mud was collected in leather buckets and taken to the building site. Here workers added straw and pebbles to the mud to strengthen it, then poured the mixture into wooden frames to make bricks. The bricks were left out in the sun to dry. After the house was built, its walls were covered with plaster, and the inside was often painted - either with patterns or scenes from nature. Inside, the houses were cool, as the small windows let in only a little light. Wealthy families had large houses. Beyond the hall were bedrooms, private apartments, and stairs to the roof. The kitchen was some way from the living rooms, to keep smells away. The ancient Egyptians held parties in their homes, which the children enjoyed as much as their parents.

AROUND THE POOL
A pool was often the central feature of a wealthy family's garden. It was stocked with lotuses and fish, and the water was renewed regularly to keep it fresh. Poolside borders were planted with shrubs and trees such as sycamore figs, date palms, and acacia trees.

HOME COMFORTS
This is a typical home belonging to a successful official, the royal scribe Nakht. The walls were made of mud bricks and coated with limestone plaster. Grille windows high on the walls let in only a little sunlight and dust, and vents trapped the cool north wind. In front was a garden with a pool and trees, in which Nakht and his wife could relax.

SOUL HOUSE
This model shows the house of a poorer family. The model would have been placed in the tomb of the owner, for use in the next life, so it is known as a "soul house." The entrance is through a low arched doorway. A window lets in a little light, and a stairway leads to the roof, where a vent could catch the cool north breeze that the Egyptians loved so much. Food is stored around the walled north courtyard of the house.

Empty vessels

A variety of cups, jars, and pots has survived from ancient Egypt. Among the earliest were stoneware vessels, some made over 5,000 years ago, before the first pharaohs ruled Egypt. These were often superbly crafted from attractive mottled stone. Later, a widely used material was faience, made by heating powdered quartz in a mold. Many different designs were made, including drinking cups and storage containers for wine; some of the jars had pointed bases, showing that they would have been set on stands.

WINE JAR
This container for wine is made of faience. Manufactured c. 1000 B.C., it is decorated with diamond and leaf patterns. Vessels like this were often used in wealthy Egyptian homes.

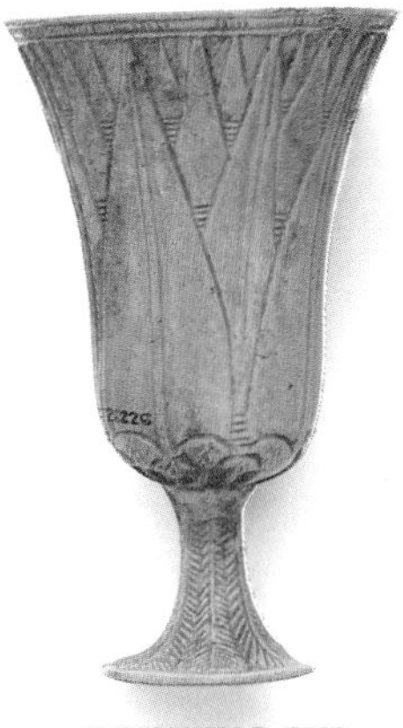

DRINKING CUP
Water, wine, or beer could have been drunk from this beautiful faience cup decorated with a lotus-flower pattern. Its broad base meant that the drinker could easily stand the cup on a convenient table or mat.

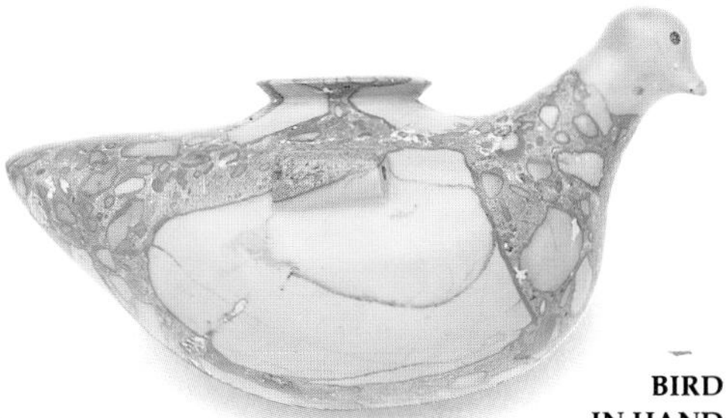

BIRD IN HAND
Carved over 5,000 years ago, this vase is a container for oil or other liquids. The contents could be poured in and out through the hole above the wings. It is made of a mottled stone called breccia.

FRUIT BASKET
Baskets were easy to make from either palm leaves or strips of papyrus. Some were patterned with abstract designs or pictures of people. They were often used as household containers - this one holds two doom palm fruits.

FANNING THE FIRE
This household servant is squatting near some charcoal, which he is fanning to make a fire. As well as heat for cooking, the fire provided a focal point for servants to gather around and talk.

This side view shows the graceful carved profiles of some typical Egyptian chairs

BUTCHERS AT WORK
An ox was slaughtered by tying three of its feet together, pushing it on its side, and cutting its throat. The free leg was cut and sometimes given as a religious offering.

Food and drink

THE FERTILE MUD deposited by the annual Nile flood allowed farmers to grow barley and emmer wheat, the mainstay of the Egyptian diet. Stored in granaries, these crops were eventually turned into bread or beer. Egyptian farmers grew vegetables such as onions, garlic, leeks, beans, lentils, and lettuce. There were also gourds, dates and figs, cucumbers and melons, but no citrus fruits. Egyptian bakers made cakes of many shapes and sizes, sweetened by dates or by honey gathered from conical pottery beehives. Grapes grown in the Nile delta or oases of the western desert were plucked for wine-making or drying into raisins. Poorer people would have less meat and poultry, and more fish. The spread at banquets was extremely varied - from ducks, geese, and oxen to oryx and gazelles. There were also pigs, sheep, and goats, which could be boiled or roasted.

IN THE VINEYARD
Two men pluck bunches of grapes from the vines. This job was often given to foreign settlers or prisoners from the Middle East or Nubia. The grapes would then be taken to be crushed by treading.

BREAD
More than 3,000 years old, this bread was baked from barley dough. Its texture was tough: flour often contained grit that got in during grinding. Studies of mummies have shown how coarse bread made Egyptians' teeth wear away.

STRAINER
This wooden syphon with its perforated mouthpiece was used for making beer taste better. Made from mashed loaves of barley-bread, Egyptian beer was very thick and needed to be strained either through a basket or with a syphon.

Perforations for straining

A Syrian soldier serving the pharaoh Akhenaten is sitting drinking beer through a syphon

GRAPES
The Egyptians grew most of their grapes in the north, just as they do today. Both red and green grapes provided the fermented juice for wine. They also imported wine from Syria and Greece.

DELICIOUS DATES
Dates were eaten fresh at harvest time in August or were dried or conserved in a sweet mash. Date wine was also made from both the fruit and the tree's sap.

BABOON WHO DOES NOT GIVE A FIG!
The fruit of the sycamore fig was held in high esteem in ancient Egypt. The modern examples are easily identifiable as the same as those on this sketch. Baboons loved figs and are often shown helping themselves from bowls or straight from the trees.

Modern fig

PALM-TREE FRUIT
These doom-palm fruits come from a 3,000-year-old tomb offering. The fruit has a gingery taste. The outer case of the nut is so tough it could be used as the top end of a drill handle.

EGYPTIAN BANQUET
Scribes and nobles were able to enjoy a wide variety of meat, poultry, and fruits. This rich and colorful display of food and drink is from a party scene at a Theban banquet. Wine jars are fixed with their pointed bases in racks and garlanded with leaves. The courses included cakes, baskets of figs and bunches of grapes, the head of a calf, the heart and foreleg of an ox, a plucked goose, and a twist of onions.

POMEGRANATES
The pomegranate was introduced to Egypt from the Middle East and its fruit was soon popular. This dish contains pomegranates that were originally part of a tomb offering. The shape of the fruit was used as a model for jewelry and drinking cups. The skin may have been used to produce a yellowish dye.

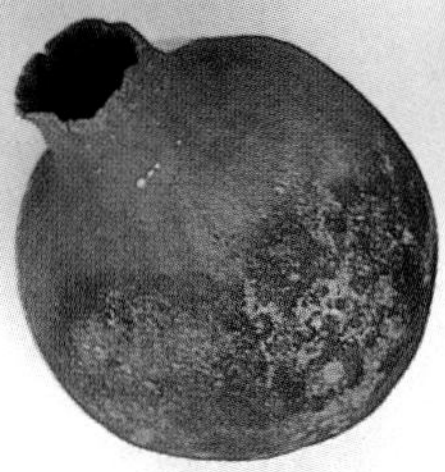

Ancient fruits

Large pomegranate produced by modern agriculture

Song and dance

THE EGYPTIANS ENJOYED LIFE to its fullest. Party scenes on tomb walls, songs on papyri, and musical instruments show us how much music and revelry meant to them. They had great public festivals, at which much wine was drunk and thousands of people were entertained with singing and music from flutes, harps, and castanets. Music was also performed on everyday occasions. Vintners pressed grapes for wine while men clapped rhythm sticks together; farm workers sang to their oxen as the oxen threshed the corn with their hooves; a princess would play the harp while her husband relaxed on a divan; dancers would turn somersaults alongside every procession. We do not know exactly what Egyptian music sounded like, but a small orchestra at a banquet could have string, wind, and percussion sections, and the music probably had a strong beat.

SONG AND DANCE
This section from a tomb painting shows a group of dancers and an orchestra of women playing a song in praise of nature. The frontal view shown in this picture is very unusual in Egyptian art.

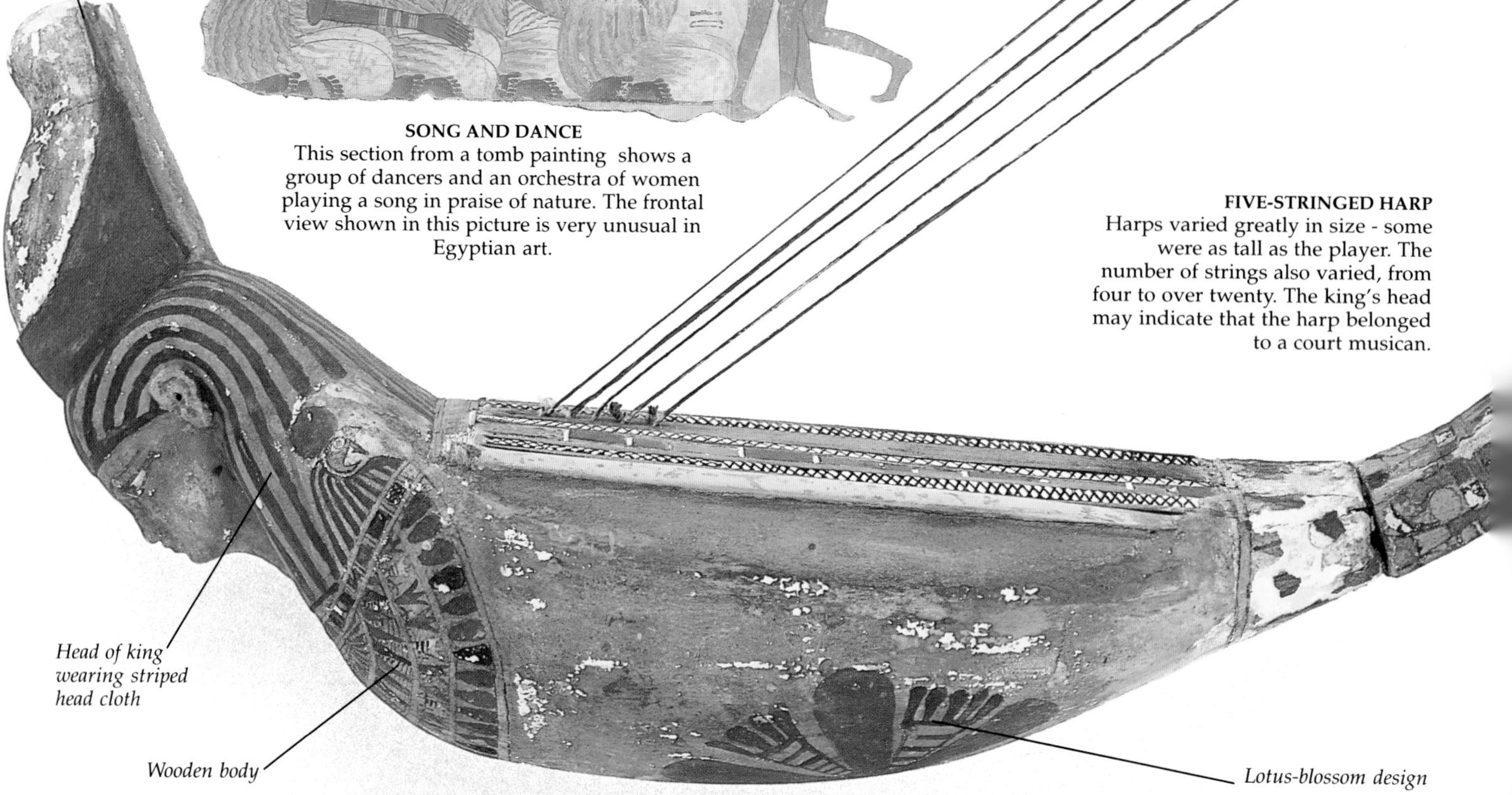

FIVE-STRINGED HARP
Harps varied greatly in size - some were as tall as the player. The number of strings also varied, from four to over twenty. The king's head may indicate that the harp belonged to a court musican.

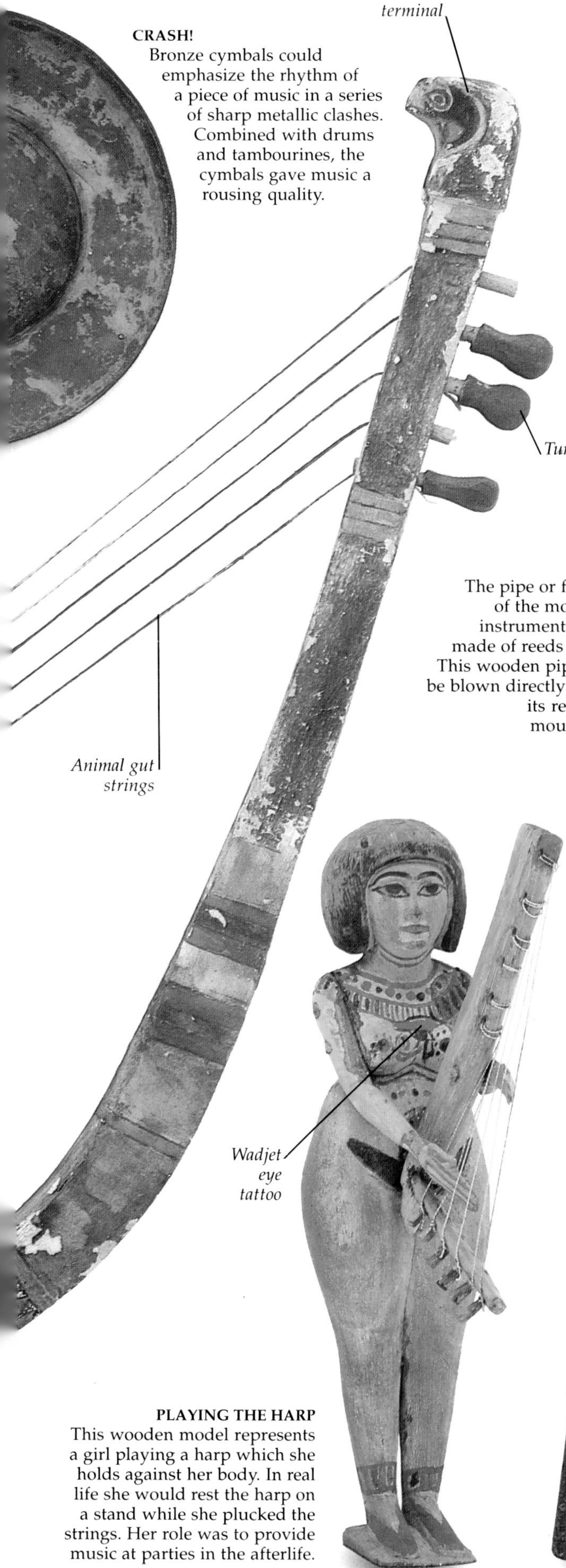

CRASH!
Bronze cymbals could emphasize the rhythm of a piece of music in a series of sharp metallic clashes. Combined with drums and tambourines, the cymbals gave music a rousing quality.

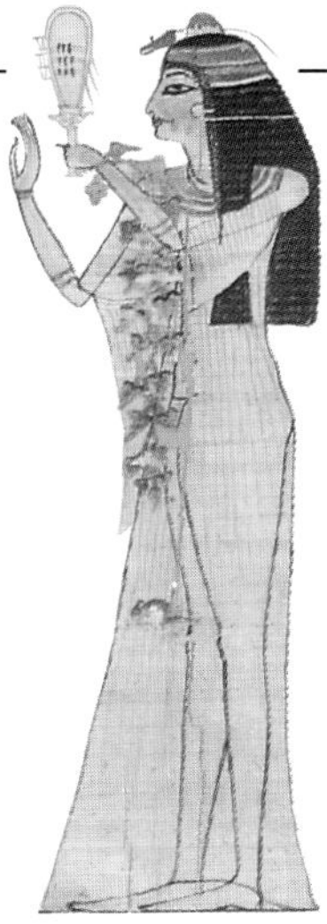

Priestess carrying a sistrum

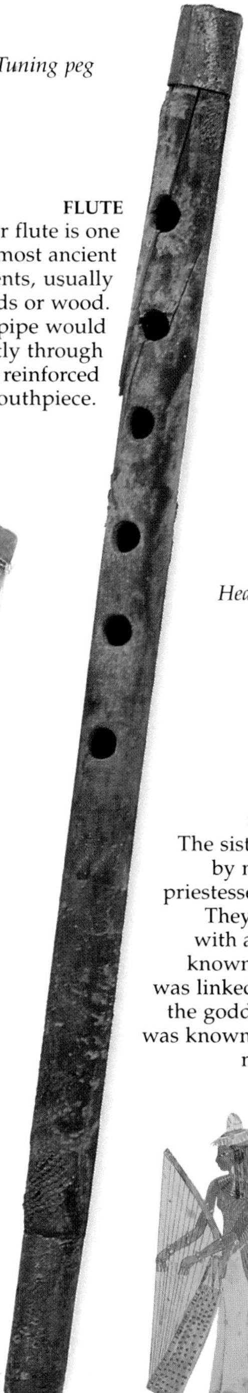

FLUTE
The pipe or flute is one of the most ancient instruments, usually made of reeds or wood. This wooden pipe would be blown directly through its reinforced mouthpiece.

SACRED RATTLE
The sistrum was carried by noblewomen and priestesses at ceremonies. They used it together with a sacred necklace known as a "menat." It was linked with the cult of the goddess Hathor, who was known for her liking of music and dance.

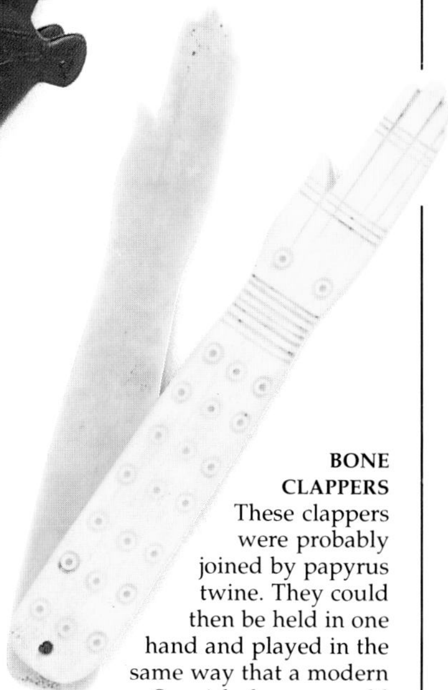

BONE CLAPPERS
These clappers were probably joined by papyrus twine. They could then be held in one hand and played in the same way that a modern Spanish dancer would use castanets.

PLAYING THE HARP
This wooden model represents a girl playing a harp which she holds against her body. In real life she would rest the harp on a stand while she plucked the strings. Her role was to provide music at parties in the afterlife.

Lyre and double-flute players from a painting at Thebes

Toys and games

GAME PIECE
This carved lion's head could have been used as a counter in a number of games

EVEN AS CHILDREN, the ancient Egyptians enjoyed life. Some of the games they played are still loved by children today, such as "khuzza lawizza," or leapfrog, and tug-of-war. There are also Egyptian paintings showing boys playing soldiers and girls holding hands in a sort of spinning dance. Then there were board games, like snake and the more complicated senet, and a number of toys, including balls, dolls, and toy animals. The Egyptians were also great storytellers, and kept their children amused with popular tales of imagination and enchantment. In one example, a magical wax toy crocodile turns into a real one when thrown into the water - a relevant story for people who lived under the threat of being eaten by crocodiles every day of their lives.

BALLS OR RATTLES?
These colorful balls are made of clay. They were originally filled with seeds or small beads of clay, so that they rattled as they were thrown.

DOLL OR GIRLFRIEND?
The Egyptians made dolls out of wood, with hair of clay beads attached to lengths of twine. Dolls like this one may have been for children, or they may have been made to put in someone's tomb, to act as a companion in the afterlife.

BALL GAMES
A popular pastime, especially for girls, was throwing and catching balls. Ball games were played while standing, or on piggy-back or leaping high into the air.

HORSE ON WHEELS
The Egyptians used horses on hunting trips and to pull their chariots and also on hunting trips. Horseback riding became a favorite pastime of the pharaohs. This toy horse, dating from Roman Egypt, has a saddle mat thrown over it. It was pulled along by a rope through the muzzle.

TOY MOUSE
This wooden mouse had a string fitted to it, which a child could pull to make the tail go up and down.

String to move lower jaw

ROAR OR MEOW?
This roughly carved wooden toy does not seem to know whether it is a cat or a lion. Its main attraction is its movable lower jaw, attached to some string.

The game of senet

The board game senet symbolized a struggle against the forces of evil that tried to prevent you from reaching the kingdom of the god Osiris. Images on each of the thirty squares of the board stood for advantages like "beauty" or "power," or for perils, like the spearing of a hippo. There were two sets of counters, and moves were made according to the way throw sticks landed.

YOUR MOVE
This papyrus from the Book of the Dead of the scribe Ani shows Ani and his wife Tutu playing senet. In spite of the fact that the artist has drawn Tutu sitting behind her husband in a rather formal pose, both seem to be enjoying their game.

SPINNING TOPS
A vigorous twist of the fingers or a tug on some papyrus twine wound around the cone would set these tops spinning. They were made of powdered quartz formed in a mold and then glazed. Toys of cheap materials like this meant that even the poorest families could give their children a few amusing games.

FIT FOR A KING
Tutankhamun was buried with four senet boards, of which this ebony and ivory board is the finest. It is fitted with a drawer for the counters and fixed on legs that have been delicately carved in the shape of bulls' feet.

Hieroglyph of pharaoh's name

Stone counter used in the snake game

THE GAME OF SNAKE
One of the earliest board games discovered in Egypt was called "snake" because the stone board represented a serpent coiled with its head in the center. The winner was the first to move his or her counter around the squares on the snake's body to the center. The stone counters are sometimes carved with the names of some of Egypt's earliest pharaohs.

From fabric to finery

MAN AND WIFE
This worker wears a pleated calf-length kilt; his wife wears a cloak. Their finely braided wigs have perfume pomades (p. 114).

LINEN, made from flax (plant fiber) provided clothing materials for everyone in ancient Egypt. The earliest picture of a loom in Egypt is on a pottery bowl dated to c. 3000 B.C. and flax was used for thousands of years after that. A pharaoh would have exceptionally fine linen; workers wore loincloths of coarser fabric. The Egyptians had clever ways of reducing wear on linen clothes - soldiers would cover the rear of their kilts with leather netting; domestic servants wore nets of cheap but colorful beads over their dresses. The basic courtier's kilt consisted of a linen cloth wrapped around the waist and secured by a knot, often elaborately tied. Cloaks gradually developed for use as overgarments. Women wore long, close-fitting dresses, often with beautifully pleated cloaks. There are still only vague ideas about how the Egyptians put pleats into their clothes - perhaps they used a board with a grooved surface. The number of pleats is probably exaggerated in many statues. The Egyptians learned the art of dyeing their clothes in colorful patterns from the Middle East, but the technique was never widespread.

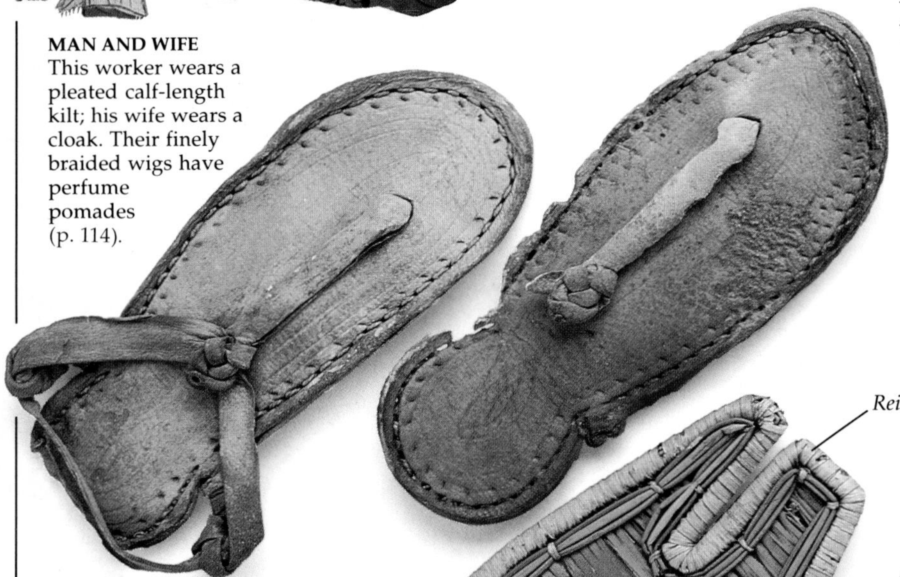

LEATHER SANDALS
These sandals are made from strips of ox leather stitched together with papyrus twine. Leather is an unusual material for Egyptian footwear.

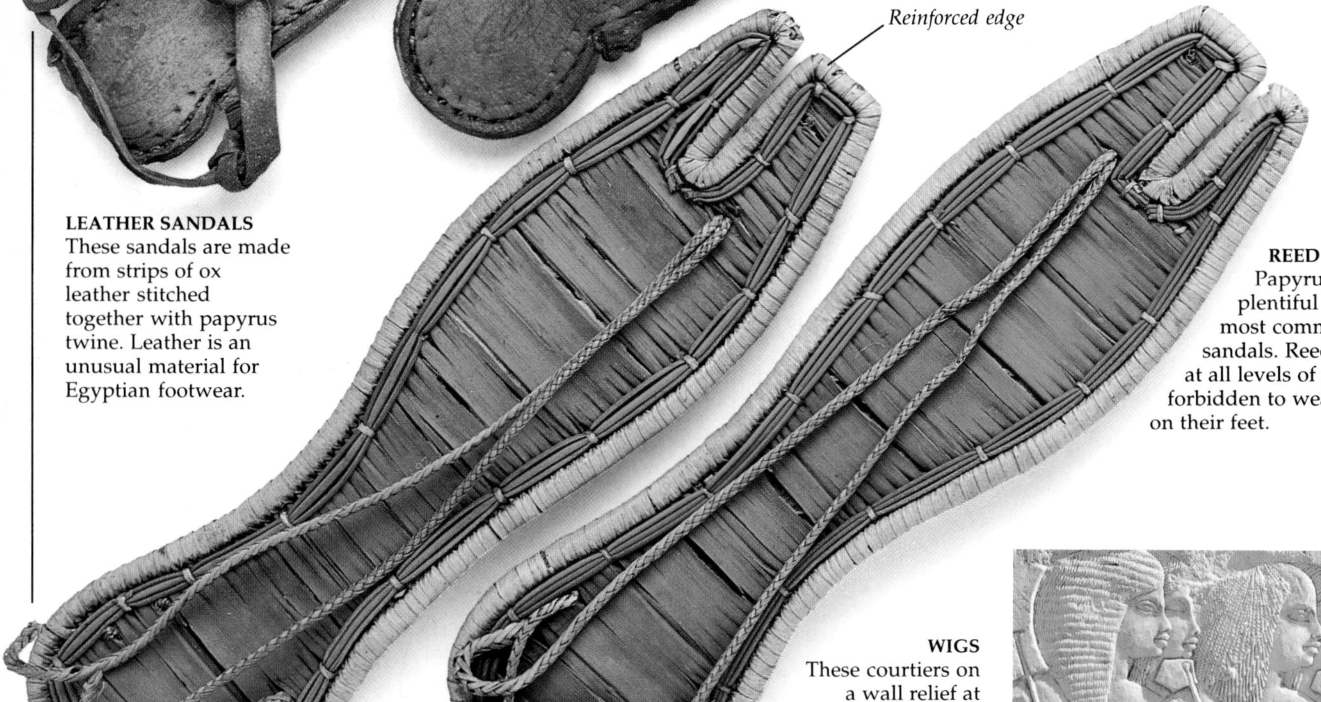

REED SANDALS
Papyrus and other reeds, in plentiful supply, were the most common materials for sandals. Reed sandals were worn at all levels of society; priests were forbidden to wear any other material on their feet.

WIGS
These courtiers on a wall relief at Memphis are wearing typical wigs and costumes with billowing sleeves. The wigs were made of human hair kept in place with beeswax.

PRINCESS OR QUEEN?
This statue is one of many intriguing works of art that survive from the reign of Akhenaten (p. 10). It represents Akhenaten's queen, Nefertiti, or one of her daughters. She is shown wearing a very fine garment of royal linen. The dress would have had many pleats, but probably not as many as shown by the sculptor.

IN THE GROOVE
This grooved board may have been used for pleating. The damp garment would be pressed into the grooves.

FLAX COMB
The first stage in making linen was to remove the flax heads with a long comb like this one. Then the flax stems were soaked and beaten to separate the fibers from the stalk and combed again to prepare them for spinning.

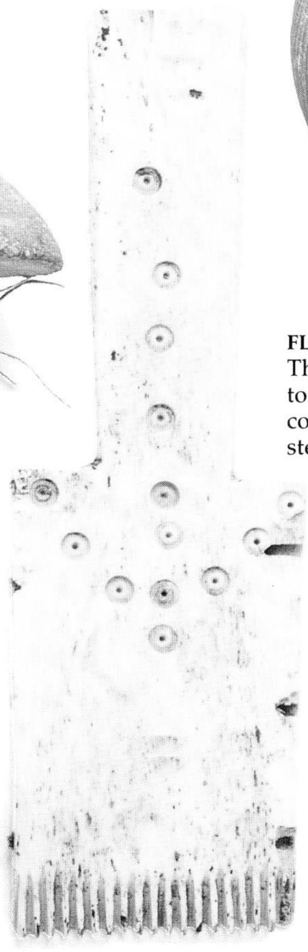

LINEN SHEET
Types of linen in ancient Egypt ranged from coarse material like this, which most people would have used, to the finest gauze worn by kings and queens.

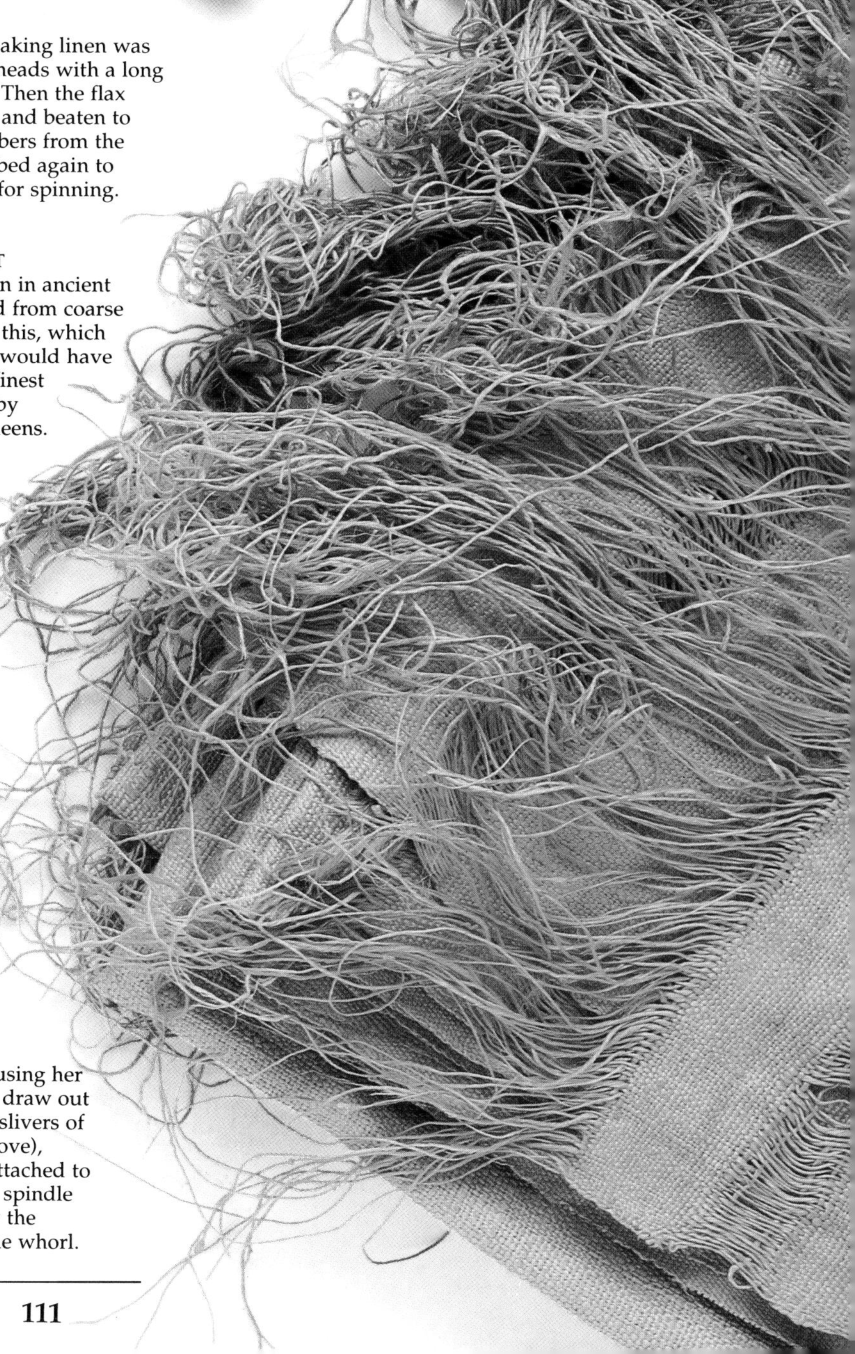

SPINDLE
The flax fibers were spun on sticks, or spindles, which had a weighted circular whorl on one end. Whorls dating from around 3000 B.C. have been discovered.

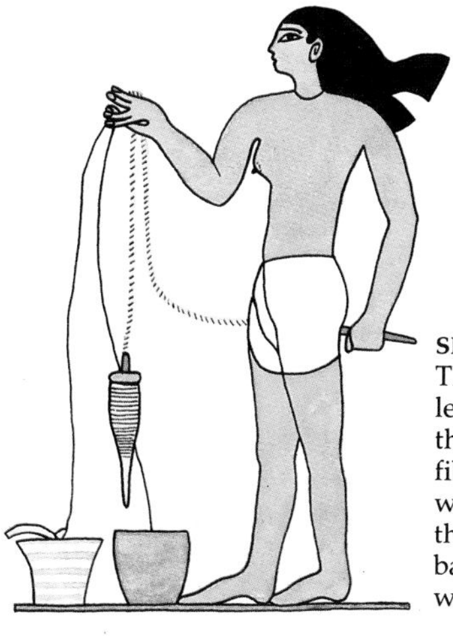

SPINNER
This girl is using her left hand to draw out the twisted slivers of fibers (the rove), which are attached to the rotating spindle balanced by the weight of the whorl.

All that glitters

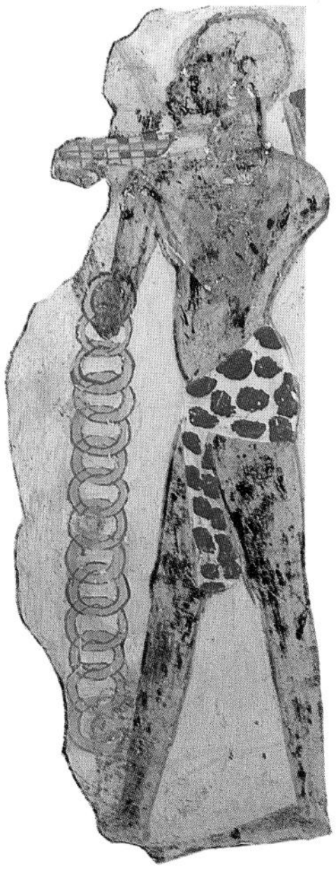

Rings of gold being brought to Egypt from Nubia

YOU CAN SEE the glint of gold everywhere in Egyptian jewelry - mines between the Nile and the Red Sea coast yielded large quantities of this precious metal. The gold could be beaten into shape or cast in molds. Goldsmiths also made patterns using a method called granulation, in which tiny grains of gold were attached to an object by soldering. Egyptian jewelers had access to many semiprecious stones from the deserts - orange-red carnelian, green feldspar, and mauve amethyst. They also imported stones. From mines in the Sinai peninsula came light blue turquoise and trade routes from Afghanistan brought rich blue lapis lazuli to Egypt. But Egyptian jewelers had no knowledge of precious stones like diamonds, emeralds, and rubies.

ROYAL BRACELET
This bracelet, made for Prince Nemareth, has a central design showing the god Horus as a child (p. 83). He is sitting on a lotus and is protected by cobras. Like many children in Egyptian art, he is portrayed sucking his finger.

Hieroglyphs give name of owner

Cowrie shell shows desire of wearer to have children

LUCKY BELT
This is the surviving section of a belt. In addition to cowrie shells made of electrum (a mixture of gold and silver), the belt contains beads of carnelian, amethyst, lapis lazuli, and turquoise.

A STAR IS BORN
This gold star was worn on the fore-head as a diadem. It dates from the Roman period of Egypt. The Roman mummy mask shows a priest wearing a diadem.

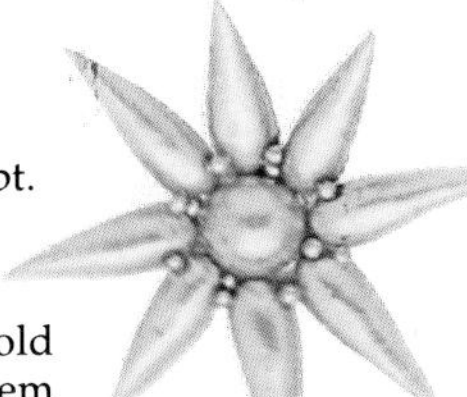

Gold diadem

Gold earrings

EAR ORNAMENTS
Middle Eastern influence led the Egyptians to have their ear lobes pierced and wear earrings. These earrings show how large the holes had to be to fit these studs of the 14th century B.C.

Faience stud

Glass stud

Jasper stud

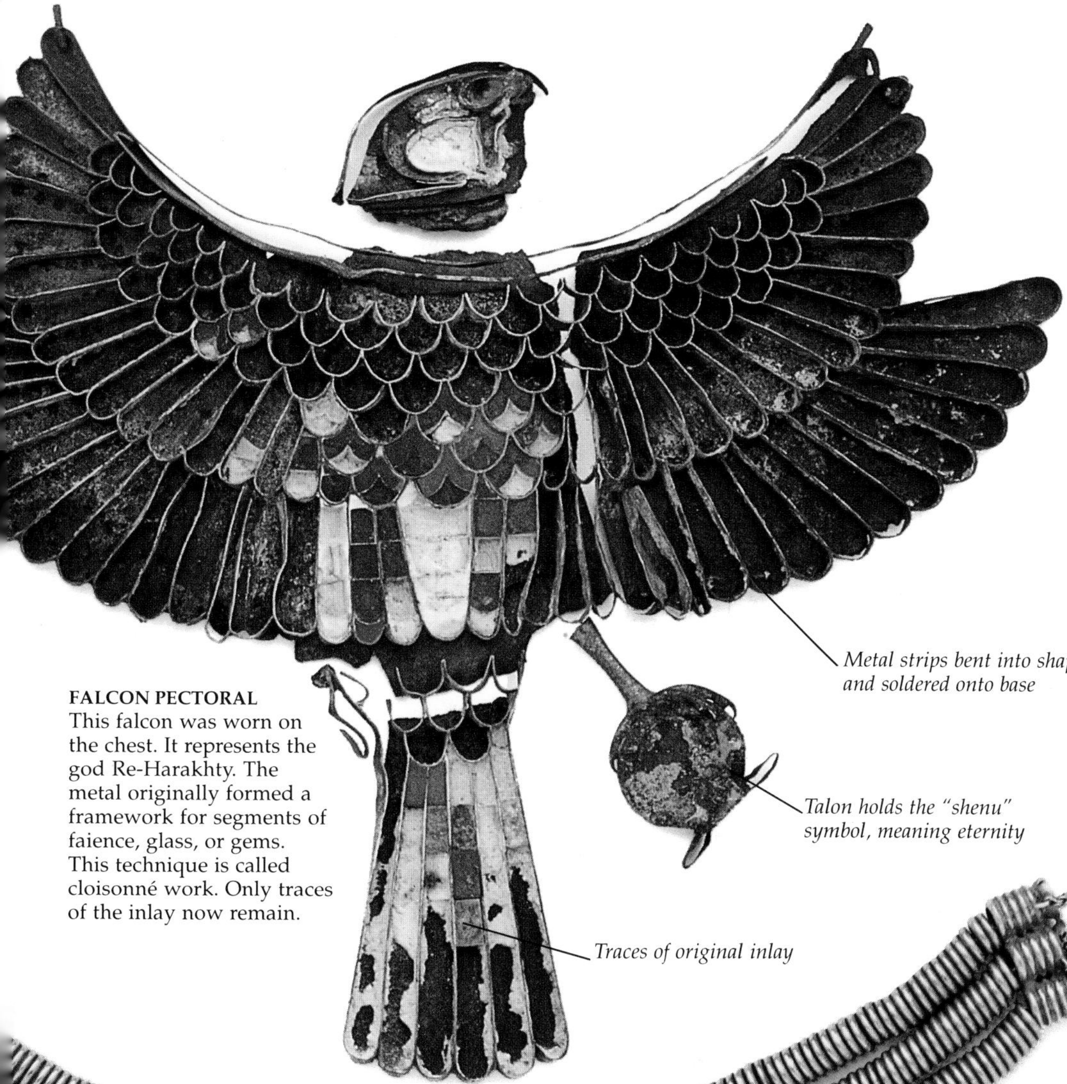

Metal strips bent into shape and soldered onto base

Talon holds the "shenu" symbol, meaning eternity

Traces of original inlay

FALCON PECTORAL
This falcon was worn on the chest. It represents the god Re-Harakhty. The metal originally formed a framework for segments of faience, glass, or gems. This technique is called cloisonné work. Only traces of the inlay now remain.

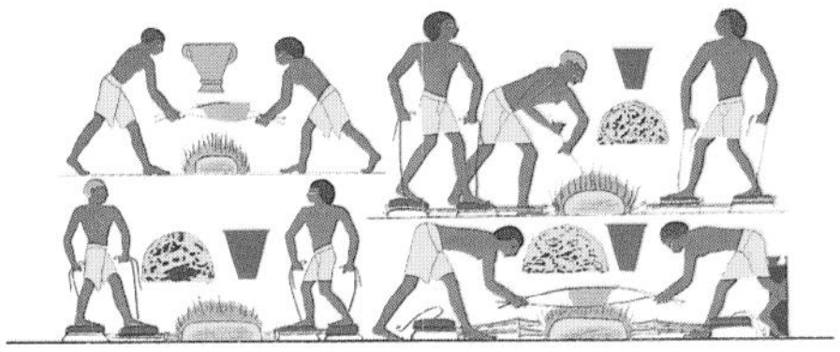

JEWELERS AT WORK
Many metal objects were made by casting - heating the metal until it was liquid (top) and then pouring it into molds (above) in the shapes of the objects required.

GIFT OF A KING
Outstanding service to the state was rewarded by a gift of jewelry from the king. He would lean out of a window and drop bracelets or collars to the nobles waiting respectfully below. This collar of honor has three rows of gold rings threaded tightly together on twine. It was tied in position at the back of the neck. Sometimes the pharaohs themselves wore collars like this.

FINGER RINGS
Rings often incorporated a swiveling stone in the shape of a scarab beetle (p. 78). The underside was carved with a name or good-luck design. These scarabs are made of steatite (soapstone), an easy material to carve.

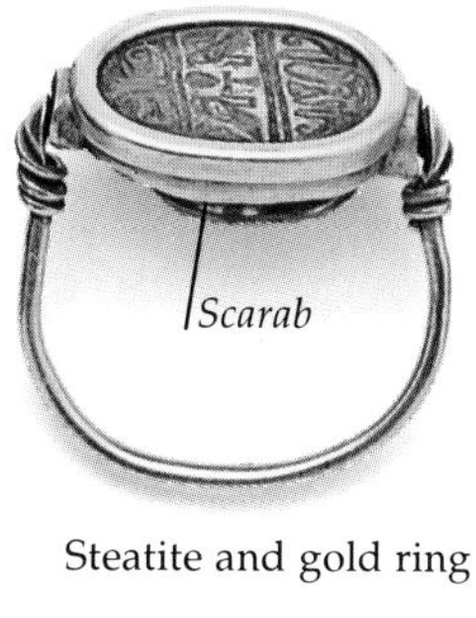

Scarab

Steatite and gold ring

Steatite and gold ring

Silver ring

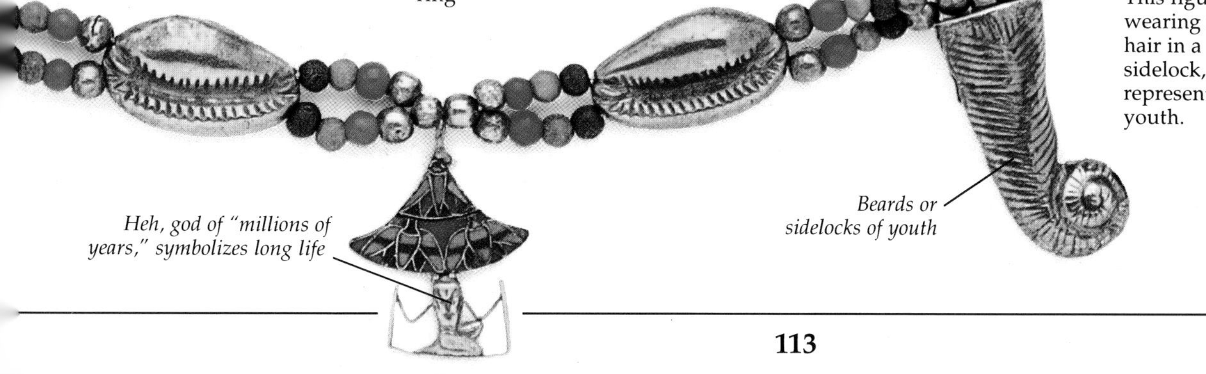

Fish amulets, to prevent drowning

Beards or sidelocks of youth

Heh, god of "millions of years," symbolizes long life

This figure is wearing its hair in a sidelock, to represent youth.

Adorning the body

THE EGYPTIANS were lovers of beauty and fashion. Many of their personal names are based on the word "nefer," meaning "beautiful" - for example, Nefret, Nefertiti, and Nefertari. The goddess associated with adornment was "Hathor the Golden," who is seen as the ideal of beauty in love poetry of the time. Egyptian men and women used eye paint, which was made from minerals ground on fine slate palettes. They went to great lengths in adorning themselves with cosmetics, wigs, floral garlands, and fine linen. Many objects like combs and mirrors have survived and show how important personal appearance was to the Egyptians. "Put myrrh on your head and dress up in beautiful clothes" says one song.

Malachite

Tube with royal inscription

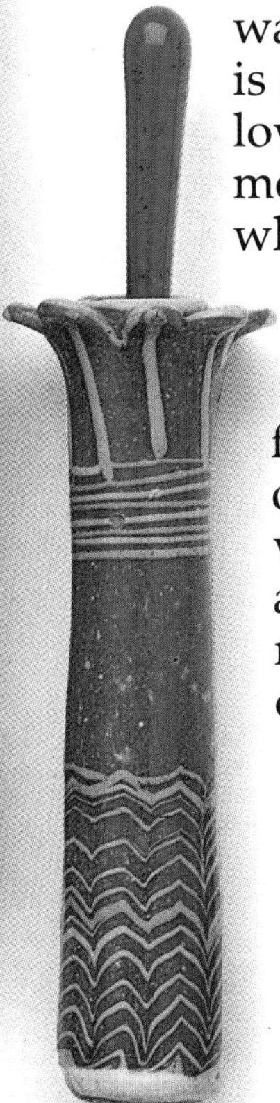

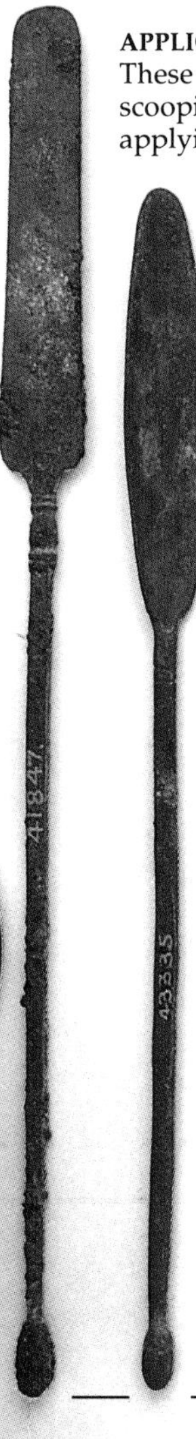

APPLICATORS
These were used for scooping, mixing, and applying pigment.

CRAFTSMAN'S MASTERPIECE
The mother duck's back wings slide across to give access to the face cream inside.

CONTAINERS
Ground mineral for eye paint was mixed with water and kept in tubes like these. The one with the royal inscription may have been a gift to a courtier.

Pot made of the rare stone anhydrite

PERFUME POMADES
Courtiers tied cones of scented animal fat to their wigs, sometimes with a lotus blossom. The fat would melt and slide down the wig.

MIRROR
Courtiers used polished bronze or copper mirrors. Here a naked servant girl holding a bird forms the handle, suggesting love and beauty.

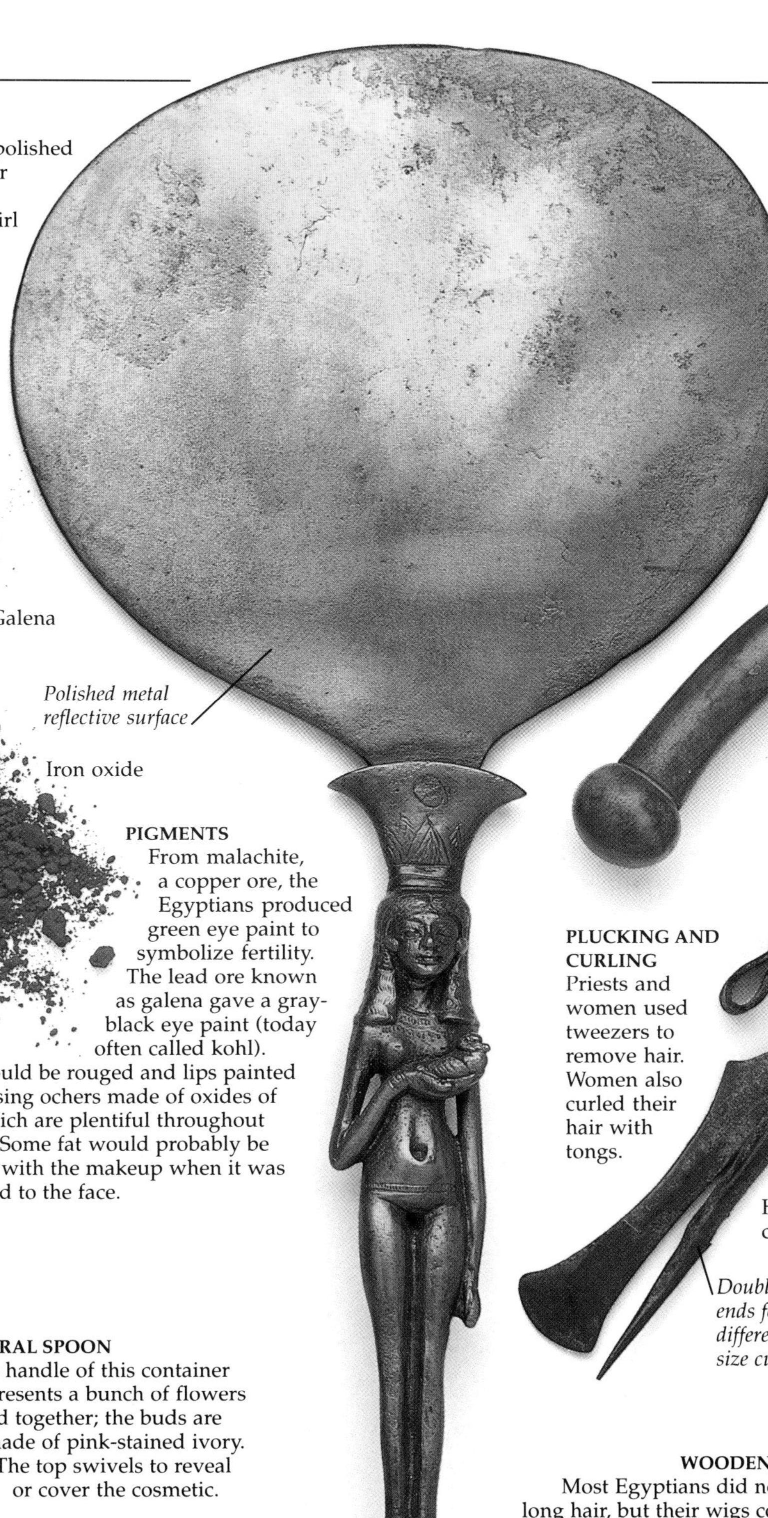

Polished metal reflective surface

BATH AND MASSAGE
This noblewoman kneels on a mat while a friend holds a flower for her to smell. Her bath is symbolized by water being scattered over her; she is also being given a shoulder massage.

Galena

Iron oxide

PIGMENTS
From malachite, a copper ore, the Egyptians produced green eye paint to symbolize fertility. The lead ore known as galena gave a gray-black eye paint (today often called kohl). Cheeks could be rouged and lips painted red by using ochers made of oxides of iron which are plentiful throughout Egypt. Some fat would probably be mixed with the makeup when it was applied to the face.

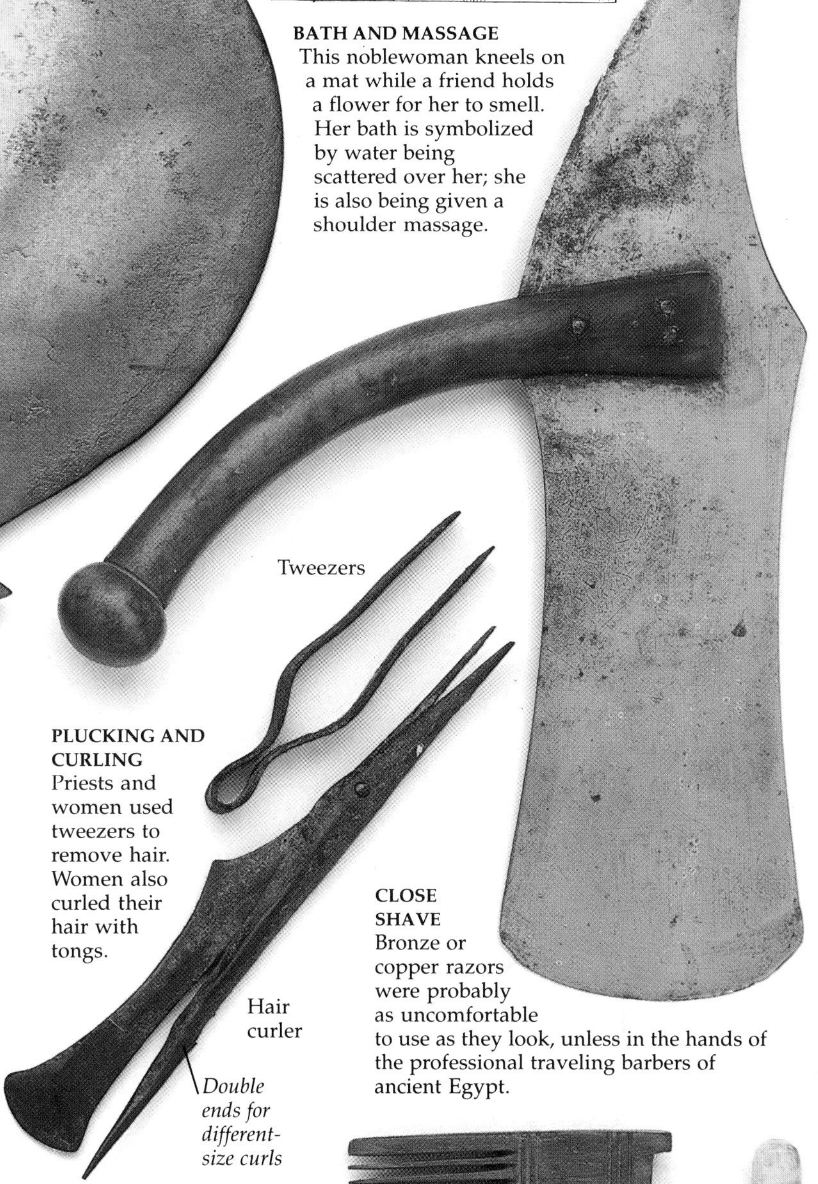

Tweezers

Hair curler

Double ends for different-size curls

PLUCKING AND CURLING
Priests and women used tweezers to remove hair. Women also curled their hair with tongs.

CLOSE SHAVE
Bronze or copper razors were probably as uncomfortable to use as they look, unless in the hands of the professional traveling barbers of ancient Egypt.

FLORAL SPOON
The handle of this container represents a bunch of flowers tied together; the buds are made of pink-stained ivory. The top swivels to reveal or cover the cosmetic.

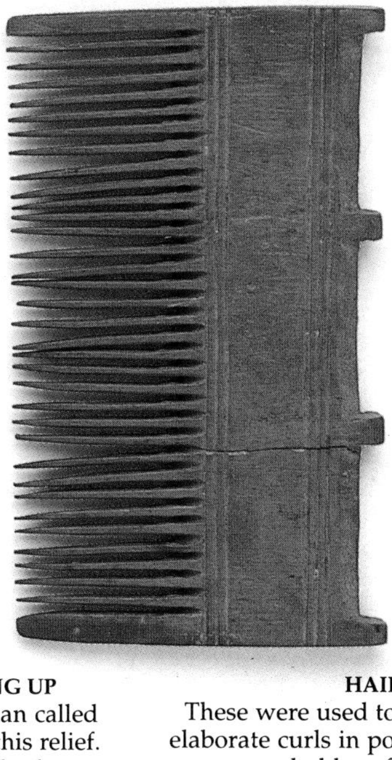

WOODEN COMB
Most Egyptians did not have long hair, but their wigs could be quite long and heavy, sometimes with three different layers of curls and fringes, so ivory and wooden combs were a necessity.

TOUCHING UP
A noblewoman called Ipwet appears in this relief. She holds a mirror while she dabs powder onto her cheeks.

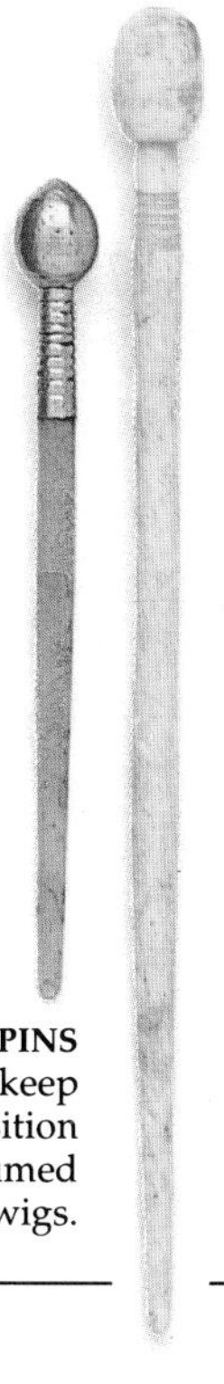

HAIRPINS
These were used to keep elaborate curls in position or hold perfumed pomades in place on wigs.

Animals of the Nile valley

LION
The lion represented strength and domination, and so became an emblem of the god-king himself. Rarely is the lion shown being hunted by any other person than the pharaoh. This gold lion was originally part of a necklace.

THE ANCIENT EGYPTIANS shared their environment with many different beasts, birds, reptiles, and fish. Out in the desert east and west of the Nile valley you would find ferocious lions and wild bulls as well as timid antelopes and gazelles. These animals either hunted their prey or grazed on the borders of the flood plain. The stillness of night would suddenly be broken by the eerie howls of scavenging hyenas and jackals fighting over carcasses. In the papyrus thickets beside the Nile there would be nests of birds like pintail ducks, cormorants, pelicans, and hoopoes. Lurking on the river banks would be crocodiles, and in the water you might see hippos with Nile perch and catfish darting around them. Animals appear on many ancient Egyptian objects. They were thought of as part of the "world system" made by the sun god, and as the earthly versions of many gods. Animal symbols were also used in hieroglyphics.

PEEK-A-BOO
The goddess Hathor was often portrayed as a cow in the papyrus marshes.

ANIMAL ANTICS
Satirical papyri show the topsy-turvy Egyptian sense of humor. On this example, two enemies, the antelope and the lion, are enjoying a friendly game of senet (p. 109). A jackal playing a double flute escorts a herd of goats while a cat lovingly attends to some geese. The lion at the right end seems to be amused by the antics of an ox on a couch.

WILD SHEEP AND NONCHALANT CAT
On this cosmetic container a wild sheep, or mouflon, is stepping carefully over a crouching cat that is clearly determined not to move. Rams symbolized some of the most important gods in ancient Egypt. A curly-horned ram could represent Amun-Re, king of the gods.

Crown of Osiris, made of ram's horns, reeds, and ostrich feathers

CROCODILE GOD
The peril of being snatched and eaten by crocodiles led the Egyptians to try to get these dangerous creatures on their side. Consequently the crocodile became the symbol of the god Sobek, and priests used to decorate sacred crocodiles with jewelry and mummify them when they died.

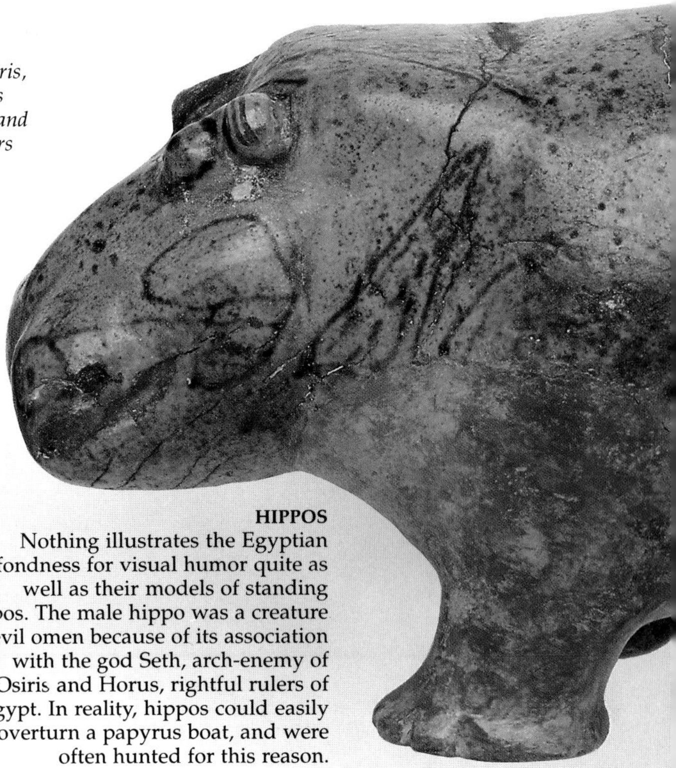

HIPPOS
Nothing illustrates the Egyptian fondness for visual humor quite as well as their models of standing hippos. The male hippo was a creature of evil omen because of its association with the god Seth, arch-enemy of Osiris and Horus, rightful rulers of Egypt. In reality, hippos could easily overturn a papyrus boat, and were often hunted for this reason.

FISH FLASK
This glass fish was made by molding the glass over a core. The ripples are meant to indicate the fish's scales. The flask was designed to hold perfume, which could be poured out of the mouth into the owner's hand. Objects like this show the beauty of the fishes of the Nile and the Red Sea.

GEESE ON PARADE
These geese are part of a very early tomb painting and were meant to ensure that the supply of food in the afterlife would not run out.

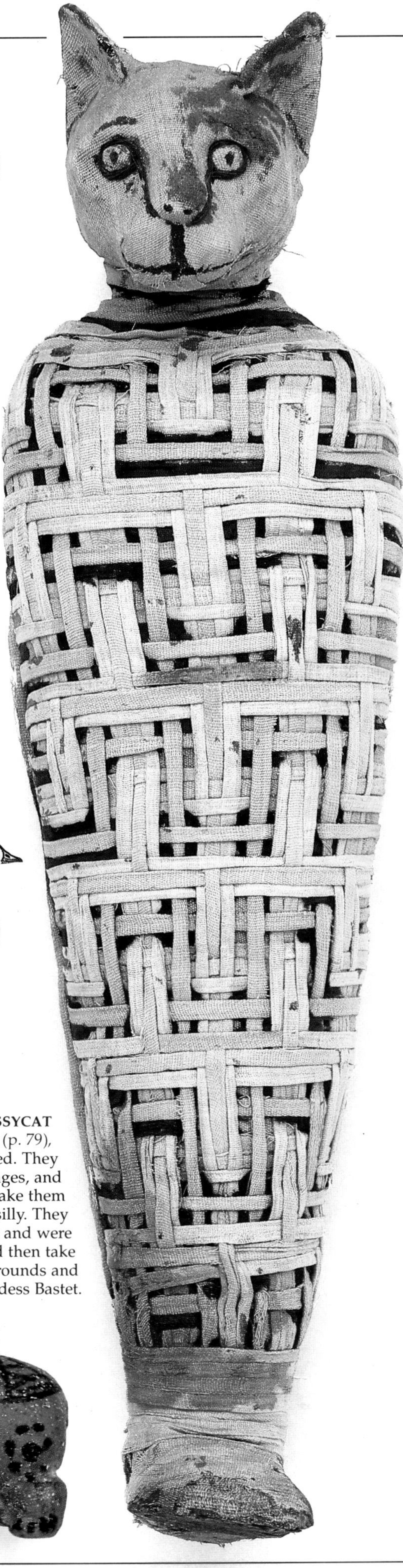

PUZZLED PUSSYCAT
Cats, sacred to the goddess Bastet (p. 79), were mummified when they died. They were wrapped in linen bandages, and their faces were painted to make them look bewildered - or just plain silly. They were put in cat-shaped coffins and were sold to temple visitors, who could then take them to the temple burial grounds and dedicate them to the goddess Bastet.

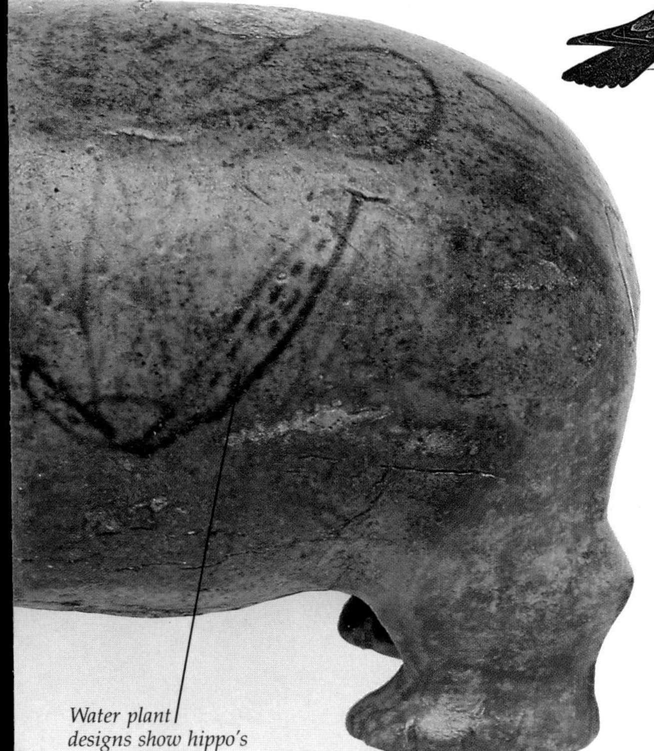

Water plant designs show hippo's aquatic habitat

Small faience hippo

Animal mummies

THE ANCIENT EGYPTIANS MUMMIFIED many animals with the same care they took for people. Favorite pets were occasionally mummified and put in the tomb with their owners to keep them company in the afterlife. But most beasts were embalmed for religious reasons. Animals were thought to be representatives or spiritual messengers of the gods. Many gods became naturally associated with one or more animals that shared the same qualities. The cow, for instance, which took such tender care of its young, was associated with Hathor, the goddess of love and motherhood. Special places became the centers of worship for major gods and goddesses. Here the animals sacred to these gods were mummified and buried in enormous cemeteries. By the later period of ancient Egyptian history, a huge religious industry flourished and millions of animals were bred just to be mummified.

Mummy of a wild dog or jackal, sacred to Anubis, the god of embalming (pp. 14, 17, 35).

SACRED BULL
When he died, the sacred Apis Bull (p. 29) was embalmed with the same care and ceremony shown to a pharaoh.

Bronze case for the mummy of a shrew mouse, sacred animal of the god Horus (p. 22)

ROYAL SERPENT
Bronze container for the mummy of an eel or cobra. The snake's beard and crown show its association with royalty.

TWINS
These two falcons were embalmed and mummified together, to strengthen their magical association with the god Horus (p. 22).

A limestone case for a mummified scarab beetle, the smallest creature to be embalmed

ROLLING ACROSS THE SKY
The scarab beetle rolls up balls of dung and pushes them around. The Egyptians believed the beetle god Khepri rolled the sun across the sky in the same way.

Unwrapped mummy of a crocodile

ON THE MENU?
An unwrapped mummified fish. Fish were sacred in some parts of Egypt, where they were never caught or eaten. In other areas, they were on the menu. This often led to violent conflicts between neighboring towns.

IN THE NILE, CROCODILE
In ancient times, the River Nile was full of crocodiles, which were feared for their ferocity. They were sacred to Sobek, a god of the water. Tame crocs were kept in luxury, fed on fine meats and wine and dressed in gold jewelry. The largest mummified crocodile ever found was 15 ft (4.6 m) long.

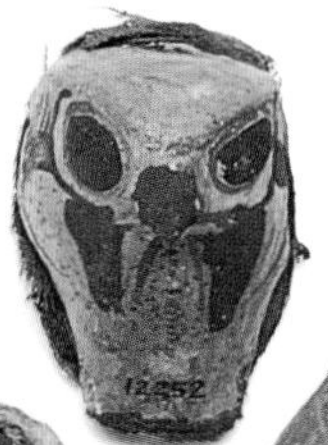

Painted plaster mask for a falcon mummy

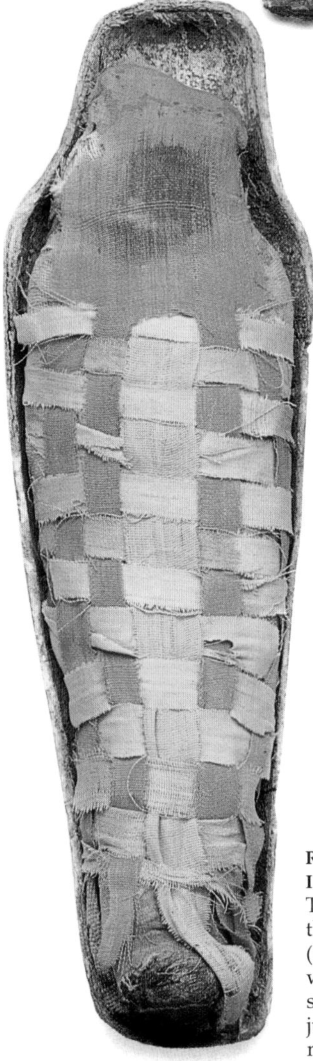

ROOST IN PEACE
The mummy of a falcon lies in this coffin made of cartonnage (p. 20). The lid is richly painted with a floral collar and a winged scarab beetle. The designs are just like the ones on human mummy cases.

Head of a mummified goose, sacred to the god Amun

SACRED IBIS
Three kinds of ibis were found in ancient Egypt. The migrant species with brown plumage still visits the country every year. But the bronze-colored crested ibis and the beautiful sacred ibis (right) are now extinct there.

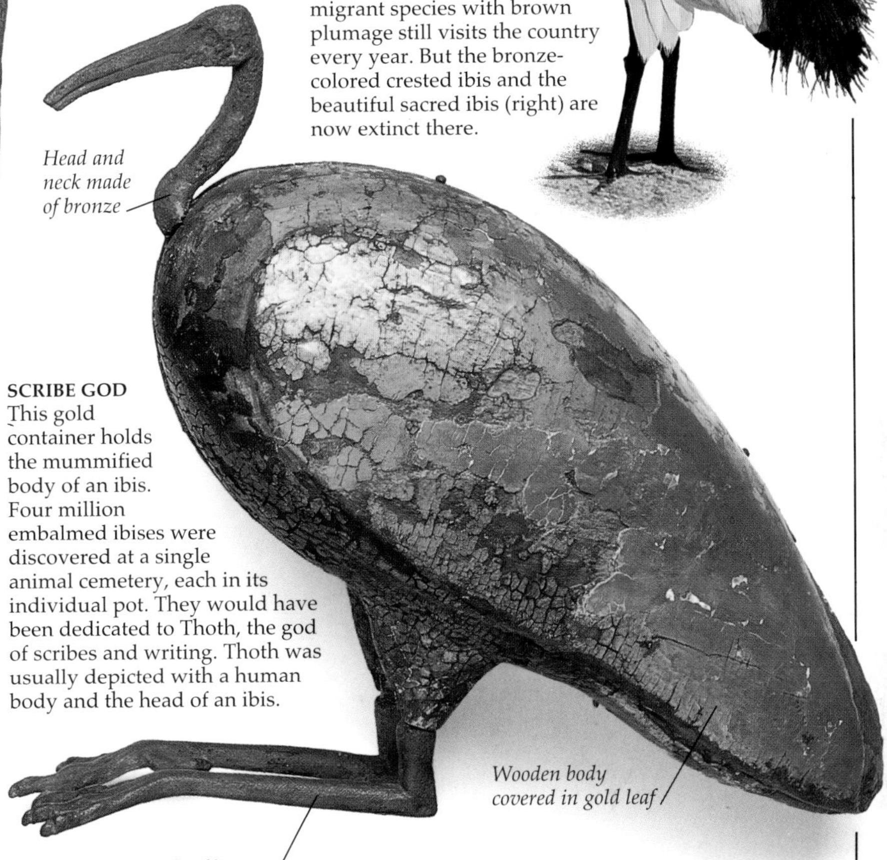

SCRIBE GOD
This gold container holds the mummified body of an ibis. Four million embalmed ibises were discovered at a single animal cemetery, each in its individual pot. They would have been dedicated to Thoth, the god of scribes and writing. Thoth was usually depicted with a human body and the head of an ibis.

Unwrapping the mummy's secrets

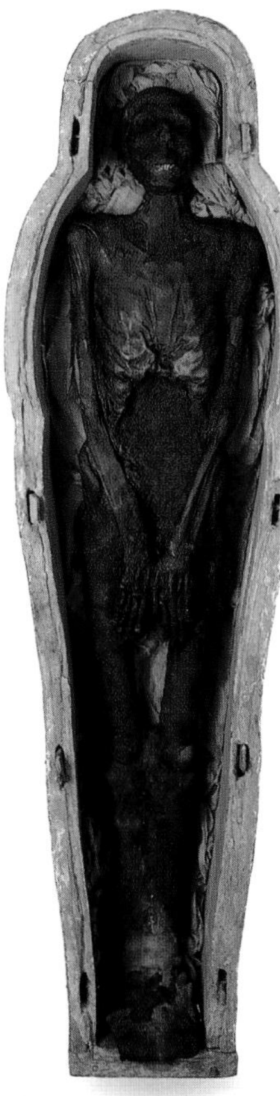

ESTIMATING AGE
This mummy of a man is lying in a coffin made c. 1000 B.C. for Tawuhenut, a female singer. Studies of the man's teeth and bones put his age at 20 to 35. More accurate estimates can be made for mummies who died before the age of 25, when their teeth and bones were still growing.

THE SCIENTIFIC STUDY OF MUMMIES does more than reveal how the ancient Egyptians embalmed their dead. Autopsies of ancient bodies can also show how people lived, what they ate, and what diseases they suffered from. In the 19th century, many mummies were unwrapped by surgeons. But their findings were limited by the technology of the age. Nowadays ruining the careful bandaging and dissecting the body is considered destructive and disrespectful. The invention of X-ray analysis in 1895 meant that mummies could be electronically "unwrapped" without being damaged. Early equipment was heavy and awkward. But by the 1960s, powerful, mobile X-ray units that could be brought into museums had been developed. The latest scanning equipment can "see" through the bandages and create complex, three-dimensional images of the body within. A small tissue sample from the mummy can be rehydrated (made wet again) and its cell structure studied. Even DNA, a person's basic genetic structure, can be identified. Some scientists believe that genetic analysis of mummies may one day help find a cure for modern viruses.

CAIRO AUTOPSY
Daniel Fouquet, a French doctor, unwraps the mummy of Tawedjatra, a priestess who died around 1000 B.C. This historic autopsy took place at the Cairo Museum in 1891. It was attended by the leading French Egyptologists of the day, along with several society women.

THE MANCHESTER TRADITION
In 1908, Dr. Margaret Murray (second from right) and her colleagues unwrapped and dissected a mummy at Manchester University in England. They kept some tissue samples. These were examined in the 1970s as part of a major mummy survey led by Dr. Rosalie David. When rehydrated and viewed under a microscope, the tissues revealed evidence of a lung disease called silicosis. Desert sandstorms and the dusty climate may have caused breathing problems like silicosis for many ancient Egyptians.

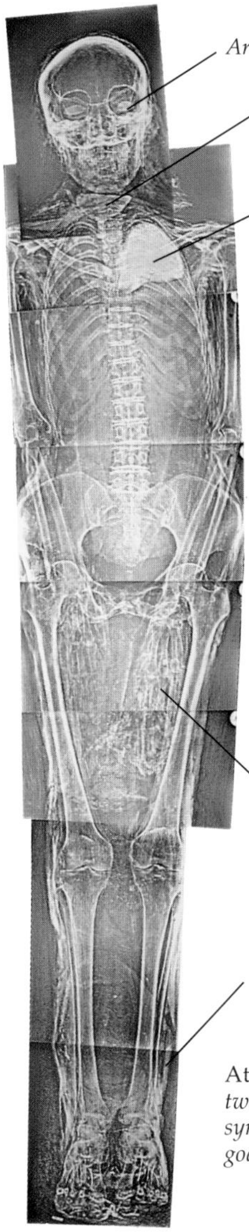

ALL IS REVEALED
This is a xeroradiograph (a special high-definition X-ray) of a mummy wrapped around 1000 B.C. Unlike normal X-rays, xeroradiographs emphasize edges, so that outlines of shapes are easier to see. This makes it easier to locate amulets (pp. 22–23), wrapped organs, and bones. This image revealed a lot of packing material which was pushed under the skin to make the shrunken body appear more lifelike.

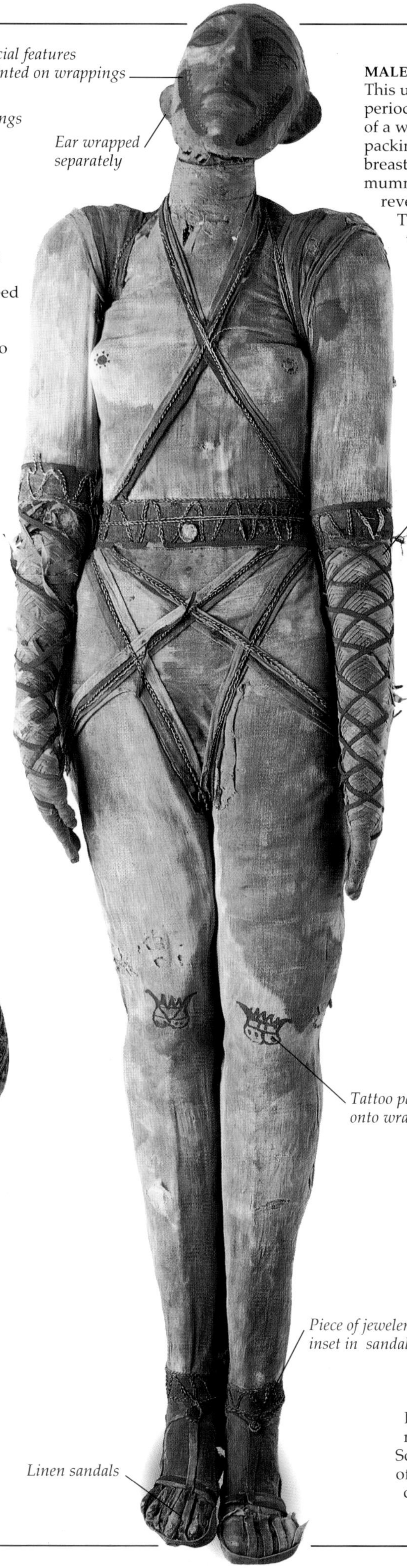

MALE DANCER
This unusual mummy from Egypt's Roman period (pp.20–21) was found lying in the coffin of a woman dating from much earlier. From the packing, which emphasizes the shapes of the breasts and thighs, it was assumed that the mummy was female. But X-rays taken in the 1960s revealed a man's body beneath the wrappings. The paintings on the linen represent body tattoos. He may have been a dancer who performed at religious ceremonies and banquets, because such dancers are known to have had similar tattoos. The embalmers wrapped the mummy with great care, packing it to give it the shape of a living body. The facial features were painted on, in the style of Old Kingdom mummies. The fingers and toes are all wrapped separately, even in the outer layers. This is very rare.

Side view of Roman mummy, showing careful wrapping of individual fingers

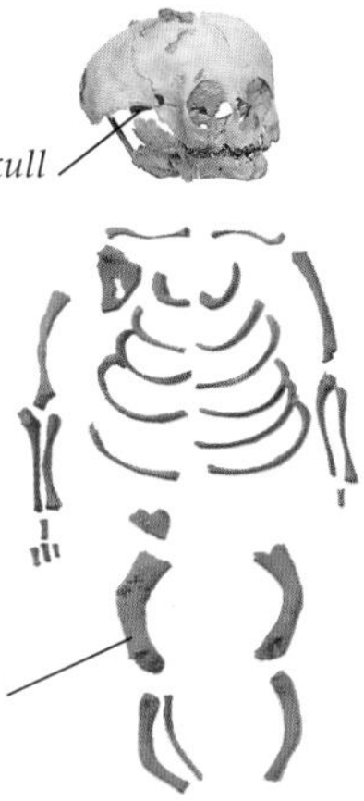

BONE DISEASE
This cartonnage coffin from the 22nd Dynasty (945–715 B.C.) once held the mummy of a child. All that remains of the body is a skeleton. Medical experts found that the strange deformities in the skull and other bones were caused by a rare bone disease called osteogenesis imperfecta. This would have afflicted the child while still in the mother's womb. He or she must have been born with brittle bones and probably died soon after.

MUMMY FINGERPRINT
Even after 3,000 years, it is still possible to take a mummy's fingerprints. Police forensic experts at Scotland Yard in London, England, have the prints of an Egyptian mummy in their records of modern criminals. They took the prints from a mummy's hand lent to them by the British Museum.

Continued on next page

Continued from previous page

ROYAL VISIT TO PARIS

In 1974, experts in Egypt discovered that Ramses II's skin was being destroyed by a mysterious infection. The royal mummy was flown to Paris three years later for medical treatment. International regulations required him to have a passport, which gave his occupation as "King (deceased)." When he arrived in France, a team of conservators successfully cured the infection, which turned out to be a fungus. A total of 102 specialists, including radiographers, police forensic scientists, botanists, and textile experts, examined the ancient pharaoh's body.

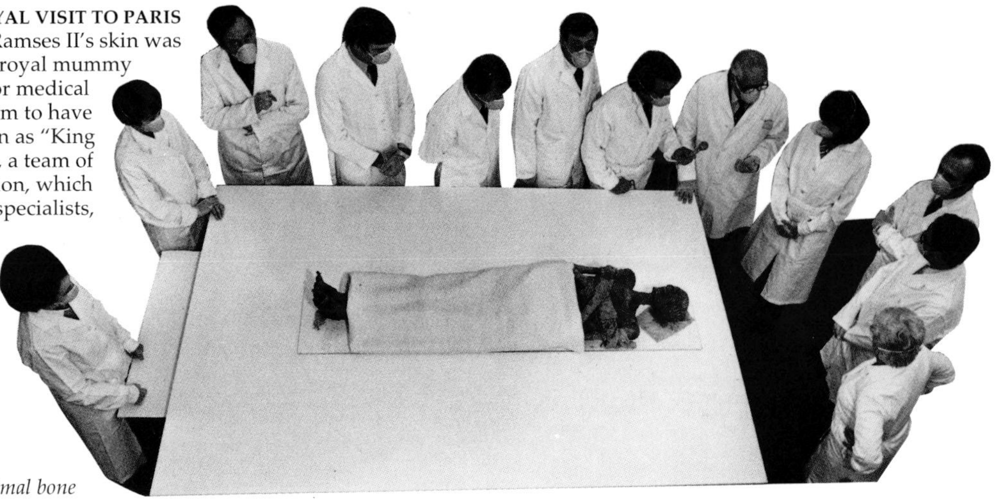

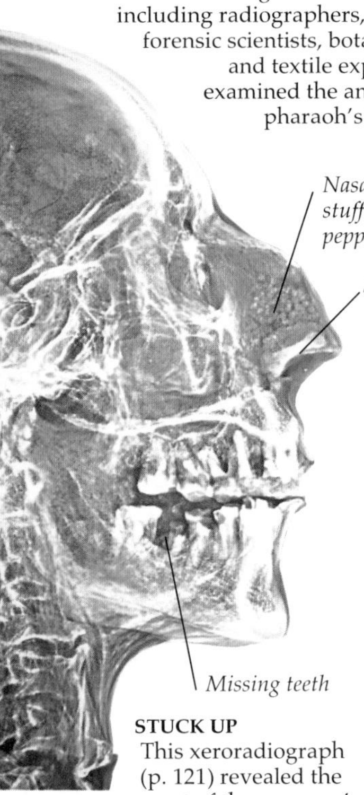

STUCK UP

This xeroradiograph (p. 121) revealed the secret of the mummy's dignified profile. The embalmers had kept the king's nose in the air by packing it with peppercorns and propping it with a tiny animal bone.

Ramses the Great revealed

The mummy of Ramses II was found in 1881 (p. 70) and has been resting in the Cairo Museum ever since. A special trip to Paris in 1977 gave medical experts from around the world a unique chance to examine the dead pharaoh's body. It is interesting to compare their findings with the historical records of his 67-year reign. X-rays showed a battle wound on one shoulder and signs of a healed fracture in one toe. The king may have suffered these injuries in an accident in the desert, an event described in ancient records. Close examination revealed a tiny piece of blue and gold fabric stuck to the mummy's skin. This was probably part of the king's clothes. Traces of unusual sand suggest that he may have been embalmed near Per-Ramesse, the king's northern capital. Analysis of resins identified the herbs and flowers used to embalm him. Ramses's body was especially rich in camomile oil. It was also coated with an extract from a wild tobacco plant, possibly added to keep insects off the body.

THE LIVING PHARAOH

This is Ramses II as he may have looked in life. Painted by Winifred Brunton in 1920, it was based on a comparison of his mummy and ancient sculptures. There is a striking physical resemblance between Ramses II, his father, Seti I (p. 30), and his son, Merenptah. The mummies of the three kings all have large, hooked noses.

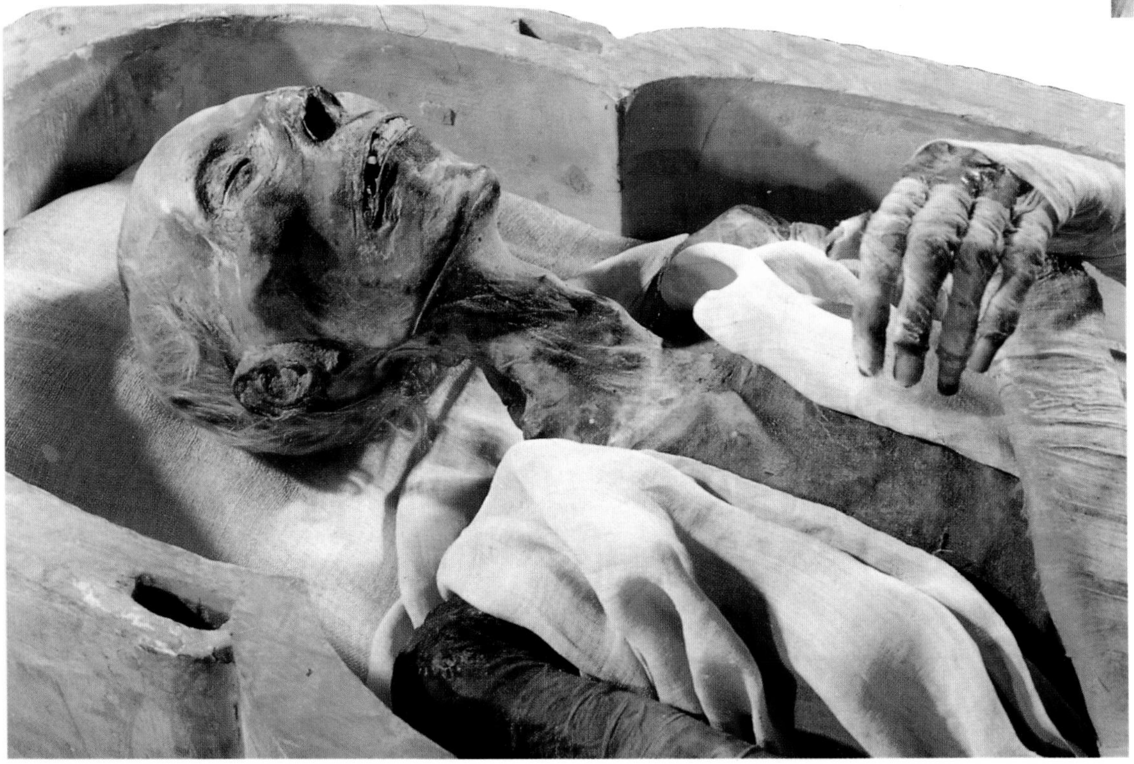

REDHEAD

Considering he is more than 3,260 years old, Ramses II is in very good health. His hair was probably dyed with henna but seems to have been naturally red. His slightly open mouth reveals a good set of teeth. Abscesses in his jaw must have caused him great pain. The king also suffered from blood circulation problems and severe arthritis in the hips. This must have made it hard for him to get around in his last years. He was probably in his nineties when he died and had a bent back. To keep his head up, the embalmers had to break his spine.

CAT scanning

Since 1977, doctors have been examining mummies with the help of an advanced X-ray process called CAT scanning. CAT stands for Computerized Axial Tomography (the last word means "cut" or "section"). A normal X-ray produces one flat view of an object. But a CAT scan takes many thin views, each one like a slice of bread. These are then processed by a computer and put together to produce the whole loaf – a three-dimensional image of the object and all its surfaces, inside and out. It is possible to zoom in on one slice or isolate a particular part of the mummy to study it in more detail. The thickness of the slices can also be varied to give more information on one area like the skull or teeth. In 1991, doctors at St. Thomas' Hospital in London, England, began a mummy scanning program with the British Museum. The first mummy they studied was Tjentmutengebtiu, a priestess who died around 900 B.C. She is enclosed in a beautiful cartonnage case that would be damaged if it were opened.

Cartonnage mummy case of Tjentmutengebtiu

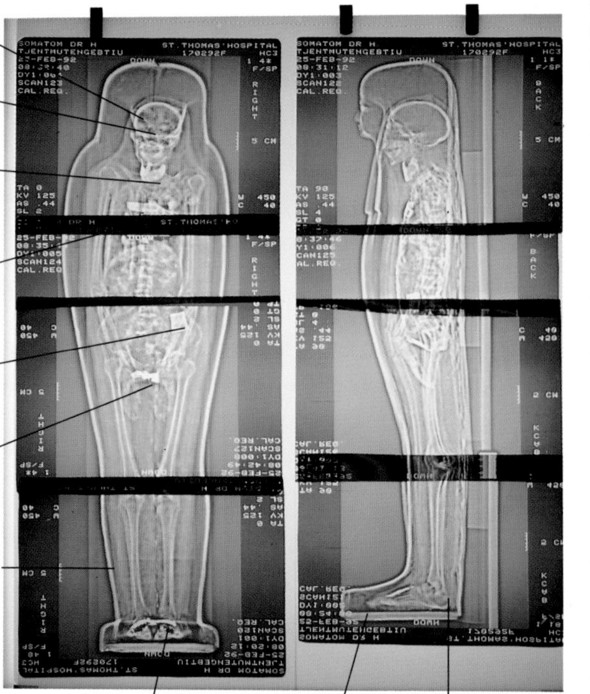

X-RAY VIEWING

The CAT scanner can also simulate normal, flat X-ray images (above). Dense structures like bones are shown in white. Less dense materials like bandages come out dark blue or black. These X-rays show the skeleton inside the mummy and the mummy lying inside its case. The mummy mask, artificial eyes, various amulets, and an embalming plate can also be seen.

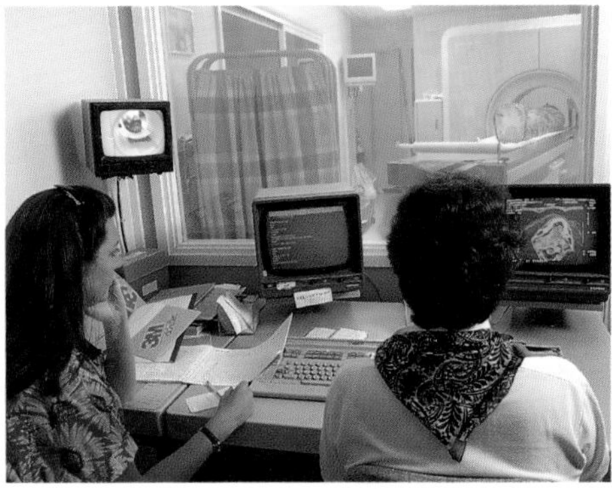

TV CELEBRITY

Radiographers view the scanning process on high resolution television screens in a separate observation booth. They can control the thickness of the individual slices. The radiographers took slices 0.1 in (2 mm) thick of Tjentmutengebtiu's head and neck and 0.2 in (4 mm) thick for the rest of her body. It took a total of over 500 slices to scan the mummy from head to toe.

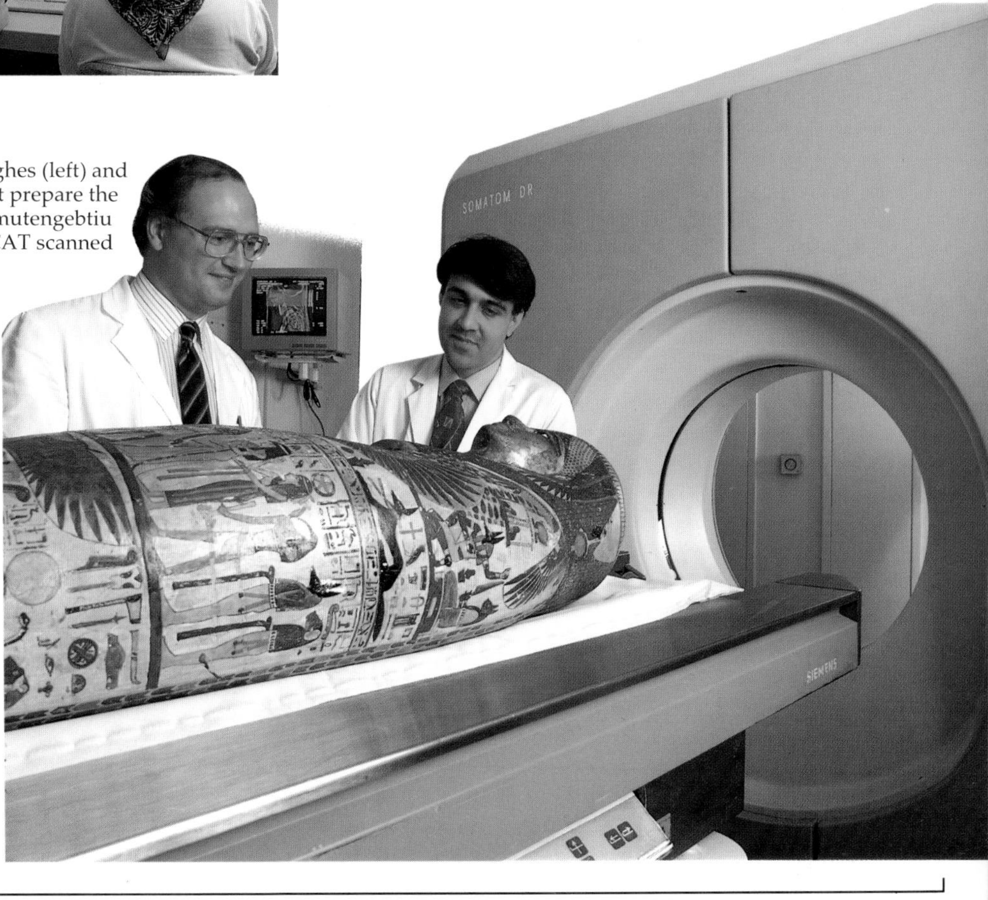

Dr. Stephen Hughes (left) and Dr. Ajit Sofat prepare the mummy of Tjentmutengebtiu to be CAT scanned

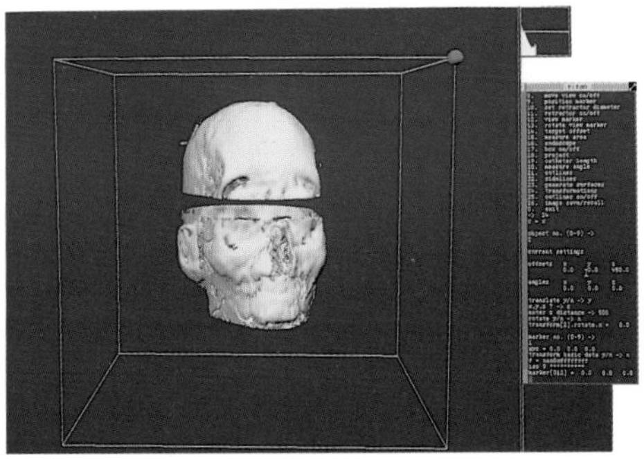

COMPUTER GRAPHICS

CAT scans tell doctors a lot about the density of objects hidden beneath the surface. Different tissues like bone or skin have their own distinctive densities. Once these have been calculated, one tissue can be isolated from the others. This is the skin on Tjentmutengebtiu's skull. The doctors can even look inside her skull and see details like the sinus cavities. Information on density can also reveal if an object like an amulet is made of clay or metal.

Egypt after the pharaohs

CLEOPATRA
Queen Cleopatra VII was the last in a line of Greek rulers of Egypt. Her suicide was famous, but there is no historical evidence to back up the familiar story that she died of the bite of a snake called an asp.

EGYPT WAS INVADED by foreigners several times in the last 1000 years B.C. The invaders included the Sudanese, the Persians, and the Macedonians under Alexander the Great. Alexander was followed by his general Ptolemy, who founded a dynasty that ruled from Alexandria. These rulers spoke Greek and worshiped Greek gods and goddesses, but on temple walls they were portrayed as traditional Egyptian rulers. In 30 B.C. Egypt passed into Roman hands, and gradually, following the conversion to Christianity of the Roman emperors, churches and monasteries replaced the temples. The Arab invasion of the 7th century A.D. turned Egypt into the mainly Muslim country that it is today.

The Romans

The Roman world took grain from Egypt's fields and gold from its mines. But although the Romans exploited Egypt, they also built temples. The names of emperors like Augustus and Tiberius were written in hieroglyphs just like those of the pharaohs, and the emperors were sometimes pictured wearing elaborate Egyptian crowns.

EMPEROR AS HORUS
Just as the Egyptian pharaoh was identified with the god Horus (p. 83), so the Roman emperors were sometimes portrayed as this hawk-headed god. The hawk's feathers suggest metal armor, and the figure wears Roman sandals and a toga.

Mummy of Artemidorus

Roman child's mummy

ROMAN MUMMIES
Mummies of the Roman period often had lifelike portraits of the deceased. The coffin above shows its owner, Artemidorus, painted in typical wide-eyed Roman style. The pigment was mixed with beeswax to give bright colors. The idea of these portraits was to help a person's spirit identify the body to which it belonged. They look toward you as if they had been called by name.

The Christians

Egypt officially turned to Christianity with the conversion of the Roman Empire in A.D. 324, although there were Christian hermits living in caves in Egypt before that. The version of Christianity that eventually triumphed in Egypt was called Coptic. It still flourishes in the country today and Coptic monks still live in thriving monasteries. Recently the relics of Saint Mark, who is said to have introduced Christianity into Egypt, were sent back from Venice to Cairo.

SURVIVOR
Qasr Ibrim, a mountain in Nubia, was the center of a Christian diocese that was stormed by Muslim troops. This silver cross was one of the items to survive the attack.

WARRIOR SAINT
The image of the god Horus on horseback spearing his rival Seth was adopted by the early Christians in Egypt to portray warrior saints like St. George and St. Menas.

Tapestry roundel showing the victorious St. George

STREET SCENE
Until the 19th century the streets of Cairo contained stalls - each selling the products of one craft - running alongside the walls, minarets, and domes of the mosques.

Brass openwork design

The Muslims

Arab armies, skilled in warfare on horseback, conquered Egypt in the 7th century A.D. They ruled though the existing, mainly Christian, bureaucracy. But Islam became the state religion, Arabic the official language, and the new city of el-Qahira later became the capital, Cairo. Eventually Egypt was conquered by the Turks, and it was not until the 1960s that the country was again governed by a native Egyptian.

INCENSE BURNER
This vessel, made about 1,000 years ago, was used in a mosque. Burning incense was part of the ritual of purity observed by Muslims, which included removing shoes and washing upon entering a mosque.

Index

Acknowledgments

Dorling Kindersley would like to thank:

The staff of the Department of Egyptian Antiquities, British Museum, London, for providing artifacts for photography, in particular James Putnam, John Taylor, Stephen Quirke, Carol Andrews, Jeffrey Spencer, Virginia Hewitt, Tony Brandon, Bob Dominey, and John Hayman; the British Museum Photographic Department, especially Ivor Kerslake; Celia Clear of British Museum Publications; the Departments of Oriental Antiquities and Medieval and Later Antiquities, British Museum for providing extra objects for photography; Ian Mackay at the Museum of Mankind, London; Angela Thomas and Arthur Boulton of the Bolton Museum; John Saunders, Stephen Hughes, and the staff of the Department of Medical Physics, St Thomas' Hospital, London (p. 123); Martin Atcherley in Germany; Robert Bauval; Don Brothwell; Martin Davies; Reg Davis; Maria Demosthenous; Guita Elmenteuse; Joyce Filer; Jean-Phillipe Lauer; William and Miranda MacQuitty; Mitsouko Miyazaki in Japan; Peter Nahun; George Bankes at the University of Manchester; Theya Molleson at the Natural History Museum, London; the Seventh Earl of Carnarvon; the Egypt Exploration Society; Belinda Rasmussen; Nicholas Reeves; and Morgan Reid.

Design, research, and editorial help:
Helena Spiteri, Linda Martin, and Lester Cheeseman for editorial help. Sharon Spencer, Manisha Patel, Susan St. Louis, Isaac Zamora, and Ivan Finnegan for design help.

Maps: Simone End (36r).

Illustrations: Eugene Fleury (8cl); Thomas Keenes (88br, 89bl, 99t, 111bc); Gillie Newman (17tc); James Putnam (27tr); and John Woodcock (46bl, 49t, 65c).

Index: Hilary Bird and Judith Ann Smith.

Additional photography:
by Peter Anderson (53tr, 62–63, 65br); Stan Bean (40–41); Geoff Brightling; Michael Dunning; and Karl Shone.

Editorial Co-ordinator: Marion Dent
Assistant Editors: Julie Ferris & Nicola Waine
Assistant Designer: Iain Morris

Picture credits
(t = top, b = bottom, c = center, l = left, r = right)

Agyptisches Museum / Photo: Staatliche Museen zu Berlin 104bl.
Ancient Art & Architecture Collection: 10bl, 10bc, 11tr, 11bl, 14tr, 63tr, 65tr, 84–85t.
Anglo Aquarium Plant Co. / Barbara Thomas 82cl.
Ardea, London Ltd: 25tc; / John Mason 118bc; / Peter Steyn 119tr.
Ayeshah Abdel-Haleem: 50br.
Stan Bean / Egyptian Museum, San José, Ca: 40–41b.
Bridgeman Art Library: 78tr, 84tl, 84br.
British Museum: 6b, 9tr, 10c, 11c, 14br, 15tl, 15tc, 15br, 25tl, 30tl, 31tr, 31br, 34c, 35t, 35br, 68tl, 80tr, 82cr, 83tl, 83cr, 84c, 85r, 86cr, 88, 89, 90c, 91cr, 96tl, 97t, 97bc, 100c, 101tl, 102l, 102b, 105bl, 106c, 107tc, 109tc, 112tl, 112bl, 113br, 114bc, 115bc, 116tr, 116–117c, 118tr, 124bl, 124bc, 125tr.
British Museum / Nina M. de Garis Davies: 95c, 104cr, 107b, 117c.
Jean-Loup Charmet: 70tl.
Peter Clayton: 82tl, 94c.
Bruce Coleman Ltd: 97cr.
Reg Davis: 121tl, 122tl.
Vivien Davis: 74cl, 74–75 b.
Michael Dixon, Photo Resources: 10tr, 79tl.
Egypt Exploration Society, London: 110br.
Egypt Tourist Office: 17bc.
Egyptian National Museum, Cairo / Giraudon / Bridgeman Art Library, London: 72cl.
e.t. archive: 31tl, 50cl, (detail) 67bl.
Mary Evans Picture Library: 16tr, 19br, 31bcl, 44tl, 45cr, 48bl, 50tl, 70bl, 73c, 113tr, 124tr.
Francis Firth / Royal Photographic Society, Bath (The Southern stone pyramid of Dahshoor from the South West): 42cr.
Gallimard Jeunesse: 45tr, 46c.
Griffith Institute, Ashmolean Museum, Oxford: 26tl, 69b, 72br, 81cb.
Robert Harding Picture Library: 12cl, 13bl, 31tcl, 69cr, 72bl, 72c, 72tr, 73tl, 73tr, 73br, 78bl, 92–93b, 95tr, 98tl, 109cl, 110tl.
George Hart: 69c, 85c.
Michael Holford: 31tc, 97br.
Hulton-Deutsch Collection: 18bl, 28br.
Hutchison Library: 9cr.
H. Lewandowski / Photo-R.M.N.: 37tl.
Jürgen Liepe: 39br, 46tl, 46cr.
Louvre, Paris / © Réunion des Musées Nationaux: 111tc.
Manchester Museum, University of Manchester: 120b.
Mansell Collection: (detail) 49bcr, 63cr.
© Metropolitan Museum of Art, Gift of Edward S.Harkness, 1914 (14.3.17): 64l.
Daniel Moignot, P.L.J. Gallimard-Larousse: 63tl.
Museum Expedition. Courtesy of Museum of Fine Arts, Boston: 47r.
Courtesy of the Oriental Institute of the University of Chicago: 100–101b.
Pelizaeus-Museum, Hildesheim: 16b.
Popperfoto: 94tl.
James Putnam: 45tl, 47tl, 48tr, 49c, 66cl, 67cl, 87cl.
Photo R.M.N.: 27tl, 29c, 53br.
John Ross: 40tl.
Staatliche Museen zu Berlin Preussischer Kulturbesitz Agyptisches Museum / Photo - Margarete Busing / Bildarchiv: 76tr, 76b, 76c, 77t, 77b, 77br.
Sygma: 70br, 72tl, 122tr, 123bl.
Uni-Dia Verlag: 99cl.
University College, London 68b, 91cl.
Werner Forman Archive: 8tr, 42tr, 43tl, 50bl, 57cl, 58cr, (detail) 61cl, (detail) 61tc.
Roger Wood: 88tl.
Verlag Philipp von Zabern / Cairo Museum: 8–9b.

Every effort has been made to trace the copyright holders of the photographs, and we apologize for any unintentional omissions. We would be pleased to insert the appropriate acknowledgment in any subsequent edition of this publication.